PATRISTIC MONOGRAPH SERIES, NO. 3

CONSOLATION PHILOSOPHY

Greek and Christian Paideia

in

Basil and the Two Gregories

by

Robert C. Gregg

Published by

The Philadelphia Patristic Foundation, Ltd.

1975

TABLE OF CONTENTS

Contents ii

Preface iii

Chapter 1. The Consolatio in Antiquity: Origins
           and Development 1

Chapter 2. Form in Consolatory Letters, Orations
           and Sermons 51

Chapter 3. The Problem of "Appropriate Grief":
           ἀπάθεια and μετριοπάθεια 81

Chapter 4. Basil the Consoler: The Convergence
           of Hellenic and Christian Tra-
           ditions in the Consolatio 125

Chapter 5. Cappadocian θεολογία as παραμυθία :
           Death as Separation from the
           World and Ascent to God 219

Bibliography 265

Indices 281

PREFACE

Faced with the task of composing a consolatory letter for a friend or acquaintance, a modern becomes aware of two impressions which are curiously contradictory: he has no contemporary literature upon which he might model his consolation, and yet many of his attempted phrases and sentiments strike him as hackneyed and trite. The situation was not at all the same for the ancient citizen. Even if he found it as difficult as we do to advance a genuinely original consolatory argument or proposition, the literature of consolation was available to him as a branch of popular philosophical writing. Within this literature old and new answers were given to the puzzles and questions surrounding death -- the significance of human existence, the possibilities of afterlife, the dread of dying, the means of assuaging grief, the suitable ways to honor the deceased, and the preferred or "philosophic" attitude one ought to cultivate toward his own approaching death.

When the new oriental religion which proclaimed Jesus its savior insinuated itself into the Greek-speaking world of the Mediterranean, it brought with it germs of distinctive answers to the questions with which Hellenic consolers had been occupied for ages. Because Christianity came to maturity in this setting, its spokesmen and writers naturally added portions of the Greek philosophical tradition to their heritage of Hebraic wisdom and lore.

The following chapters attempt to analyze and understand the consolatory letters of a Greek-speaking Cappadocian Christian of the 4th century by viewing them against the background of the ideas and kinds of literature emanating from both the Hellenic and biblical worlds. Within the extensive correspondence of Basil of Caesarea (329-379), there are preserved nineteen letters of consolation. When

examined in conjunction with letters and orations
(or sermons) composed on the same subject by his
brother, Gregory of Nyssa, and his lifetime friend,
Gregory of Nazianzus, Basil's epistles provide ample
material for a thorough study of consolation style
and argumentation as practiced by educated Greek
Christians in the generation following the recogni-
tion of the church by Constantine. This project,
originally a University of Pennsylvania doctoral dissertation, endeavors to answer a specific need, for
although several works have been produced which treat
Latin Christian contributions to the literature of
consolation,[1] comparable attention has not been given
to the consolatory and funeral writings of Greek
Christianity. Among the Greek Fathers, Basil's correspondence and the collected writings of the Gregories represent the earliest substantial materials
of this type. As such, the writings of the Cappadocians were not without influence on contemporaries
and successors in the West (notably, Ambrose, Jerome
and Augustine).

The present work is comprised of five chapters.
The first sketches the emergence and development of
consolatory literature and philosophy in Greek let-

---

[1]Charles Favez, La Consolation Latine Chrétienne
(Paris: J. Vrin, 1937). Favez apparently devoted
his attention to the Latin Christian consolers,
among other reasons, because writers like Gregory
of Nyssa and Gregory of Nazianzus do not emphasize
so sharply as their western counterparts "l'élément
chrétien" in consolation (p. 2). M.M. Beyenka,
Consolation in Augustine (Washington: Catholic University of America Press, 1950), p. x, writes: "Particularly for the Greek Fathers, there is need of a
systematic study which will give a complete picture
of their handling of the theme of consolation under
both the traditional and peculiarly Christian
forms."

ters and in the Greek and Latin writings of the Hellenistic period. It is followed by an analysis of the formal characteristics of the <u>consolatio</u> and the funeral oration, and an attempt to delineate the extent of indebtedness to the established rhetorical forms observable in the works of Basil and the Gregories. A third chapter treats a particular problem which pervades consolatory writings, and frequently is the issue which divides consolers into separate philosophical camps -- the question whether or to what extent grieving is permissible. The final chapters concentrate upon Cappadocian writings. Chapter four examines the predominant consolatory <u>argumenta</u> utilized by Basil and his colleagues, and seeks to establish both the points of contact with the established Hellenic consolation tradition and the departures from this tradition which were prompted by the influence of the Bible, practices and ideas stemming from the Christian community, and the like. The concluding chapter seeks to identify certain themes and motifs within these consolation writings which may be recognized as distinctive Cappadocian <u>theologoumena</u>, and are capable both of being set in a broader context of thought and of being evaluated as the authors' peculiar contributions to a genre in which the appearance of truly new ingredients is a rarity.

Another prefatory word: for their encouragement at various points during the preparation of this study, I wish to thank Donald Winslow, Dennis Groh and William Schoedel. It was my special privilege to receive guidance, good criticism and a sense of the joy of research from Robert Evans before his death. Above all, for a fine mixture of patience and saving distraction I am grateful to Mary Layne and our children.

June 18, 1975   R. C. G.
                                       Durham, N.C.

CHAPTER 1:
THE CONSOLATIO IN ANTIQUITY:
ORIGINS AND DEVELOPMENT

> But what should one feel concerning a law
> of God which has held sway from ancient
> days, that one who came to birth departs
> at the appropriate time?

With these words to Maximus, a man who mourns the
death of his wife, Basil of Caesarea (Ep. 301) gives
voice to the question which is at the core of all
efforts to combat grief. It comes as no surprise
that Basil's manner of expressing the dilemma bears
the marks of a long history of consolation, for the
question and the attempted responses are as old as
human experience. A double fact -- death, which
demands that sense be made of the life now ended,
and grief, which disorients and impedes the lives
of those who survive the dead -- dominates the
literature of consolation, from the earliest poet-
mourners to the later collectors of stylized sentiments. This double fact of death and grief elicits
a bewildering range of responses: cries of reproach
to the gods for their cruelties, utterances of worn
resignation from sages who have perceived the logic
of Fate, the tentative speculations about possibilities of life beyond the tomb, and the expansive
visions of after-life in blessed fields or around
blessed thrones, drawn in picturesque and confident detail.

Among the papyri found at Oxyrhynchus is a
brief letter which dates from the second century,
A.D. It is sent from a certain Irene to a man and
wife who have apparently suffered the loss of their
son. This simple note, made more poignant by the
author's reference to her own similar misfortune,
closes with these words:

1

ἀλλ' ὅμως οὐδὲν δύναταί τις πρὸς τὰ τοιαῦτα.
But truly there is nothing anyone can do
in the face of such things.[1]

The unwillingness of many a poet, philosopher and
theologian to concede the woman's point makes the
following study possible.[2] Indeed, Basil, a fourth
century Christian bishop, when he composes epistles
of consolation, finds himself the heir of a stream
of arguments and musings traceable to the beginnings of Greek thought and letters. Clues about
the sources of the stream are made available to
us in the quotations from poets and playwrights, for
these were employed by consolers of subsequent eras
to lend antiquity (and thus, authority) to their
attempts to relieve the grief-struck. From the
works of Hesiod, Homer and Euripides come passages
touching upon misfortune and human disposition in
the face of travail -- these reveal the earliest
Greek literary traces of a theme destined to become
a literature of its own. The first example of
written consolation has been located in the speech
of Achilles to Priam in the twenty-fourth book of
the Iliad. Achilles, having described the two jars
of evils and blessings from which Zeus dispenses
the lot of mortals, advises:

---

[1]POxy., 115. Text given in George Milligan,
Selections From the Greek Papyri (Cambridge: University Press, 1927), pp. 95-6.

[2]Rudolf Kassel, Untersuchungen zur Griechischen
und Römischen Konsolationsliteratur, Zetemata, Heft
18 (Munich: C.H. Beck'sche Verlagsbuchhandlung,
1958), p.4, (Hereafter referred to as Konsolationsliteratur) remarks that the authors of the Greek and
Latin consolations are far removed from "so ruhrender
Hilflosigkeit," and in fact make it their task to
create statements with which to confront "such things."

But bear up, nor mourn endlessly in your
heart, for there is not anything to be
gained from grief for your son; you will
never bring him back; sooner you must go
through yet another sorrow.[1]

This and similar pieces of poetry stand at the
beginnings of the art of consoling mankind, and utterances of this kind retain their place, if not their
original liveliness, throughout the history of the
genre consolatio. A detailed recounting of the
emergence of consolation is not within the compass
of this study, though it should be mentioned that
everyone who approaches the subject is in debt to
C. Buresch's thorough study of nearly a century ago.[2]
It will be profitable, however, to sketch this literary tradition by mentioning those authors who figured

---

[1]Homer Iliad 24.549-51, in The Iliad of Homer,
trans. by Richmond Lattimore (Chicago: University of
Chicago Press, 1951), p.489. A.D. Nock writes:
"...as early as Homer, the suffering of others and the
inevitability of suffering are used in words of consolation: the speech of Achilles to Priam is our first
example of the παραμυθητικὸς λόγος or consolation
which developed as a literary genre." Arthur Darby
Nock, "Orphism or Popular Philosophy?", Harvard Theological Review 33 (1940), p.309. See also the remarks
of W.C. Greene, Moira (Cambridge, Mass.: Harvard University Press, 1944), pp. 27ff. For treatment of
passages from playwrights, see Kassel, Konsolationsliteratur, pp. 5ff. The Homeric passage in question
appears in Plutarch Cons. ad Apoll. 7.

[2]Carolus Buresch, Consolationum a Graecis Romanisque Scriptarum-Historia Critica, (Hereinafter, Consolationum) Leipziger Studien zur Classischen Philologie (Leipzig: J.B. Hirschfeld, 1886). For the
outline and for much of the information of this survey of early consolation writings, I join many others
in my indebtedness to Buresch's study.

importantly in it, and by describing, however summarily, the character of their writing.

The initial stirrings of consolatory craft are sighted in the oldest type of funeral song (ἐπικήδειον) and in the lamentation (θρῆνος), as well as in certain poetic works.[1] It was the philosophers, however, who provided the outlines of a discipline within the field of ethics. Within this area of ethical thought and practice, there developed arguments designed for the consolation of the whole spectrum of human misfortunes -- exile, destruction of patria, physical disability, and that subject of the vast majority of such writing, death.[2] Claiming the con-

---

[1]Ibid., pp. 4-5.

[2]Ibid., p. 6. Eudorus of Alexandria, a philosopher of the new Academy, made room in the third division of his moral philosophy for a section περὶ τῶν ἀλλοτριούτων ἀπό τινῶν πράξεων which he called παραμυθητικός. This type of writing is closely akin to the protrepticus, or exhortation, as we see in the works of some orators and philosophers, e.g., Cicero De Or. 2.12.50, Quintilian Inst. 10.1.46, Seneca Ad Lucilium 95. Favez, La Consolation Latine Chretienne, pp. 10-11, writes:

"Nous connaissons, par exemple, Areus, le 'philosophe' d'Auguste, et nous savons par Sénèque que c'est auprès de lui que Livie chercha, lors de la mort de son fils Drusus, le réconfort dont elle avait besoin. Prodigues de leurs conseils, ces médecins de l'âme accourent auprès des malheureux, même sans être appelés. On en voit qui, recourant a la publicité, annoncent par un écriteau qu'ils connaissent des paroles propres à soulager la doleur. En même temps, ils rivalisent d'ingéniosité, distinguant entre le souci, l'abattement, l'angoisse, le deuil, le

dition of the soul as their proper province of study,
philosophers sought to treat its disturbances in their
capacity as moral practitioners, and to prescribe for
the maladies (grief, anger, lust, envy, etc.) their
healing counsels. Faith in reason and reasonings as
central to the restoration of the soul's equilibrium
led ultimately, as we learn from Dio Chrysostom,[1]

---

désespoir, et cherchent à chaque mal le remède
approprié. Les maux les plus importants qu'ils
s'efforcent de guérir sont la maladie, la
vieillesse, l'exil, la pauvreté et surtout la
mort. Ils ont, pour chacun de ces malheurs,
des arguments soigneusement catalogués et
devenus classiques."

[1]Dio Chrys. Or. 27.7-9 (trans. J.W. Cohoon, LCL
Vol. II, 1939, pp. 352-5): "...people are, as a general rule, not willing to listen to the words of the
philosopher until some affliction visits them, something which men consider serious....And if it is
[a man's] misfortune to lose any of his relatives,
either his wife, or a child, or a brother, he asks
the philosopher to come and speak words of comfort,
as if he thought it were only then necessary to consider the future." On this function of philosophers,
the remarks of C. Martha are interesting: "Dans
l'antiquité, c'est la philosophie qui exerça les
délicates fonctions qui, depuis, appartiennent à
la religion. Les prêtres païens demeuraient étran-
gers à la science de l'âme et même n'y prétendaient
pas. Ils n'étaient que les officiers du culte,
chargés d'offrir selon les rites les hommages tout
extérieurs que les hommes adressaient aux dieux,
des magistrats de police réglant les rapports entre
la faiblesse humaine et la puissance divine, des
collecteurs préposés surtout à la rentrée des rede-
vances que la terre devait au ciel. A la philosophie
seule revenait le soin d'instruire, d'exhorter et

to the custom of summoning a philosopher to scenes
of mishap and tragedy, where he was called upon to
practice his profession as consoler, as ὁ τῆς ψυχῆς
ἰατρός.

In his treatise On Those in Hades, Democritus
(c. 460-c. 370) comes into view as the first philosopher, apparently, to turn his attention to the theme
of consolation. Hé argues (along lines to reappear
in Epicurean teaching) that since death marks the end
of all sensation, fear of death is vain.[1] The story
of Democritus "consoling" King Darius by challenging
him to produce the names of three people who never
mourned, it is said, derives from one of Democritus'
own works.[2]

---

même de consoler." B. Constant Martha, Études
morales sur l'antiquité (Paris: Hachette et cie,
1905), p. 140 (Hereafter, Études). The tradition
that Antiphon the sophist (5th C. BC) practiced consolation (τέχνη ἀλυπίας) if not apocryphal, points
to a long history of this "service" by philosophers.
See W.C. Greene, Moira, pp. 232ff.

[1]See Buresch, Consolationum, pp. 7-8, n.8,
where Stobaeus Flor. 120.20 is cited. For the
"demythologizing" of the torments of the underworld
in Epicurean teaching, see Lucretius De rerum nat.
3. 978. Democritus' views on the gods, and his doctrine of images and effluences are reported in Diogenes Laertius Vitae phil. 9.7.34-49, and are commented upon in Eduard Zeller, Outlines of the History of Philosophy, ed. Wilhelm Nestle, trans.
L.R. Palmer (13th ed.; Cleveland: The World Publishing Company, 1965), pp. 82-6.

[2]On the legend involving Democritus and Darius
(and variations on the theme), see Julian Ep. 69 (To
Himerius), Pliny's allusions to the story in his
H.N. 7.189, and Lucian Demonax 25.

No part of life is free from pain, and the
infant's initial crying is a signal for all that lies
ahead -- tyranny at the hands of teachers in youth,
military campaigns and wounds in manhood, the loss
of hearing, sight and sense which old age introduces.
This cheerless survey of the evils which fill the
span of life is attributed to Prodicus, the fifth
century sophist, who is better known to us from his
discourse on "The Choice of Heracles," preserved by
Xenophon.[1] Mention of Prodicus introduces us directly
to what is perhaps the earliest extended consolatory
writing to have come down to us, for it is in the Ps.
Platonic Axiochus that Prodicus' catalogue of life's
troubles appears.[2] Though the authorship and dating
of the Axiochus are debated,[3] the influence of this
remarkable document upon the development of the consolatory genre is not questioned. The work is set in
the form of a dialogue in which Socrates persuades
Axiochus, who is at "death's door," that his fear of
dying is vain -- indeed, after striking eschatological prospects are unfolded before Axiochus, he

---

[1]On the grounds that the pessimistic views
attached to his name are "hard to reconcile with the
buoyant tone of the famous 'Choice of Heracles,'" W.
C. Greene doubts whether the Axiochus accurately portrays Prodicus. Greene, Moira, pp. 242-43.

[2]Ps. Plato Axiochus 366C-376C. The standard
topos asserting that death concerns neither the
living nor the dead (the living are not yet dead;
the dead have no awareness) is also put at the door
of Prodicus in Axiochus 369B.

[3]The early critical debate over the authorship,
date (and quality) of the Axiochus is both recounted
and supplemented by Buresch, Consolationum, pp. 9-17.
He concludes that the work is the product of Aeschines
and belongs to the Socratic age. Cf. W.C. Greene,
Moira, pp. 241ff.

admits to a change of mood about his death. What had been feared is now desired![1] This change of attitude which in later consolations and funeral orations is adopted as a device of the writer or speaker, is but one of the many topoi which this work, subtitled περὶ θανάτου, fed into the stream of consolatory ideas. Our analysis of the writings of the Cappadocian Fathers will give us reason to return more than once to items found within the Axiochus. At this point only a few of the ideas need to be mentioned: the suggestions of Socrates that life is but a sojourn,[2] that the soul pines for the heavenly atmosphere, its original home,[3] the teaching that those loved by the gods are taken from life early[4] (a commonplace which persists in our day in the form, "The good die young"), and that afterlife holds for the philosopher the promise of conducting his searches πρὸς ἀμφιθαλῆ τὴν ἀλήθειαν .[5]

---

[1]Ps. Plato Ax. 372 A: τοσοῦτον γὰρ ἀποδέω τοῦ δεδοικέναι τὸν θάνατον, ὥστε ἤδη καὶ ἔρωτα αὐτοῦ ἔχειν. οὕτως με καὶ οὗτος ὁ λόγος, ὡς καὶ ὁ οὐράνιος, πέπεικε, καὶ ἤδη περιφρονῶ τοῦ ζῆν, ἅτε εἰς ἀμείνω οἶκον μεταστησόμενος.
Worthy of note here is the emphasis on the words of the wise man. Kassel, Konsolationsliteratur, p. 11. points out that the rhetorical element, which is by no means a peripheral element in later consolation writings, stems from sophistic origins. The sophistic power of speech provides the background for confidence that grief can be systematically combatted by inspirational or hortatory utterance.

[2]Ps. Plato Ax. 365B.

[3]Ibid., 366a, 365E.

[4]Ibid., 367C.

[5]Ibid., 370D.

Among the three Platonic writings which contain materials bearing upon consolation, the arguments and wide popularity of the teachings of the Apology and the Phaedo require no particular comment. The Menexenus is noteworthy in that it purports to preserve the funeral oration of Aspasia, the mistress of Pericles. Several features of Plato's treatise -- an exhortation to the fathers and mothers who survive their war-wasted sons, a warning about excessive grieving (μηδὲν ἄγαν),[1] and the conceit of presenting within the oration the last words of heroes to their families as an inducement to courageous behavior -- serve to remind us that from an early date, and manifestly in the period of late antiquity in which the funeral orations and sermons of men like Libanius and Gregory of Nyssa drew notice, the history of the ἐπιτάφιος λόγος is in fact an important part of the history of consolation literature.[2]

In another writing which centers on the figure of Socrates, Xenophon places upon the lips of his hero several solacia which later writings demonstrate to have had great durability. In the Apology, Socrates tells weeping followers that his impending death would be a cause of grief if his life were filled with blessings. As it is, he continues, the future portends only further troubles, and his demise ought to cheer all.[3] He goes on to suggest that the time and

---

[1]Plato Menexenus 247C-E, 248C.

[2]See Buresch, Consolationum, p. 7; Beyenka, Consolation in Augustine, pp. 6-7; Johannes Bauer, Die Trostreden des Gregorius von Nyssa in ihrem Verhältnis zur antiken Rhetorik (Marburg: Universitats-Buchdruckerei, 1892), throughout.

[3]Xenophon Apology 27. This theme is present in Axiochus 367B, and is elsewhere attributed to Euripides and Sophocles. Important for Buresch's argument that Xenophon is the author of the Apology is

circumstances of his death are by no means accidental
(an assertion which figures prominently in numerous
writings of later date, pagan and Christian): "Perhaps God in his kindness is taking my part and
securing me the opportunity of ending my life not only
in season but also in the way that is easiest."[1]

Aristotle (364-322) and his successor as head of
the Peripatetic school, Theophrastus (372-287), have
left traces of their attention to consolatory matters.
Nothing of Aristotle's tribute to his friend Eudemos
survives, except the story of Silvanus' answer to ·
Midas, which carries the lesson that the best thing
(τὸ πάντων ἄριστον)is not to be born, the next best
thing to die quickly.[2] A similarly baleful saying is
preserved from Theophrastus' περὶ πένθους : life consists of Fate's frustration of our labors and the
interruption of our seeming tranquility.[3]

We pass over the Cynic consolers[4] in order to

---

the presence of this topos in the 28th Discourse of
Dio Chrysostom, who proclaims himself an imitator of
Xenophon (Or. 18). See the elaborate case built by
Buresch, Consolationum, pp. 21-33.

[1]Xenophon Ap. 7, (trans. O.J. Todd, LCL, Vol. IV,
1968, pp. 644-45).

[2]Plutarch Cons. ad Apoll. 115B.

[3]Ibid., 104D: "ἄσκοπος γὰρ ἡ τύχη," φησὶν ὁ
θεόφραστυς, "καὶ δεινὴ παρελέσθαι τὰ προπεπονημένα καὶ
μεταρρῖψαι τὴν δοκοῦσαν εὐημερίαν, οὐδένα καιρὸν
ἔχουσα τακτόν."

[4]Antisthenes wrote several works on the subjects of dying, those in Hades, etc. Diogenes of
Sinope is mentioned in Jerome's Ep. 60.5 as one "who
tried to alleviate mourning by letters and books."

·

take note of the contributions of the Stoa to the
literature of consolation. In the case of the early
Stoics, the poverty of our sources does not bear
adequate testimony to the impact of their doctrine
upon much consolatory argumentation. As a consequence,
we are dependent upon the reports of Cicero, Plutarch,
Diogenes Laertius, Stobaeus and others for much of
what we are able to reconstruct of their teachings
concerning consolation. Chrysippus of Soli (281-208),
the successor to Cleanthes, evidently did not compose consolation literature as such, but his work
περὶ παθῶν , of which book four was entitled θεραπευτικός, clearly belongs to the area which concerns
us. No record exists of any specifically consolatory
writings by Zeno or Cleanthes, but Jerome (Ep. 60)
lists Posidonius among those known for their consolations, and Panaetius' work περὶ εὐθυμίας is praised on
two occasions by Plutarch.[1] Stoic notions concerning the rational faculty and the affections have a
direct bearing upon the question of mourning and the
therapy to be offered the grieving, and differences
of opinion regarding what might pass as "appropriate"
sorrow can be seen as a persistent source of contention throughout the long history of written consolations. Consequently, we shall want to say more in
Chapter 3 about Stoic doctrines concerning the
πάθος of grief, about the passions generally, and
about the ideal of freedom from "affects" (ἀπάθεια)
attributed to these teachers of the Porch.

Insofar as the genre consolatio can be said to
have a "father," the title belongs to the Academician
Crantor (c. 330-268), who traveled from his birth-

Perhaps Teles' (3rd C.) name should be joined with
those above. His work, περὶ εὐπαθεύας, judging from
preserved fragments, bears some similarity to portions
of the Plutarchian consolation for Apollonius. See
Buresch, Consolationum, p. 38.

[1]Plutarch De cohib. ir. 463D; De tranq. an.
474E. Cited by Buresch, Consolationum, p. 38.

place in Sicily to Athens, where he became a student of Xenocrates and an associate of Polemo and Crates. Joining the debate revolving around the proper interpretation of Platonic doctrines concerning the nature of the soul and the meaning of the mythic elements in the writings,[1] Crantor is credited with having composed the first commentary on the Timaeus.[2] Further evidence of the range of his pursuits is the reputation he earned as an ethicist,[3] and we are fortunate to have a fairly substantial piece of his writing preserved in the work Against Ethicists by Sextus Empiricus.[4] It is chiefly as consoler, however, that Crantor is commended in ancient letters, for his

---

[1] Eduard Zeller, Plato and the Older Academy, trans. by Sarah F. Alleyne and Alfred Goodwin (London: Longmans, Green & Co., 1888), p. 618, notes that Crantor, along lines similar to those taken by his mentor, Xenocrates, argued against the notion of the soul having a beginning in time, and favored a non-literal (in this case, non-temporal) interpretation of the creation account of the Timaeus. For these points, see Plutarch De an. procr. 2-3, and Proclus In Tim. 85A.

[2] Proclus In Tim. 24A.

[3] Horace Ep. 1.2.4. considers Crantor to be an ethicist of the same caliber as Chrysippus: "qui quid sit pulchrum, quid turpe, quid utile, quid non, planius ac melius Chrysippo et Crantore dicit."

[4] Sextus Math. 11 (Adv. Eth.) 51-8. Here Crantor is credited with a "delightful illustration" concerning the rank and value of "goods." As all Greeks assemble in a common theatre, ὁ πλοῦτος, ἡ ἡδονή, ἡ ὑγεία, ἡ ἀνδρία vie in turn for the first prize, which by a progression of arguments enumerating the limitations and values of each, is awarded ultimately to the last-mentioned.

περὶ πένθους became a model for many of the major consolationes which followed. This treatise On Grief Crantor wrote in the form of an epistle to one Hippocles upon the death of his children,[1] and this collection of solacia was, as C. Martha put it, "une sorte de fontaine publique ou l'antiquité allait sans cesse soulager ses doleurs."[2] Attempts to reconstruct the lost περὶ πένθους have long occupied scholarship, proceeding by means of a comparison and compilation of ideas of Crantor alluded to in later writings, and more recently, through a thorough source- and form-analysis of these works.[3] Beyond the references to Crantor by name, it is considered proven that many of the more popular consolatory themes which appear in Greek and Latin writings in the Hellenistic period and after have their origins in what Cicero called his "small, but golden" book.[4] Specifically, the consolation letters ascribed to Plutarch, the Tusculan Disputations of Cicero, and the well-known epistles of Seneca to Marcia, Helvia, and Polybius are believed to preserve for us, both explicitly and indirectly, much of the content of Crantor's teachings on the subject of grief. Because it will be necessary to speak in greater detail below of an important aspect of Crantor's thought, (namely, his insistence that grief could not be suppressed)

---

[1] See Plutarch Cons. ad Apoll. 104C; Diogenes Laertius Vitae phil. 4.27; Cicero Acad., 2.44.135.

[2] B. Constant Martha, Études, p. 143.

[3] Horst-Theodor Johann, Trauer und Trost: Eine quellen- und strukturanalytische Untersuchung der philosophischen Trostschriften über den Tod, Studia et Testimonia Antiqua V (Munich: Wilhelm Fink Verlag, 1968).

[4] Cicero Acad. 2.44: Aureolus...ad verbum ediscendus libellus.

let us simply mention here several of the topoi which are customarily traced to his work.

Crantor's enthusiastic use of examples was responsible, it seems, for establishing the names and feats of certain legendary personages as common stock in the literature of condolence. Elysius of Terina seeks an explanation for the death of his son, and while visiting "a place where the spirits of the dead are conjured up," experiences a vision in which he is told: "Dead now Euthynous lies; destiny so has decreed. Nor for himself was it good that he live, nor yet for his parents."[1] In a similar vein, Anaxagoras, upon receiving word of his son's demise, is reported to have lapsed into silence for only a moment before remarking, "I knew that I had begotten a son who was mortal."[2] Crantor appears to have provided his friend Hippocles with similar accounts of "philosophical" acceptance of the death of loved ones in further examples of Telamon, Pericles and Xenophon, and one can observe that this string of heroes is being extended in the productions of Plutarch and Cicero. Examples of a different kind are likewise employed by Crantor, and thereby pass into the lore of consolation: for her excessive mourning, Niobe was turned to stone,[3] and the priestess of Argos, who besought the gods to grant to her two sons the "greatest boon" discovered her prayer fulfilled in

---

[1]Plutarch Cons. ad Apoll. 109D (trans F.C. Babbitt, LCL, Vol. II, 1962, pp. 148-49). Cf. Cicero Tusc. 1.48.115. The series of Crantorian topoi, by no means exhaustive, are drawn from Buresch, Consolationum, pp. 39=57. See also, Johann, Trauer und Trost, esp. part 3, pp. 127ff.

[2]Plutarch Cons. ad Apoll. 118D; Cicero Tusc. 3.24.58.

[3]Plutarch Cons. ad Apoll. 116C; Cicero Tusc. 3.26.63; Jerome Ep. 60.14.

their immediate deaths![1]

A number of popular consolatory ideas and maxims stem from, or are transmitted by Crantor. In the latter category, we spot the teaching familiar to us from the Axiochus, that just as nothing affects us before birth, so will it be also after death,[2] and we meet once more the doctrine of the divine (or heavenly) origin of the soul.[3] Also among Crantor's teachings we find the proposition that when once a person realizes how little his mourning accomplishes he will be able to bring it to an end.[4] He seems to have offered a three-part argument intended to relieve those in adversity: anticipation of mishaps removes the bite from misfortune;[5] one gains comfort by understanding that the lot of man is to be borne in a human manner (φέρειν καὶ τὰ ἀνθρώπινα ἀνθρωπίνως);[6] and (finally) there is solace to be gained from the truth that there is no evil except guilt, and "there is no guilt when the issue is one against which

---

[1]Plutarch Cons. ad Apoll. 108F-109D; Cicero Tusc. 1.47.113-15.

[2]Ps. Plato Ax. 369B; Plutarch Cons. ad Apoll. 109F; Cicero Tusc. 1.38.91. Cf. also Lucretius De rerum nat. 3.830. Buresch, Consolationum, pp. 39-57, argues compellingly that Crantor was the medium between the Axiochus and Plutarchian and Ciceronian consolations. Note that in Ax. 370DE and in Tusc. 1.47.112, the listener is led from fear to desire of death.

[3]Ps. Plato Ax. 370B; Cicero Tusc. 1.25.61-3, 68-70.

[4]Plutarch Cons. ad Apoll. 102CE.

[5]See below, pp. 17-8, on the Cyreniac emphasis on premeditation of possible evils.

[6]Plutarch Cons. ad Apoll. 118C.

a man can give no guarantee."[1] This brief glimpse of
Crantor's thought is perhaps best concluded in the
quotation of his estimate of human life: "the lot
of man has been bewailed by many wise men who have
felt that life is a punishment and that for man to
be born at all is the greatest calamity."[2]

We learn from a passage in the Tusculan Disputations of yet other contributions from the Academy.
Cicero records that he read "the book which Clitomachus sent by way of comfort to his captive fellow
citizens after the destruction of Carthage."[3] Within
Clitomachus' work were pages of a lecture once
delivered by his predecessor, Carneades (b. 215 BC),
in which he refuted the proposition that a wise man
"would feel distress at the fall of his country."
Central to the consolation offered by both men, it
appears, was a teaching destined to gain wide use.
It had to do with the safeguard of premeditation --
the anticipation of misfortunes. As Cicero phrases
it: "...we have on the tip of our tongues as a rule
the words 'nothing should seem unexpected.'"[4] This

---

[1]Cicero Tusc. 3.16.34 (trans. J.E. King, LCL,
1966, pp. 268-69). The text reads: "adversis casi-
bus triplici consolatione sanetur: primum quod posse
accidere diu cogitavit, quae cogitatio una maxime
molestias omnes extenuat et diluit; deinde quod
humana humane ferenda intelligit; postremo quod
videt malum nullum esse nisi culpam, culpam autem
nullam esse, cum id, quod ab homine non potuerit
praestari, evenerit."

[2]Plutarch Cons. ad Apoll. 115B (trans. Babbitt,
LCL, Vol. II, 1962; pp. 176-77).

[3]Cicero Tusc. 3.22.54 (trans. J.E. King, LCL,
1966, pp. 290-91). Clitomachus was the successor of
Carneades, who belonged to the new academy.

[4]Ibid., 3.23.55 Stobaeus Flor. 98.67 attributes

dogma, however, which warns men against being caught
unaware by a τύχη whose only constancy is its bewildering inconstancy,[1] became associated particularly
with philosophers of the Cyreniac school. By Cicero's
time, the notion that the sting can be taken from
evils by forethought is considered to be "the Cyreniac view."[2] One adherent of the Cyreniac philosophy,
Hegesias, is represented as having developed the doctrine of ἡδονή into a thoroughgoing pessimism.[3] Concluding that the body (and the soul, by virtue of its
sharing in the fortunes of the body) is so beset with
troubles that happiness is impossible, Hegesias held
that "life and death are each desirable in turn."[4]

---

the same teaching to Clitomachus: οὐδὲν τῶν ἀνθρωπίνων
βέβαιόν ἐστιν, ἀλλὰ πάντα φέρεται φορᾷ τινι παραλόγῳ.

[1]Buresch, Consolationum, p. 59, writes in reference to Stobaeus' two citations of Clitomachus:
"Utrum que ad consolationis sollemnem et sexcentis
modis uariatim locum perinet quo monemur ne in hac
misera uita semel conlocati uicibus fortunae cuius
constantia sit summa inconstantia frangi nos patiamur."

[2]Cicero Tusc. 3.22.52. The philosophers of the
Cyreniac school are known to have quoted as a "proof-
text" these lines from Ennius' Telamo, in which Telamon speaks of his warrior sons Ajax and Teucer:
    "I begat them and begetting knew that them
    for death I reared. Also when to Troy I
    sent them to Greece to fight for and defend,
    Well I knew to deadly warfare not for feast-
    ing sent I them."
Cited in Cicero Tusc. 3.13.28 (trans. J.E. King, LCL,
1966, pp. 260-61). For a more detailed study of this
topos, see Johann, Trauer und Trost, pp. 63-84.

[3]C.J. De Vogel, Greek Philosophy, I (3 vols.,
Leiden: E.J. Brill, 1953-1959), 169.

[4]Diog. Laert. Vitae phil. 2.93 (trans. R.D.

This viewpoint earned for him the nickname ὁ πεισιθά-
νατος, and was considered sufficiently pernicious by
Ptolemy I to warrant Hegesias' expulsion.[1] It is not
surprising to discover that Hegesias was also known
to have given time to the literary enumeration of
life's evils, a consolatory invention already known
to us from Prodicus' words in the Axiochus.

The traces we have just seen of the logical connection between Hegesias' philosophical "bearings"
and the tone of his teachings concerning consolation
provide some insight into the apparent need of the
different schools to develop their own solacia, to
fashion at least some arguments consonant with their
distinctive precepts. Among the Epicureans, signs
of this correlation between the school's basic tenets
and its style of consolation abound. Epicurus himself discounted the value of anticipating evil, and
on two grounds. It is impossible for men, he taught,
not to register distress, regardless of any exercise
of praemeditatio, if in fact they are, or believe
they are, "encompassed by evil." Secondly, sorrow
or pain can be best assuaged by a "recall [revocatio
is the term Cicero employs] to the consideration of
pleasures."[2] It is the teacher's assumption that
reason can summon the afflicted back from preoccupa-
tion with sorrows and train his gaze upon pleasures --
both those recollected and those waiting to be
enjoyed.[3] The atomist philosopher views mortality as
the dissolution of the being, and consequently urges
men not to invest hope in promises of immortality.

Hicks, LCL, Vol. I, 1931, pp. 222-23).

[1]Buresch, Consolationum, p. 59.

[2]Cicero Tusc. 3.15.33 (trans. J.E. King, LCL,
1966, pp. 266-67).

[3]Greene, Moira, p. 335.

But this argument serves to achieve one of the primary goals of consolation, as was dramatized in the person of Axiochus -- it serves to dispel the fear of death. Numerous elements of Epicurus' consolatio are to be found in the De rerum natura of Lucretius. While the extended consolatory passage in Lucretius (3.830-1094) reveals awareness of certain older arguments, especially those attributed to Prodicus in the Axiochus,[1] the section is consistently colored by Epicurean assumptions and emphases. Most illustrative of these are the words to an aging man which Lucretius imagines on the lips of Nature:

> All life's prizes you have enjoyed and now you wither. But because you always crave what you have not, and condemn what you have, life has slipped by for you incomplete and ungratifying, and death stands by your head unexpected, before you can retire glutted and full of the feast....Come, depart with dignity; thus it needs be.

Endorsing Nature's reproach, Lucretius continues:

> ...the old order always passes thrust out by the new, and one thing has to be made afresh from others; but no one is delivered into the pit of black Tartarus: matter is wanted, that coming generations may grow... This therefore is a mirror which nature holds up to us....Is there anything horrible in that?...Is it not more peaceful than any sleep?[2]

---

[1] Buresch, Consolationum, pp. 60-1, notes the use of Prodicus' argument that "death is nothing to us."

[2] Lucretius De rerum nat. 3.955-75 (trans. W.H.D. Rouse, LCL, 1931, pp. 236-37.

A few other Epicurean themes which proved useful in consolation should be mentioned. The attempt to obliterate fears of underworld punishments (mentioned above, but treated fully in De rerum natura 3.978-1023) is thought to stem from Epicurus himself. Similarly the suggestion belongs to him that "like a banqueter fed full of life."[1] one should withdraw from existence satisfied and take rest.

Our survey moves now into the period of the Second Sophistic, with its display of self-conscious literary and oratorical flourishes, even though the man who first gains our notice for his consolation writings is known for the fact that he counted style a matter of secondary importance.[2] Two consolatory writings are connected with the name of Plutarch (46-120 AD) --the letter to his wife upon the occasion of the death of their daughter, Timoxena, and the letter to Apollonius. Several ingenious explanations of the dissimilarity of the Consolatio ad Apollonium to other Plutarchian writings (and especially to the

---

[1]Ibid., 3.938. E.E. Sikes, Lucretius (Cambridge; University Press, 1936), pp. 124-25, writes: "...Epicurus was not alone in denying a Hell. The Stoic Chrysippus ridiculed the Platonic myths of reward and punishment, holding that the hell of a wicked man was his own life on earth. We do not know how far Epicurus thought it necessary to combat the popular views about a Future Life; but it seems improbable that he took them very seriously: all 'myths' were to be disdained by the philosopher, and superstitions about the Hereafter were part of this δεισιδαιμονία."

[2]See H.J. Rose, Handbook of Greek Literature (New York: E.P. Dutton & Co., Inc., 1960), pp. 401-9; Eduard Norden, Antike Kunstprosa, I (Stuttgart: B.G. Teubner, 1958), 351-92; J.M. Campbell, The Influence of the Second Sophistic on the Style of the Sermons of St. Basil the Great. (Washington, D.C.: Catholic University of America, 1922).

other consolatory letter) have not succeeded in dis-
arming doubts of its authenticity. Neither the suggestion that this lengthy and ragged treatise represents the effort of the adolescent Plutarch, nor the
hypothesis that we are dealing with an "original rough
draft" of the missive eventually sent to Apollonius
have inspired confidence.[1] What is undeniable, and
what no doubt accounted for the early attribution of
the work to the prolific author from Chaeronea, is
the similarity of tone, subject matter, and some doctrinal emphases to other known works by Plutarch. It
is legitimate to speak of the Consolatio ad Apollonium
as "Plutarchian," then, even if one harbors doubts
about whether it came from Plutarch's hand. Further,
there is a sense in which significance attaches to
this treatise-letter by virtue of a pedigree unrela-
ted to authorship, for it clearly stands in the
middle of the stream of consolation, conveying among
its basket-full of solacia many of the lessons of
Crantor's περὶ πένθους, and we know it to have been
a popular source for later Greek consolers, non-
Christian and Christian.

We shall have reason to return to certain passages in the Plutarchian writings when we consider
the consolatory writings of the Cappadocians. It is
worthwhile to review here some of the prevailing tendencies in Plutarchian consolation thought. Opinions
and assumptions of virtually all contemporaneous
philosophies spice the lectures of Plutarch -- while
attacking the Stoics for their rigorism, he employs
their techniques, and while doing battle with Epicurus' conception of a pleasurable life, he finds

---

[1]Buresch, Consolationum, pp. 65ff., was enticed
to this view of Plutarch's adolescent literary talents
by Wyttenbach. The latter contention belongs to F.C.
Babbitt, in Plutarch's Moralia, trans. F.C. Babbitt,
LCL, Vol. II, 1962, p. 106.

things in his opponent's system he can use.[1] But the predominant energies in Plutarch's thought consist of a revived Platonism, especially as it conceives the nature of the mind and of God, and a Pythagoreanism, which nourishes an expectant attitude towards super-natural phenomena.[2] For the purposes of our study, it is instructive to see how this orientation prompted a reaction to the Epicurean teaching which regarded death as annihilation. To Plutarch's way of thinking, Epicurus, in showing the terrors of the underworld to be vacuous myths, had left for the mortal a still more dreadful prospect -- the vacuum itself.[3] That death holds no horrors, argued Plutarch, is no satis-factory consolation to the mass of men, for man's "love of being, the oldest and greatest of our pas-sions,"[4] is not answered or "resolved" by nature's

---

[1]Martin P. Nilsson, Geschichte der Griechischen Religion, Handbuch der Altertumswissenschaft, II (Munich: C.H. Beck'sche Verlagsbuchhandlung, 1961), 402-3. We note that Plutarch has recourse to Epi-curus' method of allaying grief in his Cons. ad uxor. 8.

[2]See Samuel Dill, Roman Society from Nero to Marcus Aurelius (Cleveland: The World Publishing Co., 1969), pp. 520ff.

[3]Plutarch Non posse suav. viv. sec. Epic. 1091 (trans. B. Einarson and P.H. De Lacy, LCL, Vol. XIV, 1967, pp. 41-51).

[4]Ibid., 1104 (trans. Einarson and De Lacy, XIV, 130-31): "The great majority, however, have an expectation of eternity undisturbed by any myth-inspired fear of what may come after death; and the love of being, the oldest and greatest of our passions, is more than a counterpoise for that childish terror. Indeed when men have lost children, a wife, or friends, they would rather have them exist somewhere

promise of emptiness or sleep however sweet the
dreams. The Platonist must argue further that the
hope of afterlife, even with attendant risks of
punishments, is an irrepressible impulse of the human
mind, as well as the rationale and the goal for the
life which pursues virtue and truth.[1] Plutarch's
letter to his wife is not the least bit ambiguous
concerning the fate of their young daughter, and
interestingly it invokes the authority of both ances-
tral teachings and the mysteries in which they are
initiates:

---

in hardship and survive than be utterly taken away and
destroyed and reduced to nothing; and they like to
hear such expressions used of the dying as 'he's
living with us' or 'going to dwell elsewhere' and all
that represent the soul as changing but not perishing
in death..."

   [1]Ibid., 1105 (trans. Einarson and De Lacy, XIV,
138-39): "Hence in abolishing belief in immortality
they also abolish the pleasantest and greatest hopes
of ordinary men....What then do we suppose they do to
the pleasures of the good, whose lives have been just
and holy, who look forward to nothing evil in that
other world but instead to all that is most glorious
and divine?...no one impassioned for the truth and
the vision of reality has ever been fully satisfied
in this world, since the light of reason, veiled by
the body as by a mist or cloud, is wavering and
indistinct; but like a bird that gazes upward, they
are ready to take wing from the body to some luminous
expanse, and thus they lighten and disburden the soul
of the fear of mortality, taking philosophy as an
exercise in death. They regard death as so great and
so truly a blessing since they hold that in that
other world the soul will have a real life, whereas
now it is not fully awake but is living instead in a
kind of dream."

Furthermore, I know that you are kept from
believing the statements of that other set,
who win many to their way of thinking when
they say that nothing is in any way evil or
painful to "what has undergone dissolution,"
by the teaching of our fathers and by the
mystic formulas of the Dionysiac rites, the
knowledge of which we who are participants
share with each other. Consider then that
the soul, which is imperishable, is affected
like a captive bird.[1]

In the conclusion of the epistle he draws this inference from the legal prohibitions surrounding the
deaths of children:

...Our people do not bring libations to
those of their children who die in infancy,
nor do they observe in their case any of
the other rites that the living are expected
to perform for the dead, as such children
have no part in earth or earthly things;
nor yet do they tarry where the burial is
celebrated, at the graves, or at the laying out of the dead, and sit by the bodies.
For the laws forbid us to mourn for infants,
holding it impiety to mourn for those who
have departed to a dispensation and a
region too that is better and more divine.[2]

Such steady confidence in immortality is not to be
found in the letter to Apollonius, which is not at
all personal in tone, and appears to be something
more in the order of a collection of topoi. In both

---

[1]Plutarch Cons. ad uxorem 10 (trans. P.H. De
Lacy and B. Einarson, LCL, Vol. VII, 1959, pp. 600-
1).

[2]Ibid., 11 (trans. De Lacy and Einarson, VII,
604-5).

letters there is a clear appreciation of the many
follies of human existence, although the note of pessimism is more sharply struck in the Consolatio ad
Apollonium. Nowhere is this more evident than in the
quotation of Crantor in a striking passage to the
effect that from our birth from mortal seed, evil is
linked with our lives and manifests itself in the
soul's unfitness, bodily diseases and finally in the
μοῖρα θνητῶν.[1] Of course we have already observed
(for example, in considering the Axiochus and De
rerum natura) that the grim cataloguing of life's
evils, and for that matter, pessimism itself, are by
no means the exclusive property of a philosopher who
stands on one or the other side of the debate about
afterlife. The letter to Apollonius is different from
Plutarch's letter to his wife in respect to just this
issue of immortality. As S. Dill has remarked, "the
author of the Consolation to Apollonius seems at
times to waver, as Seneca did, between the idea of
extinction at death and the hope of eternal beatitude."[2] It is provocative to note, nonetheless, that
towards the end of the letter, the author resorts to
a Platonic piece of eschatology resplendent with the
imagery of judgment, and adds the assertion that
"death is...nothing else than the severing of two
things, soul and body, from each other."[3] Finally,

---

[1]Plutarch Cons. ad Apoll. 104CD.

[2]Dill, Roman Society, p. 520. See Plutarch
Cons. ad Apoll. 119-20 and 109E-110E.

[3]Plutarch Cons. ad Apoll. 121DE: ὁ θάνατος
τυγχάνει ὤν ... οὐδὲν ἄλλο ἢ δυοῖν πραγμάτοιν διάλυσις,
τῆς ψυχῆς καὶ τοῦ σώματος ἀπ' ἀλλήλοιν. Plutarch's
interest in things eschatological is well-known. His
treatise De ser. num. vind. defends divine Providence
against the complaint that postponed judgment serves
as encouragement to the unjust while the just suffer-
ers are discouraged in the delay. In the same work

the father of Apollonius is assured that his son is "with the gods and is feasting with them."[1] The impression that the author is double-minded with regard to what follows death derives more from the nature of the document, I believe, than from any trauma of belief, for we are dealing here with a "crazy-quilt" of consolatory topoi collected from many quarters.

Although we are able to treat additional features of Plutarchian consolation only as they emerge in other contexts, some mention should be made of the freedom with which traditional argumenta are used in the two letters. The topos which compares the state of man after death to that before birth is shifted by Plutarch and applied to the grieving mother, who is exhorted to recall the time before Timoxena was hers.[2] We have already seen another indication of Plutarch's willingness to improvise in his turning of the well-known topos that burial procedures are of no importance to the soul.[3] We might mention finally, the appearance of what, in Plutarch's eyes, represents the Lieblingstugend, φιλανθρωπία.[4] Because this attri-

---

(566-67D), we find his story of Thespesius of Soli, who, after a life of evil, fell from a height to his death, but on the third day revived, bringing from his "sleep" a vision of the torments in store for the wicked in the realm of the dead.

[1]Plutarch Cons. ad Apoll. 121F: νῦν μετὰ θεῶν ὤν καὶ τούτοις συνεστιώμενος.

[2]Plutarch Cons. ad Apoll. 610D. See the introductory remarks in Plutarch's Moralia, trans. De Lacy and Einarson, LCL, VII, 577-78.

[3]Above, p. 24.

[4]Nilsson, Geschichte, II, 402.

bute does greatest honor to its possessor, it is given high place in the encomiastic portions of the two consolatory letters -- Apollonius was one who "loved his fellow men" (118 A), and the two year old Timoxena, more memorably, is recalled as having attempted to share her nurse's milk with other children and even her dolls![1]

Two other Greek letter-writers deserve our attention. Apollonius of Tyana, the thaumaturge and Pythagorean philosopher whose fascinating career is chronicled by Philostratus, is credited with several letters of consolatory type.[2] Epistle 55, though it professes a sorrow which makes the writing difficult, is actually bent upon convincing Apollonius' brother to remarry after the death of his wife -- the family needs a son![3] The letter to Valerius (Ep. 58) is more interesting, for its primary argument is a philosophical one. Death, and for that matter, birth, are appearances -- the former is a passing from nature to essence, the latter from essence to nature, "though in truth a thing neither comes into being at any time nor is destroyed."[4] Proceeding on the assumption that a personal identity upon death passes back into the divine substance, the author asserts that although people lament "as soon as ever God arises out of

---

[1]Plutarch Cons. ad uxorem 608D. For this theme in Plutarch, see the passages collected in de Vogel, Greek Philosophy, III, 393-96.

[2]On the question of the authenticity of these letters, see Eduard Norden, Agnostos Theos: Untersuchungen zur Formengeschichte Religiöser Rede (Leipzig: B.B. Teubner, 1929), pp. 337-42.

[3]Apollonius Ep. 55.

[4]Apollonius Ep. 58 (trans. F.C. Conybeare, LCL, Vol. II, 1912, pp. 454-55).

mankind"[1] (via a death), the more appropriate response
would be to honor death and resign to God the person
who had appeared to exist. Here we can discern the
earmarks of neo-Pythagorean philosophy turned to the
purposes of consolation (and perhaps an example in
microcosm of that school's often-touted attempt to
combine Platonic dualism and Stoic monism).[2] Moving
somewhat arbitrarily over several centuries, we focus
upon a letter of the Emperor Julian (331-363), whose
zeal for the preservation of antiquity's religion
and folkways also expressed itself in the attention
he paid to the rhetorical arts. In an epistle to
Himerius, written to console him over the death of
his wife, Julian furnishes us with a model Greek consolatio of the fourth century.[3] We find within the
letter the kind of elaborate simile and flattering
admonition which characterizes the literature of the
new sophists: Himerius' deceased wife is likened to
a brilliant torch whose flame has died down, and
the consoler, in the course of saying how unnecessary
the traditional paramythetic topoi are for so wise a
person, manages to utilize a good number of them.[4]
The anecdote retold for Himerius by way of an example
is that account of Democritus' harsh therapy to the
mourning Darius (above, page 6), although once again
Julian denies that his friend needs such a lesson,
for unlike the barbarian Darius, he is a Greek, a
learned man whose rationality is capable of curbing

_____

[1]Ibid., (trans. Conybeare, II, 456-57).

[2]Zeller, Outlines, pp. 301-5. On the place of
Philostratus' Apollonius in the neo-Pythagorean
school, see Nilsson, Geschichte, II, 415-26.

[3]On the identity of Himerius and the debate concerning the authenticity of the letter, see Julian,
(trans. W.C. Wright, LCL, Vol. III, 1923, pp.
xlviii-xlix).

[4]Julian Ep. 69.

grief.[1]

Even though we shall soon need to take a closer
look at the rules and conventions of funeral oratory
in the era of the Cappadocians, we cannot proceed to
the Roman consolations without some remarks on the
influence of the oratorical tradition upon consolation. The funeral speech, or λόγος ἐπιτάφιος,
was, in its Greek beginnings, devoted to the dead of
a city or state and consisted largely of elements of
praise for the heroes.[2] Of such a type is the speech
of Aspasia already described in connection with Plato's Menexenus. Orations devoted to individuals are
to be found in the fifth century B.C., and the Encomium on King Evagoras (the work is more truly a
treatise on Kingship) by Isocrates (436-388), along
with the Epitaph composed by Hyperides (389-322),
Demosthenes' imitator, are frequently cited as "show-
case" funeral oratory.[3] In the early years of the
Christian era, during the reigns of Domitian and
Trajan, a Stoic-Cynic philosopher with a penchant for
touring the empire to deliver popular lectures composed three speeches which warrant our attention.
The twenty-eighth and twenty-ninth discourses of Dio
Chrysostom concern a young boxer named Melancomas.

---

[1]Ibid.

[2]Gorgias of Leontine (5th C. B.C.) is noted for
an oration before the Athenians which preserves to
us traces of the Gorgian σχήματα.   See Rose, Greek
Literature, p. 279.

[3]See Stephen Usher, "Oratory," in Greek and Latin
Literature, ed. J. Higginbotham (London: Methuen and
Co., Ltd., 1969), pp. 365-6, and Beyenka, Consolation in Augustine, p. 7. The ninth oration of Isocrates for Evagoras, as Buresch pointed out long
ago, is not an ἐπιτάφιος λόγος in the strict sense,
though ancient rhetoricians so classified it. The

After extolling his virtues at considerable length,
both pieces allude to the poet Menander's statement
(which consolers never tired of using): "He whom
the gods love dies young."[1] Of greater interest is
the discourse, set in the form of a dialogue, which
bears the name of the person mourned, Charidemus.
The scheme of the writing revolves around Dio's dis-
covery that the deceased had composed, just prior
to his death, a consolatio for the comfort of his
family and friends. Charidemus' "last words" offer
three explanations (which are at the same time estimates) of human existence. According to the first,
the world is "a prison prepared by the gods"[2] in
which the natural elements, soul and body with their
attendant anxieties, etc., conspire to punish us
until death permits an escape. A second view, which
Charidemus is more eager to relate, conceives of
the community of man as a colony established by the
gods, regulated by shadowy imitations of the ideal
laws which hold sway in the city of the deities.
In the early years of the experiment the gods visited
and supervised human affairs, but later "permitted
us to manage for ourselves as best we could"[3] -- hence
the onset of injustice and crime. The final image
portrays the universe as the setting for humanity's

---

oration was delivered before Nicocles, the son of
Evagoras, eight years after his father's death.
See Buresch, Consolationum, p. 89.

[1]Plutarch Cons. ad Apoll. 119E: ὃν οἱ θεοὶ
φιλοῦσιν ἀποθνῄσκει νέος.

[2]Dio Chrys. Or. 30.11: δεσμωτήριον ὑπὸ τῶν θεῶν
κατασκευασμένον (trans. Cohoon, II, 408-9). Cf.
Plato Phaedo 62B, where the term used is φρουρά.
According to Charidemus' theory, humanity's descent
from the Titans is the cause of the gods' vindictive-
ness.

[3]Dio Chrys. Or. 30.27 (trans. Cohoon, II, 422-
23).

festival, prepared by the king. The labors of our
lives, it is said, are no more than reaching for something on banquet board. The measure of enjoyment by
each is according to his own nature (the drinking
habits of Intelligence and Intemperance are contrasted
pointedly), and the grace with which guests take their
leave is in keeping with their bearing throughout the
feast.[1] Whether or not it is possible to see in these
"world-views" the footprints of the sophist's known
philosophical pilgrimage,[2] the Platonic derivation of
a substantial number of images is plain, and the

---

[1]Ibid., 30.43 (trans. Cohoon, II, 432-35):
"And when they have to depart, the dissolute
and intemperate are pulled and dragged away
by their slave attendants with discomforts
and spells of sickness, shouting and groan-
ing the while, and having no knowledge whatever where they have been or how they have
feasted, even if one or another remains a
very long time. But the others depart erect
and standing securely upon their own feet
after bidding farewell to their friends,
joyous and happy because they have done nothing unseemly. God, therefore, looking upon
these things and observing all the banqueters,
as if he were in his own house, how each person has comported himself at the banquet,
ever calls the best to himself; and if he
happens to be especially pleased with any
one, he bids him remain there and makes
him his boon companion; and thenceforth this
man regales himself with nectar. This resem-
bles the beverage of Sobriety, but is clearer
by far than the other and purer because, as
I think, it belongs to divine and true sobriety."

[2]See Dio Chrysostom, (trans. J.W. Cohoon, LCL,
Vol. II, 1939, pp. 395-98).

"frame" of the discourse itself is reminiscent of the
Phaedo, in which Socrates' last words comprise the
main part of the dialogue.[1]

The ninth oration of Aelius Aristeides (d. 189
A.D.), which contains some consolatory materials,
receives only a nod here, for we shall want to refer to
it in connection with the structure of the funeral
sermons of the Cappadocian Fathers. Similarly, little more than a word of gratitude can be expressed
for Lucian's περὶ πένθους. As is often the case, the
chiding of the satirist reveals a great deal about
the mourning and consoling practices of "the general
herd, whom the philosophers call the laity,"[2] and a
sampling of elements of the cynic diatribe is cleverly
supplied in Lucian's musings about what the subject of
all the wailing would say, if only he could raise
himself upon his elbow!

Three fourth century rhetoricians, all authors
of funeral orations, gained the lavish praise of the
Emperor Julian: Himerius, Themistius and Libanius.
Two of the last-named author's writings are of particular interest. In his Oration 17, Libanius created
a monody which bore the strong imprint of the Second
Sophistic -- the images and comparisons used to forti-
fy the lamentation are, by more ancient and more
modern standards, too overwrought to be compelling.[3]
Oration 18, which pretends to be a funeral speech actually delivered, shifts suddenly from lament to a supposed reproof from the deceased ruler. There follows a

---

[1]Ibid., pp. 395-6.

[2]Lucian De Luctu 2 (trans. A.M. Harmon, LCL,
Vol. IV, 1925, pp. 112-3.

[3]Libanius Or. 17. Examples are numerous, but
note especially the string of "alases" in Or.
17.27ff.

series of <u>solacia</u>, one of which argues that it is
wrong to bewail the blow of fortune which delivered
the Emperor into the company of the gods.[1] Libanius
appends the <u>topoi</u> that fate's decree is ἀνίκητα, and
that survivors of Julian must return thanks to the
gods for the manner in which he provided happiness
for all citizens by blocking the ways of destiny.[2]

Space permits only a word about the Roman <u>lau-
datio</u> at the end of this parenthetical look at the
Greek oratorical tradition. C. Buresch writes that
the Roman funeral speech did not develop into a care-
fully-tooled literary product, and seems to have
retained the feature of private rather than public
use.[3] The appearance in the West of the elaborate
funeral speech among the works of Ambrose, Bishop of
Milan (4th C.), is correctly attributed by M. Beyenka
to "the fact that he depended on the Greek Fathers
in his writings and speeches, not only for content,
but also for form."[4]

Any treatment of the earliest and most influential Latin consolation writings must come to terms
with the public and private sorrows of M. Tullius
Cicero, for to his considerable disillusion over
Roman political affairs was added the nearly incapacitating death of his only daughter in 45 B.C.
An effective consoler of others, as we learn from
his epistle to Titius (<u>Fam</u>. 5.16),[5] Cicero apparently

---

[1]Ibid., <u>Or</u>. 18.296.

[2]Ibid., <u>Or</u>. 18.298.

[3]Buresch, <u>Consolationum</u>, pp. 121-2. Also Beyenka, <u>Consolation in Augustine</u>, pp. 9-10.

[4]Beyenka, <u>Consolation in Augustine</u>, p. 10.

[5]M.E. Fern, <u>The Latin Consolatio as a Literary</u>

33

gained no comfort from his own teachings. Neither
were the best efforts of his learned friend, Sulpicius
Severus,[1] able to penetrate the grief which encompassed him at Tullia's death.[2] In these circumstances,

---

Type (St. Louis, Mo.: St. Louis University Press,
1941), p. 9, calls Cicero's letter to Titius "the
very first extant specimen of the consolatio in Latin
literature...written, it is generally supposed, in 46
B.C." Among the topoi which Cicero employs: we are
human beings, and suffering is the human lot; the grim
state of civil affairs ought to reconcile us to
departure from the world; by one's wisdom it is possible to do for oneself what time does -- lessen the
pain of grief. Cicero's inability to heed his own
consolatory arguments is explained by quotation from
the Oileus of Sophocles:
> And there is none of wisdom so possessed,
> Who with mild words has soothed another's woes,
> But does not, when a turn of fortune comes,
> Fall broken by his own calamity;
> So words, for others wise, his own need fail.
This passage is in Cicero Tusc. 3.29.71 (trans. King,
p. 309).

[1]Cicero Fam. 4.5. A comparison of argumenta
reveals that the two men drew from a common storehouse of themes.

[2]Cicero writes to Atticus of his intention to
construct a fanum to Tullia: "I want it to be a
shrine, and that idea cannot be rooted out of my mind.
I am anxious to avoid its being taken for a tomb,
not so much on account of the legal penalty as to get
as near to deification as possible." Cicero Att. 12.
36 (trans. E.O. Winstedt, LCL, Vol. III, 1919, pp.
72-3). See the remarks by Franz Cumont, After Life
in Roman Paganism (New York: Dover Publications,
1959), p. 32 (Hereafter cited as After Life).

Cicero undertook to compose his own <u>Consolatio</u>,[1] for
which task he gathered all available wisdom of his
predecessors -- especially the words of Crantor's
περὶ πένθους.[2]

Although Cicero's <u>Consolatio</u> is lost to us, the
<u>Tusculan Disputations</u> which he wrote within the year
undoubtedly contain much of its content (and quite a
bit more). This lengthy writing is a treasure-trove
of information about consolatory philosophies and
techniques. Of the five books, the first and third
are occupied with matters related to the practice of
consolation. The dialogue between the two figures
in Book One presents pro and con (that is, Platonic
and Stoic-Epicurean) arguments on the question of
afterlife, and we find Cicero the lawyer and adherent
of the New Academy's scepticism intent mainly upon

---

[1]Cicero <u>Att</u>. 12.14 H.J. Rose comments on this
passage: "...with an odd return to his usual vanity
in the midst of his very genuine sorrow, he points
out to Atticus that no one else had yet written a
consolation to himself." H.J. Rose, <u>Handbook of Latin
Literature</u> (New York: E.P. Dutton & Co., Inc., 1960),
p. 189.

[2]Neil Hultin, "The Rhetoric of Consolation: Studies in the Development of the Consolatio Mortis"
(unpublished Ph.D. dissertation, Johns Hopkins University, 1965), p. 83. Hultin points out in his study
that because neither <u>De consol</u>. nor Crantor's περὶ
πένθους, are extant, <u>it is</u> impossible to ascertain
the exact nature of Cicero's indebtedness. Fragments
of Cicero's consolation survive in Lactantius <u>Div</u>.
<u>Inst</u>. 1.5; 1.15. Buresch, <u>Consolationum</u>, pp. 95-
108, using the testimonies of Cicero's <u>Tusculans</u>,
books one and three, Jerome (whom he suggests had
access to Cicero's consolation), and the Plutarchian
<u>Consolation for Apollonius</u>, isolates passages he
believes to have been in the lost work.

airing the positions. What becomes clear as the book unfolds, however, is that the point at issue does not hinge upon the outcome of the debate over immortality. For it is Cicero's primary purpose to demonstrate that neither proposition frustrates consolation. Whether it be shown that death has no encore or that it opens upon the realm of Truth, in either case it is proved that no evil befalls the dead.[1] But it is worth asking whether Cicero, a year after his daughter's death, puts forward the proposition of afterlife with academic detachment. Does he assume that in such matters as these the critical mind can do no more than judge which argument "[approximates] more nearly to the semblance of truth"?[2] While Cicero remained an advocate of the caution of the New Academy, it is also true that his later writings, no doubt affected by the keenly felt loss of Tullia, reveal an openness -- indeed, more than an openness -- to religious and philosophical teachings about the afterlife. So it is that certain grounds for belief in immortality of the soul seen in the Tusculan Disputations (1.13.30-1.26.58) are visible in other Ciceronian works which precede and follow it: as all men believe in the gods, so also belief in afterlife is the consensus

---

[1]Cicero Tusc. 1.8.16. "M" states at the outset that he wishes to show that "non modo mallum non esse, sed bonum etiam esse mortem." Hultin, "Rhetoric of Consolation," pp. 84ff. analyzes this part of Cicero's argument most admirably.

[2]Recall this measured estimate of the debate at the conclusion of Cicero's work De natura deorum. A similar brand of wariness of dogmatic certitude, a mark of the Academicians, is seen in Cicero's remarks after a survey of view of the soul in Tusc. 1.11.23: "Which of these views is the true one it is hard for a divine being to determine; which is the most probable is a difficult question." Tusculans, trans. King, pp. 28-9.

gentium;[1] nature itself testifies for immortality in the fact that all men are deeply anxious about the future; the soul is self-moving, and quod semper movetur, aeternum est (I.23.53- a teaching for which Cicero credits the Phaedrus 245); the phenomenon of memory argues against mortality (1.24.57-9); the soul possesses divine attributes -- vigere, sapere, invenire, meminisse.[2] A particular form of this teaching is used to good effect as an inducement to patriotic and statesmanlike virtue in the Somnium Scipionis, written more than a decade before the Tusculan Disputations. In the dream, Scipio Africanus the Younger is consoled by the hope of the heavenly life awaiting all those who have lived pious lives and advanced the fortunes of their country, and C.N. Cochrane is among those who detect in Cicero's thought even at this time (ca. 54B.C.) "beliefs ...reinforced by certain intimations of personal immortality, based on philosophic fancies derived from Pythagoras and Plato."[3] In his study, After Life in

---

[1] Cicero Tusc. 1.13.30.

[2] For this summary of arguments I am indebted to the work of Hultin, "Rhetoric of Consolation," pp. 90ff. He also cites parallels in two other Ciceronian works, De senectute and Somnium Scipionis.

[3] Charles Norris Cochrane, Christianity and Classical Culture (New York: Oxford University Press, 1957), pp. 60-1, where the full statement runs as follows: "The Somnium Scipionis represents the frail embodiment of his hope for a political salvation, and in it we may perceive the sanction for that hope. This depends, in part, upon traditional Roman beliefs regarding the stock; the faith that, while the individual was the creature of a day, the 'family' was immortal; the business of its members, while they live, being to 'carry the person' of the family, showing themselves worthy representatives of the

Roman Paganism, F. Cumont suggests that Cicero's grief over Tullia drove him to the conviction that she lived among the gods, and proceeds to speak of the double impact of his study of Posidonius and his dealings with the Senator Nigidius Figulus:

> "[Cicero] gave vent to his sorrow in writ-
> ing a Consolatio, and in its preserved frag-
> ments we see him strangely impressed by the
> pythagorean doctrines: he speaks of the
> soul, exempt from all matter, as celestial
> and divine and therefore external, of the
> soul's life here below as a penalty inflicted
> on it because it is born to expiate anter-
> ior crimes....Cicero's sensitive spirit,
> troubled by the perplexing problem of our
> destiny, did not turn to the old discredi-
> ted beliefs but to the new conceptions
> which a mystical philosophy had brought from
> the East. Hortensius and the Tusculans,
> written in this period of his life, show us
> the empire which the Neo-Stoicism of his

---

ancestors whose names they bear. But, in the case of Cicero, these beliefs were reinforced by certain inti-mations of personal immortality, etc." See Cicero Somnium Scipionis 14; 20. Rose, Latin Literature, p. 186, writes of the dream: "...Cicero ends with a vision of the other world; Scipio has a dream in which he is shown the heavenly habitation of great and righteous souls and bidden to prepare himself for such a dwelling when his career on earth is ended. This eschatological passage was greatly to the taste of the fourth century A.D., the more so as it repro-duced, not pure Stoicism nor any other of the later views, but Platonizing Stoicism, of the type made popular by Poseidonius, and therefore not very much out of tune with the neo-Platonic speculations of that age." The doctrines of Cicero's De senectute 19-23 bear out the same tendency in Cicero's thought.

master and the Neo-Pythagoreanism of his
fellow senator then exercised over his mind,
saddened and disillusioned as he was, and
show us too how he sought consolation for
the private and public ills which were
overwhelming him in the luminous doctrine
of a blissful survival.[1]

The interest which the Tusculan Disputations hold for
students of consolation is, if anything, increased
by the subject of Book Three, which concerns itself
with the nature of distresses, especially grief, and
the ways in which different schools have set about
proving what Cicero firmly maintains: Est profecto
animi medicina, philosophia.[2] In addition to an
abundant supply of topoi (grief is vain; time heals;
there is no evil in death, and so on), Cicero here
informs us of the consolatory remedies (and of their
intellectual underpinnings) employed by the important
philosophical schools. We learn, for example, the
solacium for which Cleanthes was noted, that evil has
no existence. The inference to be drawn from the
proposition was that distress was unreal, and grief
unnecessary.[3] Chrysippus considered it his chief
task as consoler to disabuse people of the idea (an
idea, he says, long ago hardened into custom) that
mourning is a duty and obligation.[4] Book Three of
the Tusculans, while preserving to us much useful
information from the debate about the limits of permissible grief, points to the Stoic ingredient in
Cicero's later viewpoint. He quotes Chrysippus with
approval: "Bravery is the knowledge of enduring
vicissitudes or a disposition of soul in suffering
and enduring, obedient to the supreme law of our

---

[1]Cumont, After Life, pp. 32-3.

[2]Cicero Tusc. 3.3.6.

[3]Ibid., 3.31.76; 3.32.77..

[4]Ibid., 3.31.76.

being without fear."[1]

What we have attempted to outline in brief compass here should indicate the rich yield of Cicero's writings for those attempting to make sense of the range of ideas and energies which generate the consolation tradition. Cicero's contribution, and preeminently the Tusculan Disputations, make visible to us the several facets of an enterprise which, from Crantor's time to his own, had become a literary genre (and a philosophical depository) all its own.

The works of the Roman Stoic, Seneca, who wrote in the first century A.D., are frequently characterized as being preoccupied with the subject of death.[2] Whether as a cause or a result of this, he is responsible for several noteworthy consolation pieces. The letters of condolence, contained in the correspondence to Lucilius,[3] generally repeat certain themes which are by now familiar to us: patientia is urged upon the grieving; reason, or to say the same thing, philosophical study is said to enable one to face the issues of life; comfort is to be had in the realization that death cuts short life's ills; and the griefstruck is exhorted to recall that life is a loan to be repaid in an ungrudging spirit.[4] Seneca clearly

---

[1]Ibid., 4.24.53 (trans. King, p. 387). Cicero admits to a notion that, despite criticism of the sort that Carneades had levelled, the Stoics may be "the only true philosophers." See Greene, Moira, pp. 354-6.

[2]Max Pohlenz, Die Stoa, I (Göttingen: Vandenhoeck and Ruprecht, 1959), 305.

[3]Seneca, Seneca: Ad Lucilium Epistulae Morales, trans. by R.M. Gummere, LCL (3 vols., New York: G.P. Putnam's Sons, 1917-1930).

[4]Ibid., Eps. 13, 24, 30, 49, 63, 93, 107.

is not in full agreement with all Stoic pronounce-
ments. He draws back, when the situation requires it,
from the more austere Stoic strictures against grieving, on the grounds that such would be "inhumanitas
...non virtus."[1] In Epistle 82.9, Seneca challenges
the syllogism of "the master, Zeno," with its conclusion that death is no evil (giving the clear inference, again, that grief is irrational and illegiti-
mate).[2] But to Seneca's intriguing doctrine of immortality, if such language applies to his position, let
us return in a moment.

Three Senecan "letters," to Marcia, to Helvia
and to Polybius, in fact demand classification as
treatises. The letter to Polybius on the death of
his brother is a transparent attempt to gain an inter-
cessor with the emperor,[3] for Seneca's exile on the

---

[1]Seneca Ad Lucilium 99.15-21. Note Seneca's
distinction of tears in 18-9: "...I hold that with
the wise man some tears fall by consent, others by
their own force... When the first news of some bitter
loss has shocked us... then tears are wrung from us
by the stroke of grief, shakes both the whole body
and the eyes also, from which it pressed out and
causes to flow the moisture that lies within. Tears
like these fall by a forcing-out process, against
our will; but different are the tears which we allow
to escape when we muse in memory upon those whom we
have lost...This sort of weeping we indulge; the
former sort overcomes us." (trans. R.M. Gummere,
LCL, Vol. III, 1925, pp. 136-43).

[2]Zeno's syllogism runs: "nullem malum glorio-
sum est; mors autem gloriosa est; mors ergo non est
malum."

[3]Frank O. Copley, Latin Literature (Ann Arbor:
University of Michigan Press, 1969), p. 291: "This
was quite clearly an attempt to win the intercession

island of Corsica was becoming tedious. Somewhat
attractive is the treatise to Helvia, also written
from exile, in which Seneca sought to allay his
mother's anxieties over his plight. The work
addressed to Marcia some three years after the death
of her son deserves particular attention. Among
solacia urging moderation in grief, reminding that
mortals beget mortals, and the like, there is an
unusual passage dealing with the prospect of life
beyond the grave. Seneca assures Marcia that her
trips to the burial grounds are empty gestures, for
her son "is eternal and has reached now a far better
state, stripped of all outward encumbrances."[1] Seneca
then imagines the words of Marcia's father, Cordus,
who describes in vivid terms the life he and her son
and all the blessed enjoy -- an existence happily
free from limited vision and ignorance. Because
nothing of what the future holds is hidden to those
who dwell above, Cordus is able to reveal to Marcia
a mystery of distinctly Stoic flavor: there awaits
all souls -- those who enjoy the celestial habitation
as well as those who brave the hardships of earthly
existence -- the conflagration which must precede
the renovation of the universe.[2] It is important to

---

of Polybius with the emperor; it revealed one of the
strongest aspects of Seneca's character: he could
scarcely have thought very highly of the unprincipled
Polybius, yet in this work he was able to flatter him
in fulsome terms, apparently without feeling the
slightest twinge of conscience." Several writers,
including Buresch, have sought grounds upon which
Senecan authorship might be denied.

[1]Seneca Marc. 26.5 (trans. John W. Basore, LCL,
Vol. II, pp. 88-9).

[2]The conclusion of the letter to Marcia reads:
"And when the time shall come for the world to be
blotted out in order that it may begin its life anew,

note that τὸ ἔσχατον τοῦ πυρός[1] is considered by Stoic
thinkers to be ordered by Providence -- it occurs
κατά τινας ἑιμαρμένεις χρόνοις. Seneca thus offers
this concluding doctrine as a _solacium_ (it is not a
counsel of despair), and assures the long-saddened
mother with the final words, "Happy, Marcia, is your
son, who already knows these mysteries."[2] While this
notion of a cosmic death (more properly, a reduction
to _antiqua elementa_, as Seneca says) following upon
individual deaths may contribute to the impression
that Seneca "wavers" between denial and affirmation
of afterlife, it is overstating the case to see
Seneca here pulling the rug from beneath Platonic
notions of immortality which he clearly found attractive. We encounter here, rather, a fact of philoso-

---

these things [i.e., men, countries, mountains, seas,
etc.] will destroy themselves by their own power, and
stars will clash with stars, and all the fiery matter
of the world that now shines in orderly array will
blaze up in a common conflagration. Then also the
souls of the blest, who have partaken of immortality,
when it shall seem best to God to create the universe
anew -- we, too, amid the falling universe, shall be
added as a tiny fraction to this mighty destruction,
and shall be changed again into our former elements."
(_Ibid._, 94-7). "Chrysippus takes great pains to show
that this conflagration is not the death of the world,
for death is the separation of the soul and the body
whereas here 'the soul of the world is not separated
from its body but continually grows at its expense
until all its substance has been absorbed.'" Quoted
from Émile Bréhier, _The Hellenistic and Roman Age_,
trans. by Wade Baskin (Chicago: University of
Chicago Press, 1965), p. 50.

[1]Stobaeus _Ec._ 1.17.3, where the phrase is attributed to Cleanthes.

[2]Seneca _Marc._ 26.6 (trans. Basore, II, 96-7).

phical life in an eclectic era, the uneasy conjunction
of originally distinct motifs, and specifically the
modification of a view of immortality required, philosophically, by the Stoic eschatological dogma. As we
consider consolation writings by Christian authors,
it will be one of our concerns to determine the extent
to which doctrine and philosophy of the early church
conform to, modify, or seek to "purge" the philosophical interests borne by the time-tested consolatory
commonplaces.

We conclude our overview of the development of
the consolatio with a few remarks concerning Pliny
the Younger (61-114 AD). The works of a "very
worthy third-rate classicizer,"[1] Pliny's letters concerning the deaths of friends are valuable for our
purpose precisely because they preserve the format as
well as many of the stock arguments of such epistles.[2]
Most of Pliny's letters are intended for a wider
audience, with the result that what they lack in
spontaneity they make up in careful adherence to the
current epistolary canons.[3] A certain restiveness,
about the "received tradition" of topoi is evident
in Pliny. He asks a correspondent for "some arguments which are uncommon and resistless, that neither
the writing nor the discourses of the philosophers can
teach me."[4] Considerable attention is paid in the

---

[1]H.J. Rose, Handbook of Latin Literature, (New
York: E.P. Dutton & Co., Inc., 1960), p. 417.

[2]Pliny Eps. 1.12; 3.7,21; 5.5,16; 7.19; 8.1. A.N.
Sherwin-White, The Letters of Pliny (Oxford: Clarendon Press, 1966), p. 452: "Though Pliny writes many
letters about the deaths of friends, he never writes
a letter of consolation such as he suggests to Marcel-
linus in V, 16, 10."

[3]Sherwin-White, Pliny, pp. 16-18.

[4]Pliny Ep. 1.12 (trans. B. Radice, LCL, Vol. I,
1969, pp. 38-41).

letters to eulogy of the deceased,[1] and several solacia
recur: the subject is said to have lived a full life;
the transitory nature of existence is underscored;
time will be needed, it is written, for the mourner
to become more responsive to the usual kinds of condolence. Nor is Pliny reticent to draw from the
library of examples: he retells the tale of the tears
of Xerxes, who wept when he looked over the masses
and considered that none would be alive in a hundred
years.[2] If anything may be called distinctive in the
tone of Pliny's consolatory efforts, it is a detect-
able diminution of optimism. For him death is consistently seen as an event which robs family, friends
and the world of a laudable soul. In this it is legitimate to regard Pliny as being more dependent upon
the traditions of eulogy and lament than upon specifically consolatory themes.

It has been my purpose in this survey to sketch
the emergence of a literature. In the process I hope
to have exposed some of the motifs, ideas and themes
which were delivered by history into the hands of
three fourth-century Christian bishops of Cappadocia
who took their classical educations and their reputa-
tions as rhetors quite seriously (whatever their dis-
claimers). Certain large questions are simply the
proper subjects of the consolation, and these clearly
were not to be avoided by the consoler. Indeed, it
was his special business to deliver some penetrating
and helpful word about the imponderables of life and
death and sorrow. Perhaps it is possible for us to
reduce to a manageable number those key issues around

---

[1]See the use of eulogistic elements in Pliny's
treatment of the sensitive question of Correlius'
suicide in Ep. 1.12.

[2]Pliny Ep. 3.7. This story, first told by Hero-
dotus (7.45) is also known to Jerome (Ep. 60.18a),
who, according to Buresch, learned it from Cicero.

which themes and motifs developed. We might isolate,
in the first place, the persistent attention to man
as one at the mercy of event - he is the one buffeted
by fate. Here several kinds of motifs come into play.
Man experiences τὰ ἀνθρώπινα as cruel frustrations --
all that fills existence from birth to death is dis-
appointed hope, and the inevitable movement towards
decay and extinction. Or, man is the creature who
can discern behind the seemingly random occurrences
an unstoppable machinery which assures him of a grand
design. We meet also the tireless observation that
the "law of nature" should never come as a surprise:
men who are not gods have no excuse for forgetting
what is the μοῖρα θνητῶν. Considerations of fate
and the lot of man can be seen to prompt, then, quite
different thematic lines about the structure of events
and the nature and limits of mortal existence.

Another of the larger questions with which consolations necessarily deal is that of death's aftermath. Attempts to remove death's sting employ widely
divergent arguments. We have noted in several forms
the motif which makes death the end of all sensation,
hence nothing to be feared (Democritus, Epicurus).
More likely to crop up again in our study of Christian consolation are those consolatory motifs which
speak of the soul's existence either in the world or
in the body as an entrapment in alien territory. The
world is a prison, keeping what is essential to per-
sonhood from its original home above. Common to this
line of reasoning is the idea that at death, to use
Plutarch's image, souls flee bodies like birds
uncaged. From these considerations of death stem
particular eschatologies and quite distinct ways of
envisioning the circumstances of the person being
mourned. With regard to the former, we have noted a
view of death as the dissolution of being which pro-
duces no eschatology in the strict sense, but a picture of the return of elements to replenish the store
of matter, "that coming generations may grow" (Lucretius). We have also encountered notions of an escha-
ton of fire affecting the entire cosmos (Seneca),

46

and the conviction of a heavenly resting place,
where the soul of a young girl may join the company
of the gods (Plutarch). The blissful state of the
dead is frequently counterpoised to all that the life
of mortals entails, and even the most glowing eulogy
may function as preparation for an account of greater
riches and honors being enjoyed beyond the mundane
penitentiary.

The problem of mourning itself provokes numerous
constellations of themes. Grief, so it is argued, is
the necessary reaction of creatures capable of affection, and it is a disorder requiring the balms of
time and reason. But a contrary motif regards grief
as the liability of an unphilosophic mind -- the burden of one who has not perceived that death and
deprivation of worldly pleasures and possessions are
matters of indifference.

Another series of themes and topoi collect
around the attention given by consolers to θεραπεία,
a topic obviously closely related to the analysis of
grief, and here we mention only a few of the countless prescriptions: premeditation upon misfortunes
prevents distress; historic and mythic examples of
grief borne nobly abound, and can serve as inspi-
rations to the forlorn; reason must be trained and
encouraged, so that it might either reject or control
(a portentous "either-or," as we shall discover) the
passionate stirrings which victimize the disconsolate.
These questions, then - the dispensations of fate
(or the gods), death and afterlife, grief and its
therapies - and the motifs which consolers frame in
answer to them, are the "constants" of the genre.
It is from these materials that the Cappadocians are
to fashion their own solacia, and whatever ideas or
beliefs they choose to add to the craft of consolation, their debt to the tradition which grew up before
them will never have faded entirely from view.

At least a few general conclusions seem capable
of being extracted from our survey. The consolatio

as a genre in its own right first comes on the scene
with Crantor's περὶ πένθους, a work which collected the
lore and teachings from poets, playwrights and philosophers deemed appropriate to the purposes of consolation. Important among these sources was the pseudo-
Platonic Axiochus, whose traces can be detected well
into the Christian era. Crantor's writings, and the
consolatory notions of the Epicureans and Stoics
(though we have only fragmentary evidence bearing
upon the positions of the older Stoa) in time joined
to create an arsenal of topoi. And the genre, by
its nature, welcomed any and all argumenta by which
the fact of death might be "answered," and grief
might be overcome. The one consolatory stream divides
necessarily into two lingual branches, typified by
the works of Plutarch and those of Cicero. A Plutarchian continuation of the literary type can be said
to flow into the Greek writings of the early centuries of the Christian era. Among non-Christian
writers we may point to Apollonius of Tyana and the
rhetoricians of Athens, like Libanius; among Christian authors, most notably the Cappadocian Fathers,
whose consolations represent the earliest (extant)
collection of such writing by Eastern churchmen. In
the West, Cicero was the inspiration for Latin consolers, and here, with Pliny and Seneca, we see
traces of the genre in works of Tertullian and
Cyprian,[1] and still more thoroughgoing indebtedness in the writings of Jerome, Ambrose, and

---

[1]Tertullian's De patientia 9 treats the question
of grief, admitting its power over those who suffer
misfortune, but asserting that Christian teaching
makes grief needless. In a sermon entitled De mortalitate, Cyprian addresses himself to the ravages of
the great plague which struck in the Roman Empire in
251-255 AD. A study of Cyprian's work by M.L.
Hannan shows some striking parallels with consolatory
themes met in the writings of Cicero and Seneca. M.L.
Hannan, Thasci Caecili Cypriani De Mortalitate (Washington: Catholic University of America Press, 1933).
Consolation motifs which appear in Cyprian's De bono
patientiae 11-18 can also be shown to draw upon the

Augustine.[1] The appearance of tidiness in this
"genealogy" should not be spared a confrontation with
messier realities, as only one area of consideration
reveals. Uncharted philosophical energies, not represented by specific consolatory titles, intruded upon
and became part of the literature of consolation.
Writers like Posidonius and Epictetus were known and
used, if not named, in letters and treatises concerning death, the soul, and the problem of grief. From
the first century through the third, as we see from
the writings of Philo, Clement and Origen, Alexandrian
thinkers received and elaborated the kinds of philosophical traditions with which we have been occupied

---

tradition. We notice, for example, in ch. 12 the
statement concerning the child's first action upon
entering the world -- wailing: "By a natural foresight, the untrained soul laments the anxieties and
labours of the mortal life, and even in the beginning bears witness by its wails and groans to the
storms of the world which it is entering." Translation is from Alexander Roberts and James Donaldson,
eds., The Ante-Nicene Fathers (Hereafter, ANF) (10
vols., Grand Rapids, Mich.: Eerdmanns, 1899), V,
487. This idea is found in the Pseudo-Platonic
Axiochus 366D.

[1]For Jerome, see especially Ep. 60. Ambrose's
works occasioned by the death of his brother Satyrus
and his panegyric on the emperor, Theodosius, deserve
particular mention. It is conceded that Ambrose was
influenced in his consolation writings by the efforts
of the Cappadocians, but it is also true that he drew
upon the western branch of the tradition, as was
shown long ago in the work of K. Schenkl, "Ueber
Benutzung der verloren gegangenen Schrift Ciceros
'De Consolatione' in der zweite Rede auf Satyrus,"
Wiener Studien 16 (1894), pp. 38-46. On Augustine,
see Beyenka, Consolation in Augustine. The most
thorough study of this literature is: Charles Favez,
La Consol. Latine Chrétienne, cited above, p.4, n.2.

in this survey of the <u>consolatio</u>. At certain points,
therefore, one must back away from describing a
clearly defined "trajectory" of consolation-thought
and simply acknowledge the truth that the genre was
comprised of commonplaces -- <u>loci communes</u>.

A further reflection suggests itself. Though
it is legitimate to speak of "commonplaces", we have
observed that these teachings were not so devoid of
intellectual definition as to be usable by anyone,
regardless of his viewpoint. In more than a few
important instances, philosophical discretion determined the shape and the sound of consolation. Even
in a philosophical atmosphere of easy lending and
borrowing, the consoler was inclined towards some
arguments, and for doctrinal reasons found he was
unable to employ others. Nowhere in the literature
of consolation is this fact more clearly demonstrated than in the ongoing debate which turned on the
question whether grief is allowable - whether it is
an unavoidable or an inexcusable reaction to misfortune. Far from being an item capable of reduction
to an all-purpose commonplace, this question involved
tenets and definitions which constituted the battle
lines between philosophies. After a consideration
of the formal characteristics of consolation writings, we shall take up this issue in closer detail,
not only because of its persistent recurrence in the
literature we have been treating, but because rever-
berations from this argument are still to be found in
later Christian writings. When attention is turned
to the Cappadocian consolers, we shall want to see
to what extent the fourth century advocates of "the
true philosophy", as Clement of Alexandria called
Christianity, asserted their distinctive teachings
in a literature already dominated by inherited argument and numerous <u>solacia</u> and controlled by the conventions of rhetorical practice.

CHAPTER 2

FORM IN CONSOLATORY LETTERS,
ORATIONS AND SERMONS

It is provocative to observe that the beginnings
of the Christian movement are discovered in a collection of letters. Stirred by a vision of itself as a
holy community of unprecedented breadth and intensity,
the church's earliest activities and ideas are shown
to us in its communiqués. Missionary hopes for cities
and towns throughout the Mediterranean, the intentions
of the preacher to establish and maintain the authority of his gospel in a new community of Christians
in Asia Minor or in Rome, concern to instruct those
neophyte believers whose practice of the new-found
faith had brought rumor of excess or dispute -- for
all these purposes and more the epistle proved to be
an excellent instrument. And the mind of a Church
Father like Eusebius would have regarded it as yet
another part of the divine plan that the period from
100 B.C. to 100 A.D. saw a burgeoning interest in
epistolography in Rome[1] and more refined means of
transportation throughout the empire (facilitating,
among other things, communication by letter).[2] "So
ward der Brief die erste literarische Form der jun-
gen Religion und er blieb in grosser Beliebtheit,
auch dann, als die Christen sich eine nach der ander-
en die Formen der heidnischen Literatur aneigneten."[3]

---

[1]J. Sykutris, "Epistolographie," Real-Encyclo-
pädie der Classischen Altertumswissenschaft. Supplementband V, p. 218 (Hereafter, P-W, for Pauly-Wissowa).

[2]Dill, Roman Society from Nero to Marcus Aurelius, pp. 205-7.

[3]Sykutris, "Epistolographie," P-W, S.V, p. 219.

The setting which concerns us, fourth-century Cappadocia, confirms this remark by J. Sykutris. The epistle has become for Basil the chief means of episcopal communication. Through his letters he requests favors of those highly-placed in government (and sometimes challenges their actions!), he clarifies doctrinal matters, seeks theological allies, attacks the heterodox, chastens fallen monastics, conveys his pastoral concerns and wishes. Basil's correspondence, in short, is a window to much that is important in life within the church and the Empire from about 350 until the Caesarean bishop's death in 379. A particular kind of epistle, the letter of condolence, is the focus of our attention in this instance. Nineteen such letters, addressed to several kinds of situations, are found in the correspondence. We propose to ask how these letters compare, in terms of form, with other Greek and Latin samples of this literary type. The investigation of components and arrangement of materials undertaken here cannot rest with the letters, however, for among "die Formen der heidnischen Literatur" appropriated by the Cappadocian theologians is to be found the type of consolation so closely related to the epistle, the funeral oration or sermon.

The goals of this chapter are modest. We want to clarify those guidelines influencing the structure of consolatory compositions -- to spy out the conventions pertaining to form which exemplary Greek and Latin letter-writers and orators created and observed. Secondly, we hope to discover the ways in which Basil's epistles and the orations of the two Gregories adhere to the prevailing rules seen to be operative in the literary and rhetorical traditions. The clear purpose of consolatory writing, and the substance of the various solacia make clear lines of demarcation between form and content difficult to draw, but in this part of the study the intention is to concentrate on structural aspects of the letter and the oration. What were the necessary ingredients of a consolatio? What elements in what pattern were

52

believed to constitute an effective (and <u>correct</u>) consolatory letter or speech?

    Our knowledge of epistolary technique, especially among the Greeks, is better garnered from samples of genuine letters than from collections of τύποι ἐπιστολικά of the sort ascribed (falsely) to Demetrius of Phaleron.[1] As a consequence, the writings of several of the consolers already mentioned should provide some idea of epistolary practices which were in force, East and West, before and during the fourth century.

---

[1]Demetrius of Phaleron (ca. 350-283) is not the author of the model letters attributed to him, as Richard Bentley's study nearly a century ago proved. These letters, printed in Hercher's <u>Epistolographi Graeci</u>, pp. 1-6 are of "unknown, but later, date and authorship" (Rose, <u>Handbook of Greek Literature</u>, p. 357). The reader of Ps. Demetrius' artificial consolatory letter is struck, regardless of the lack of information about provenance of the collection, by its closeness in design to the epistles we are considering. The opening sentence reads: "When I received word of the sufferings which you met at the hands of thankless fate, I was deeply grieved, thinking that what happened had not affected you more than me." This one-sentence proem ushers in enunciation of the unhappinesses of the human condition: nature withstands neither time nor age, and for this reason one must suffer misfortunes, sometimes unexpected and often undeserved. The consoler, according to the scheme, is to exhort the bereaved to bear what has happened as lightly as possible; the future will bring relief, and reason will make the burden less troubling. We see here in very brief compass what other genuine letters of condolence reveal to be the chief ingredients: introductory comment about reception of the news, and its effect upon the consoler; lament; consolatory <u>topoi</u>; hortatory conclusion.

The letter of Plutarch to his wife serves well as an initial example of the format of an epistula consolatoria. An introductory passage (608 B-C) informs Timoxena (also the name of the deceased daughter) that Plutarch missed the messenger and heard the unwelcome news of his daughter's death from a granddaughter. Because of Plutarch's absence from home, he expresses concern for his wife's distress in a letter which presumably will reach her before he can return. There follows a section of the epistle which is taken up with praise of the two-year old (her good temper and friendliness). Within this fatherly eulogy, Plutarch takes pains to commend his wife's deportment in a time of crisis (608F-610C), creating something of a laudation within a laudation. By discussing examples of excess of lamentation, which he regards as "no less shameful than incontinence in pleasures,"[1] the author is able to render both praise and advice on how grief is borne. A clear transition to the consolatory segment of the letter is marked by Plutarch's urging that his wife project her thoughts back to the time before their daughter was born, when there was "as yet no complaint against fortune."[2] A series of argumenta is provided which invokes the memory of pleasures with young Timoxena (thus softening the force of the request he has just made), reminds of the power of reason to stabilize the distraught, and asserts an immortality doctrine as over against the view which considers death a "dissolution."[3] A concluding exhortation picks up the essen-

---

[1] Plutarch Cons. ad uxorem 609B (trans. P.H. De Lacy and B. Einarson, LCL, Vol. VII, 1959, pp. 586-7).

[2] Ibid., 610D (trans. De Lacy and Einarson, VII, 594-5).

[3] Ibid., 611 E-612 A: καὶ μὴν ἅ τῶν ἄλλων ἀκούεις οἵ πείθουσι πολλοὺς λέγοντες ὡς οὐδὲν οὐδαμῇ τῷ διαλυθέντι κακὸν οὐδὲ λυπηρόν ἐστιν....

tial thrust of the _solacia_: outward behavior should
be consonant with the laws and customs (which assume
the child's presence in "a region...that is better and
more divine"), and, through rational governance of passion the inner disposition should be kept free "from
pollution and purer and more temperate."[1]

Julian's epistle to Himerius,[2] upon examination,
bears a similarity to the Plutarchian Consolatio ad
uxorem when considered in terms of basic elements.
Again, a prefatory passage recounts how the author
heard of the misfortune, and relates how he was unable
to read the letter telling of the death of Himerius'
wife without tears (412 A). An expression of sympathy
turns upon the idea that the event is tragic in
itself, but all the more so in that it has befallen
so worthy a man as Himerius. The panegyric element
in the letter is compressed, and we find the mourning
husband as well as his wife the subject of praise.
She, Julian writes, was a "virtuous wife," like a
brilliant torch too quickly extinguished. It is
Himerius' status as orator (which is to say, in this
period and context, σοφός) which brings him commendation, and sets the stage for a string of consolatory
arguments which Julian is shortly to retract (on the
grounds that Himerius is surely sufficiently well-
versed to have knowledge of them all).[3] Having

The note on p. 601, LCL, reads: "Cf. Epicurus Ad
Menoeceum 124, and κύριαι δόξαι, II (quoted in Mor.
1103D and 1105A): ὁ θάνατος οὐδὲν πρὸς ἡμᾶς. τὸ γὰο
διαλυθὲν ἀναισθητεῖ·τὸ δ'ἀναισθητοῦν οὐδὲν πρὸς ἡμᾶς.
Death is nothing to us; for what has suffered dissolution has no perception, and what has no perception
has nothing to do with us."

[1]Ibid., 612B, (trans. De Lacy and Einarson, VII,
604-5).

[2]Julian Ep. 69.

[3]Ibid., 412C. On this artful device of Julian's,

shelved the consolatory topoi (but only after their
display!), Julian offers in their stead a story which
by itself, he dares to promise, will bring release
from suffering -- λύσιν...τοῦ πάθους (412D-413D). The
reader is surprised, even if Himerius was not, to find
so much confidence invested in the account of Darius'
consolation at the hands of "the laughing philosopher" (see above, p. 6), an anecdote neither fresh
nor far-reaching. It holds no lesson more profound
or comforting than this: life is filled with such
trials.[1] To return to the form of Julian's epistle,
though, we see that its consolatory portion ends with
the story, adding only this exhortation with its
already familiar ring: find the remedy for your distress from within, and allow reason to exercise the
power over grief which it has in common with time.[2]
In effect, Julian's letter contains a proem, eulogistic remarks about both Himerius and his deceased
wife, and a paramythetic section containing arguments
and an example (even though the author flatters his
correspondent that he is superior to these solacia).

Epistle 393 by Libanius, one of the most celebrated rhetors and men of letters of the New Sophistic, seeks to solace a certain Hierocleus upon the
loss of a favored nephew. We encounter once again
an opening statement which tells of the difficulty
of the consoler's task. Libanius' ill health accounts
for his brevity -- the circumstance calls for something of greater scope. There follows a fairly full
eulogy on Chromatius, ῥήτωρ δεινὸς καὶ ἀνὴρ χρηστός,

---

see above, chapter 1, page 28.

[1]Basil gives expression to this scarcely exalted
topos in his Ep. 5: γέμει ὁ βίος τῶν τοιούτων παθῶν.

[2]Julian Ep. 69, 413D. The same topos appears
frequently in Cicero, as for example in Att. 12.10;
Fam. 4.5.6; 5.16.6; Tusc. 3.35.

a man whom Libanius reports was a credit to his home-
land and to Athens. At intervals within the eulogy,
the writer succumbs to sorrowful outbursts (ὦ Ζεῦ καὶ
θεοί...διὰ τί πρῶτον ὀδύρωμαι).[1] Chromatius is described as one of the greatest men to have visited the
earth -- more temperate than Peleus, no less a friend
of God than Sophocles himself.[2] We meet at this point
in the letter a sharp transition of mood and idea,
for the tearful recitation of Libanius is suddenly
declared unnecessary. Consolatory topoi commence:
to have lived well, as Chromatius did, is a consolation at life's end; his fate was universal, his
achievements uncommon; such events occur in accordance
with the judgment of the deities, who are just.
Finally, Chromatius should not be mourned -- it is
better to go to the place prepared by the gods than
to waste time on earth. His fate is happy: μετε-
νειγκεῖν ἐνθένδε εἰς οὐρανόν.[3] These solacia are
concluded with an exhortation to temperate behavior,
which the author claims should not prove a difficult
charge to one so clearly in command of understanding.
The scheme, then, of Libanius' letter: proem, eulogy
and lament, consolation, and final hortatory sentences.

Similar inspections of the dominant pattern of
Latin epistulae consolatoriae do not yield significantly different results.[4] If anything, the conven-

_____

[1]Libanius Ep. 393, Libanii Opera, Vol. X, ed.
R. Foerster (Teubner), p. 381, ll. 19-20; p. 382,
1.6.

[2]Ibid., p. 383, ll. 2-3.

[3]Ibid., p. 383, ll. 15-18.

[4]See the thorough study by Sr. Mary E. Fern,
The Latin Consolatio as a Literary Type (St. Louis:
St. Louis University Press, 1951).

tions which pertain to constitutive elements and their
order in consolationes are more assiduously observed
than in Greek epistles. We find in the letters of
Cicero (note particularly his epistle to Titius, Fam.
5.16), Pliny (e.g., Ep. 1.12), and Seneca (Eps. 13,
99) the same structural outline. An exordium deals
with the grief of the writer and/or the circumstances
under which word of the death was received. A second
section of the letter is made up of a combination of
laudatio et lamentatio. The portion of the letter
which is meant to console follows, offering argumenta
and frequently, examples of persons who have borne
grief well (or badly).[1]

Generally speaking, we find these elements to be
"constants" in epistles of condolence: a proem,
offering some explanation of how the misfortune came
to the author's notice, and how he has been affected
by the news; a section of the letter constituted by
eulogistic remarks and periodic lamentations; a series
of consolatory arguments, often bolstered by tales of
the conduct of celebrated victims of misfortunes, and
concluding prayerful petitions or bits of advice to
the person addressed about how his or her travail
might best be borne.

With this pattern in mind, we turn our attention
to several representative letters of the Bishop of
Caesarea. It would be coy to set about this comparison in any suspenseful way. We shall discover in
Basil a clear indebtedness to rhetorical practices
which hold sway in the Greek tradition (and more specifically in the Second Sophistic), and it is surely
not of the sort that might have been acquired indirectly -- that is, by some sort of unconscious cultural osmosis.

---

[1]That the consolatory precepts were to precede
the examples seems to have been a firm convention.
Seneca feels obliged to apologize when he reverses
the two elements in Marc. 2.1.

The son of a professor of rhetoric of some renown in Pontus and Cappadocia, Basil trained for his
career as rhetorician (which he practiced in Caesarea
in 356-57) in Constantinople and in Athens, where he
counted among his associates both Julian and Himerius.[1]
A glimpse at the form of a few of his letters will
suffice to place him solidly within the band of practiced (and style-conscious) literary consolers. As
an example of the structure of a consolatory letter
and the clear definition of its different parts, a
better model of the type could not be found than
Basil's epistle to Nectarius (Ep. 5). The proemion
carefully recounts Basil's reception of news he prayed
would prove to be untrue. The writer joins his sorrow to that of Nectarius -- no one, he says, could
receive such tidings unfeelingly (ἀπαθῶς). Immediately Basil launches into a eulogy for the son of
Nectarius, touching upon items (prescribed, as we
shall see) relating to his family's reputation, the
hope invested in the youth by his countrymen, the
virtue of his parents. With an abruptness by which
Basil seeks to reenact, literarily, the removal of
the child from the parental embrace (ἐκ μέσου τῶν
πατρικῶν χειρῶν), the εὐλογία is broken off by a
lament: "all that happiness of home and that glad-
ness of heart has been swept away, and our whole life
has become a dismal tale." In what follows, both the
tone and the nature of the argument undergo a striking change as the consolatory portion of the letter
is begun. The παραμυθία, or consolation proper,

---

[1]Gregory of Nazianzus Oration 5.23,24. The historian Socrates reports that Gregory was a student
of Himerius (H.E. 4.26).

[2]Basil Ep. 5 (trans. Roy J. Deferrari, LCL, Vol.
I, 1961, pp. 34-5): πᾶρα ἐκείνη τοῦ οἴκου ἡ εὐθηνία
καὶ τῶν ψυχῶν ἡ φαιδρότης ἡφάνισται, καὶ ἐγενόμεθα
τῷ βίῳ διήγημα σκυθρωπόν.

is taken up in the form of several topoi, followed by
the citation of the example of Job.[1] The words of
Job 1.21 are then given a more direct application to
the tragedy at hand, and related to Nectarius' son.
A brief concluding petition speaks of the mourners'
attainment of the departed youth's purity and future
enjoyment of "repose as the children of Christ."

Basil's letter to Nectarius' wife (Ep. 6) conforms to the same pattern, and differs only in selection of commonplaces and what might be called a gentler tone. In the proem, Basil acknowledges that he
was concerned not to write too quickly, while the
injury was "inflamed," but changed his mind when he
considered the fact that he would be addressing a
Christian. A brief εὐλογία again is interrupted by
dirge-like exclamations: "O plague of an evil demon!
...O earth, that has been compelled to submit to an
affliction like this!"[2] The παραμυθία which follows
speaks, among other things, of the fact that things
which befall men are never without providential
design (ἀπρονόητα), and the letter closes with the
prayer formula we might have expected: may the
grieving mother have οἴκοθεν...τῆς παραμυθίας τὰς
ἀφορμάς.

Mention should be made of just two of the other
consolatory letters by Basil. They reveal the same
succession of formal elements: proem, eulogy and
lament, and consolation. In Epistle 206 the proem
refers to Basil's infirm condition, which alone
prevents him from presenting his consolation in
person. Though Basil's frail constitution in actuality warranted such introductory statements (they
occur with tedious frequency in his correspondence),

_____

[1]Ibid., pp. 36-7.

[2]Ibid., (trans. Deferrari, LCL, Vol. I, 1961,
pp. 40-1).

60

this particular justification for the use of letter
as substitute for an actual meeting is a commonplace
-- an epistle is understood to be "the means of conversation for those who are so widely separated in
person."[1] The consolation to Elpidius on the loss
of his grandson lacks the usual eulogistic phrases,
for the purpose of the letter is to recall the Bishop
to an "example of manliness."[2] There is in Basil's
writing here a mild reproof and an exhortation to
leave undue sorrow behind, returning to service of
"the Master." In a final example, Epistle 300 to the
father of a student who has died, we observe that all
ingredients necessary to a proper consolatio are in
place. Basil begins by recounting how he sympathized
as one "in the second rank of fathers of Christians,"[3]
until reason reminded him of τὴν φύσιν τῶν ἀνθρωπίνων. The commendation of the youth is tailored to
his accomplishments as a student, making mention of

---

[1]Basil Ep. 185 (trans. Deferrari, LCL, Vol. II,
1962, pp. 474-5). See the remarks of Klaus Thraede,
Grundzüge griechische-römischen Brieftopik, Zetemata,
Heft 48 (Munich: C.H. Beck'sche Verlagsbuchhandlung,
1970), pp. 117ff., on Basil's frequent references to
ἡ τοῦ σώματος ἀσθένεια. On the letter as a substitute for the presence of the writer, see the same
work, chapter three. See also Sr. M. M. Wagner, "A
Chapter in Byzantine Epistolography: The Letters of
Theodoret of Cyrus," Dumbarton Oaks Papers, Vol. IV
(Cambridge, Mass.: Harvard University Press, 1948).
Sr. Wagner has gathered some interesting materials
on the letter as an extension of friendship in Greek
tradition, and treats the stylized proem as "psychological propaedeutic" (pp. 129-51).

[2]Basil Ep. 206 (trans. Deferrari, LCL, Vol. III,
1962, pp. 178-9).

[3]Basil Ep. 300 (trans. Deferrari, LCL, Vol. IV,
1961, pp. 218-9).

his popularity with friends and teachers. The para-mythetic section of the letter deals in the main with the problem of an early death, which Basil attempts to transform (by his argumentation) from a misfortune to a boon: "with his soul sullied by no stain has he departed, but in purity has he withdrawn to the better lot."[1] Job's utterance (1.21), rather than a prayer, closes the letter.

A comparison of the form of Basil's letters of condolence with representative letters of other writers, Greek and Latin, puts beyond any question the derivation of his techniques and the binding force which the recognized conventions hold for him. Whatever particular features in one of Basil's consolations might owe their existence to the fact that he is a Christian, and indeed an ἐπίσκοπος with pastoral obligations and sensibilities, the schema, and the consolatory procedure which is at once fashioned and controlled by the schema are the products of prescribed rhetorical theory and practice.

This picture gains much in the way of detail when the kindred genre, the funeral oration, as composed by the Cappadocian Fathers, is subjected to a comparable synoptic analysis. It will be helpful to reconstruct here some of the findings of an 1892 dissertation by J. Bauer which illuminate our subject.[2]

Although the fourth-century sophist Aphthonius produced in his προγυμνάσματα materials having to do

---

[1]Ibid., (trans. Deferrari, LCL, Vol. IV, 1961, pp. 222-3).

[2]For the argument and analysis which follow, I am indebted to Johannes Bauer, Die Trostreden des Gregorius von Nyssa (Marburg: Universitätsbuchdruckerei von Joh. Aug. Koch, 1892). (Hereafter, Bauer, Trostreden).

with the encomium,[1] a more useful treatment is found
in the De genere demonstrativo, written by Menander
of Laodicea late in the third century.[2] In his handbook for show-piece oratory, Menander divided the
orations for eulogy of the dead into four distinct
classes: (1) τὸ καθαρὸν ἐγκώμιον-- a simple or pure
panegyric, which is not delivered in connection with
a tragedy; (2) ὁ ἐπιτάφιος λόγος-- in which the encomiastic items are coupled with laments (Dio Chrysostom's Oration 29 on Melancomas is a good example);
(3) ἡ μονῳδία-which has as its stated purpose θρηνεῖν
καὶ κατοιατίζεσθαι, to indulge oneself and the
audience in lamentation and pity (e.g., Libanius'
Oration 17, the Lament over Julian); and (4) ὁ παραμυθητικὸς λόγος-- a speech which adds the task of
consolation to various combinations of elements from
the other kinds of encomia. The remarks of Menander
about the consolatory speech hold particular interest for us, first as they relate to the orations of
Gregory of Nyssa and Gregory of Nazianzus, and retro-
spectively, as I shall suggest, for the light they
cast back upon the epistles of Basil. The παραμυθητικὸς λόγος, according to Menander, sets for itself
the initial tasks of lamenting the deceased, height-
ening the sense of tragedy (by extolling the numerous
virtues of the mourned), and exciting the feelings
of pity and remorse of the audience by the power of
speech.[3] So it is that after the proem, the consola-

---

[1]Ibid., p. 6: "Aphthonios schliesst sich den
Darstellungen der früheren Progymnasmatiker an, an
Hermogenes (in der Zeit Marc Aurel's) c. 176 C. Sp.
II, 11 und an Theon, Sp. II, 109 (vor Hermogenes,
in ersten Jahrhundert nach Christus)."

[2]Menander De genere demonstrativo, in Rhetores
Graeci, III, ed. Leonardi Spengel (Leipzig: B.G.
Teubner, 1756), 368-446). (Hereafter, Menander De
demons. in Spengel, Rhetores).

[3]The elements of a proper eulogy can be learned

tory oration calls into play many of the themes and
devices of the monody, the predominant characteristic
of which is the combination of eulogy and lament.

The second part of the oration, from which it
receives its name, is ὁ παραμυθητικός. Opening with
a well-known passage from a poet or historian, the
consolatory section includes a general philosophical
observation about the common destiny of all mortals,
or some such topos.[1] At this point in the oration,
Menander counsels the introduction of narratives
(διηγήματα) from lore and history, in order that the
point only intimated in the literary citation might
be made more explicit, and be linked with events and
personages. From considerations of death and the
afflictions which fill life, the sophist urges a
transition to the theme of the happy state of the
deceased, who is viewed as an escapee from earthly
woes to the blisses of the Elysian Fields. And
from the lips of one so blessed, what would be more
natural than a reproach of those who waste their energies in misguided lamentation below?[2] Menander's

---

from Menander's outline of the ἐπιτάφιος λόγος, under
the heading τὰ κεφάλαια ἐγκωμιαστικά: τὸ γένος, ἡ
γένεσις, ἡ φύσις, ἡ ἀνατροφή, ἡ παιδεία, τὰ ἐπιτηδε-
ύματα, ἀι τράξεις, τὸ τῆς ψύχης, αἱ συγκρίσεις πρὸς
ὅλην τήν ὑπόθεσιν.
For Menander's remarks about the desired results of
the lament and encomium, see Menander De demons.,
in Spengel, Rhetores III, 11. 6-9.

[1]Ibid., 414, 11. 2-6: καὶ φιλοσοφῆσαι δὲ ἐπὶ τούτοις οὐκ ἀπειρόκαλον καθόλου περὶ φύσεως ἀνθρωπίνης,
ὅτι τὸ θεῖον κατέκρινε τῶν ἀνθρωπίνων τὸν θάνατον, καὶ
ὅτι πέρας ἐστὶν ἅπασιν ἀνθρώποις τοῦ βίου ὁ θάνατος,
καὶ ὅτι ἥρωες καὶ θεῶν παῖδες οὐ διέφυγον.

[2]Ibid., 414, 11. 19-21: καὶ τάχα που μᾶλλον μετὰ

proposed consolatory oration, then, follows an "outline" comprised of three basic parts:[1]

    I. τὸ προοίμιον
    II. τὰ ἐγκώμια, with θρῆνος
    III. τὸ παραμυθητικὸν μέρος

By means of an examination of Aristeides' Oration 11, a funeral speech commemorating Etoneus, Bauer
demonstrated the way in which Menander's hand-book
theory was practiced.[2] The proem explains why the
oration is being delivered, and is followed by ἔπαινος
-- the commendation of Etoneus' family, training,
and love of learning. Aristeides composes a lament
which refers to traits of the young man now sorely
missed, and includes a reproach of the daemons, who
gave such joy to a household, but quickly rescinded
it. The consolatory section is introduced by the
voices of the gods, who remind the mourners that
Etoneus' death did not take place without their know-

τῶν θεῶν διαιτᾶται νῦν, περιπολεῖ τὸν αἰθέρα καὶ ἐπι-
σκοπεῖ τὰ τῇδε. Καὶ τάχα που καὶ μέμφεται τοῖς
θρηνοῦσι.

[1]The fuller scheme is presented in Bauer, Trostreden, p. 26:
    I. τὸ προοίμιον
    II. τὰ ἐγκώμια with θρῆνος
        A sequence of θρῆνος, ἔπαινος, θρῆνος
    III. τὸ παραμυθητικὸν μέρος
        1. Citation. φιλοσοφεῖν περὶ φύσεως
ἀνθρωπίνγς· διηγήματα βελτίων ἐστὶ τάχα μετάστασις
τοῦ τῇδε βίου.
        2. Application of these points to
           the deceased. Praise of same.
        3. μακαρισμός: μετὰ τῶν θεῶν
διαιτᾶται νῦν.
    IV. ἐπίλογος: ὡς θεὸν αὐτὸν μακαρίσωμεν.

[2]Bauer, Trostreden, pp. 27-9.

ledge. His death, they say, calls not for wailing, but for songs of the sort sung to heroes.

Of the dozen panegyric speeches of Gregory of Nyssa, only the orations concerning Meletius, Pulcheria and Flacilla may be classified as λόγοι παραμυθητικοί. The rest either commemorate revered personalities long dead (as, for example, in Gregory's two orations on the protomartyr Stephen), or are more accurately described as epitaphs, lacking in consolatory materials.[1] Bauer's research demonstrated how completely the three consolatory funeral "sermons" of Gregory are offspring, or better, blood-brothers of the paramythetic oration so wisely practiced by the rhetoricians. The similarity of format can be amply shown from Gregory's oration shortly after the death in 358 of Pulcheria, the young daughter of Theodosius I and Flacilla.[2] In a somewhat involved introduction, we find the preacher engaging a dilemma intended to gain the interest and empathy of the congregation: to which shock should Gregory address

---

[1] Gregory's λόγοι πανηγυρικοί can be divided into two categories -- those written in honor of Christian heroes whose lives (and deaths) have taken on the authority of hagiography, and the panegyrics written to commemorate contemporaries. In the former category, besides the two orations on Stephen, there is an oration on the martyr Theodorus, three in memory of the forty martyrs, and one on Gregory Thaumaturgus. In the latter, besides the orations concerning Meletius, Pulcheria and Flacilla, there are orations in honor of Ephraem and Basil, neither of which is a consolatory speech. They fit more naturally under the classification ἐπιτάφιος λόγος. (See Bauer, Trostreden, pp. 30-1).

[2] Gr. Nyss. Oratio funebris de Pulcheria. Citations are based on Gregorii Nysseni Opera, ed. Werner Jaeger, et al. (Leiden: E.J. Brill, 1921-).

himself -- the recent earthquake, or the death of
this young girl, precious to the whole empire? Of
course, the purpose of the gathering is not in doubt,
and Gregory uses the fictitious problem to good oratorical effect: "[The death of Pulcheria] did not
ravage the lifeless beauty of buildings, nor did it
bring well-flowered inscriptions to the ground, nor
very lovely spectacles of stone, but this quake, falling suddenly, destroyed the dwelling of her very
being, so splendid in its beauty, so luminous in
graces."[1] The use of this conceit enables Gregory to
slip gently into an encomium which concentrates, as
is usual in the case of consolations for children,
upon the virtues of the parents. Consistent with the
requirements of the genre, the praise of the Imperial
family is interspersed with expressions of sorrow.
Gregory also employs the convention of dwelling upon
the physical features of the deceased, commenting
upon the beauty of Pulcheria's eyes, the flush of her
cheek, etc. Gregory heightens the element of lamentation by adding to the customary baleful interjections his recollection of the funeral scene: "Everything visible to the eye was filled with people, as
if the whole world had come together on account of
this misfortune. That holy flower borne upon the
golden bier was set before all...How the eyes were
all filled with tears, hands being slapped together,
groanings, ... making known the heart-felt pain!"[2]

---

[1]Gr. Nyss. Pulch. (Opera, IX, 462,ll. 26ff).
Trans. author.

[2]Ibid., (463, ll. 19ff), trans. by author. In
the Oration for Pulcheria, the mention of the young
girl's features takes place in the context of a consolatory argument which seeks to answer the charge
that an early death is especially cruel. However,
the two features mentioned here, the attention to
the physical attributes of the deceased, and the
re-creation (or description, in instances where the

Gregory relates how even the gems of the bier and the
torches which lighted the path of the procession were
darkened by the sorrow of the time.[1] Of at least one
technique of the παραμυθητικὸς λόγος Gregory of
Nyssa had become a master -- recall Menander's dictum
to the effect that the purpose of the lamentation is
to magnify the tragedy and to stir up the feelings of
the audience![2]

---

speech is given at the funeral) of the gathering of
the mourners are recognized parts of the monody,
which was incorporated into the paramythetic speech.
According to the design of the monody in the De demons. of Menander, the final portion of the lament
contained two topoi, ἡ ἐκφορά, ἡ σύνοδος τῆς πόλεως
and τὸ εἶδος τοῦ σώματος . For the scheme of topics
of the monody, see Bauer, Trostreden, pp. 18-21.

[1]Gr. Nyss. Pulch. (Opera, IX, 464). Trans.
author. "It did not seem to me at the time (probably
also not to the others present then) that the gold
[of the bier] outshone the beauty emanating from her
nature. But the glitterings of the stones, and the
woven garments of gold, and the flashings of the sil-
ver, and the strong and plentiful illumination from
the fire extending on each side in an unbroken line
of lanterns -- all of these things were darkened in
mourning and all shared in the general sorrow."

[2]Menander De demons. in Spengel, Rhetores, III,
413, ll.6-9: ὁ παραμυθητικὸς δὲ λόγος ὀδύρεται μὲν
καὶ αὐτὸς τὸν πεπτωκότα καὶ ἐπὶ μέγεθος ἐγείρει τὴν
συμφορὰν αὔξων, ὡς οἷόν τέ ἐστι τῳ λόγῳ τὸ πάθος, ἐκ
τῶνάφορ μῶν ὧν εἴπομεν περὶ μονωδίας...
The "stage directions" for the one delivering the
lamentation are also provocative: οὐ μὴν φυλάξει τὴν
ἀκολουθίαν τῶν ἐγκωμίων διὰ τὸ μηδ᾽ ἑαυτοῦ δοκεῖν τὸν
λέγοντα, ἀλλ᾽ ἐξεστηκέναι ὑπὸ τοῦ πάθους.
(Cited by Bauer, Trostreden, p. 19).

The line which divides the encomium - lament
from the παραμυθητικὸν μέρος in the oration is clearly visible, and given a knowledge of the scheme of
this literary type, the appearance of a biblical quotation is not surprising.[1] Since the sermon to this
point has caused suffering to gain the upper hand over
rationality, says Gregory, "it would [now] be a propitious time for the weariness of understanding to be
strengthened afresh... by the counsel of arguments"
(τῶν λογισμῶν).[2] So he is led to paraphrase St.
Paul: "One must not grieve over those who have fallen asleep, for this is the disposition of those,
only, who have no hope" (Cf. I Thessalonians 4.13).
In the argumentation which follows, the preacher
counters the complaint against untimely death with
two lines of thought. In one, he enumerates the
sufferings which would have been in store for Pulcheria had she survived.[3] Drawing upon the gospel

---

[1]It appears likely that Gregory's paraphrase,
rather than recitation of the passage is also intended rather than casual. Menander suggests that the
quotation be well-known, and that it not be given
literally: συνήθη τοῖς πολλοῖς καὶ γνώριμα, ἀλλὰ
παραδώσεις μᾶλλον.
(413, 30-1).

[2]Gr. Nyss. Pulch. (Opera, IX, 464, ll. 11ff).
Trans. author.

[3]Ibid., (465, ll. 26ff): "...it grieves you
that it happens that she did not reach old age. What
benefit, tell me, do you see in old age? Is the dim-
ming of the eyes beautiful? The wrinkling of the
cheek? The melting away of the teeth from the mouth
and the producing of unintelligible sound by the
tongue? The trembling hand, the becoming stooped
toward the ground? The onset of stumbling, the
necessity of leaning on another's arms? Being
deranged in the heart? Murmuring with the voice?

lection for the occasion (Matthew 19.14: "Let the children come to me, and do not hinder them..."), Gregory's second consolatory "thesis" focuses upon the beatitude now enjoyed by the young princess:

> So even if your child has departed, yet she has run off to her Master. She closed her eyes to you, but opened them to the eternal light. She withdrew from your table, and was delivered to the angelic board. Here the young seedling was uprooted, but in paradise she was sown. From a kingdom she was removed to a kingdom. She took off the brilliance of the purple, but she clothed herself in the robe of the heavenly kingdom...Do you see for what things she exchanged her own? The beauty of the body which is seen no more grieves you, for you do not see the true beauty of her soul, with which she now exults in the festal assembly of the heavens.[1]

Following the consolatory precepts, as we've come to expect, the speaker provides what are meant to be instructive διηγήματα.[2] The testings of Abraham and

---

-- which sufferings necessarily come upon that stage of life." (Trans. author)

[1]Ibid., p. 465, ll. 5ff. For the beatitude theme, see Menander De demons. in Spengel, Rhetores, 414, ll. 19ff; Aristeides' Or. 11.

[2]"Die Beispiele hatten nicht nur in der Rhetorik, sondern auch in den Trostschriften der Philosophen eine grosse Bedeutung; so werden denn Abraham und Hiob von Gregor als ὑποδείγματα zur Nacheiferung empfohlen und der Heldenmut und der Glaube dieser Männer in längeren Erzählungen (διηγήματα) der Zuhörerschaft vor Augen gefuhrt." Bauer, Trostreden, p. 61.

Job are recounted in picturesque language, and Gregory extracts from the narratives the lessons appropriate to the moment -- these "noble athletes" bore
their trials philosophically, and stand as ὑποδείγματα to those who are in grief, especially to those
who have lost children. We shall postpone comment
upon the theology which the preacher places upon the
lips of Abraham, Sarah and Job, as well as his concluding topos, which centers in the resurrection
belief.[1] More pertinent to our immediate subject is
the observation we can make on the basis of a close
look at the structure of the oration for Pulcheria:
Gregory's consolatory sermon, far from being a distinctly Christian homiletic invention, conforms in
every important respect to the rhetorical guidelines
established for the formation of the παραμυθητικὸς
λόγος . A number of consolatory arguments, but what
is more to the point, the form of the work itself
is taken over by the Christian preacher from the
library of Greek oratory.[2] We discover in the

---

[1]On the quite disparate estimates of a "Christian element" within this and other consolatory writings we shall have more to say later. I would only
remark here that Bauer's close paralleling of elements in non-Christian orations of this type often
passes over without mention certain arguments in the
latter which show at least a Christianization of
Greek themes (and forms). This is particularly true
of his remarks about Gregory's Oration for Meletius,
where the παραμυθητικός in particular presents some
material for which "pagan" comparisons are not so
plentiful. On the other hand, several modern writers
intent upon asserting a transformation of the genre
by Christian writers, or that "the Christian mentali-
ty, emancipated by the Cross from dolorous mourning
into living hope" (Wagner, "Byzantine Epistolography", DOP, IV, p. 159) has left the thought of the
Greek tradition behind, have, in my view, gone
beyond what the evidence will support.

[2]See Bauer's concluding remarks, Trostreden,

<u>Oratio in funere Pulcheriae</u> precisely the sort of
outline known to us from Menander's <u>De genere demon-
strativo</u>:[1]

  I. προοίμιον - the difficulty presented by the
      subject
 II. τὰ ἐγκώμια with θρῆνος
III. παραμυθητικός
    1. biblical passage; the problem of
       overcoming grief
    2. beatification motif
    3. φιλοσοφεῖν περὶ φύσεως ἀνθρωπίνης
    4. διηγήματα - Abraham and Job
 IV. ἐπίλογος

It is worthy of comment that this does not represent
the only or even the closest proximation to the rhetorical "model." Gregory of Nyssa's Oration for
Bishop Meletius is, in terms of structural characteristics, virtually identical with Menander's guidelines and also, as Bauer took pains to prove, with
Aristeides' Oration for Etoneus.[2]

Only two of the orations of Gregory of Nazianzus
contain consolatory materials in large enough measure
to warrant the title λόγοι παραμυθητικοί : Oration
18 on the Death of Gregory (his father), delivered
in 374, and the Oration for Caesarius (his brother),
which belongs to the year 369. Although a certain
aloof freedom from the rhetorical rules is sometimes

---

pp. 85-7.

[1]Adapted from Bauer, <u>Trostreden</u>, p. 58.

[2]In discussing the elements which made up the
eulogy and the monody, Bauer says: "Was diesen
Klagereden fehlt, der Trostabschnitt, findet sich in
der Rede des Aristeides, mit welcher insbesondere
die Rede auf Meletios die grosste Aehnlichkeit zeigt"
(<u>Trostreden</u>, p. 86).

claimed for Gregory of Nazianzus,[1] the assertion does
not test well. Gregory claims in the proem of his
panegyric for Caesarius, for example, that in his
surrender of himself to the "true and highest word"
he put to the side all interest in oratorical display
or renown. He proceeds, nonetheless, to deliver himself of a consolatory oration which would satisfy the
canons of the most exacting teacher of rhetoric: the
eulogy and consolatory portions contain no surprises,
except perhaps that there is less space given to
lamentation than one might expect to find. Similarly,
Gregory's tribute to his father contains two major
sections: a eulogy which consciously replaces the
usual panegyric topoi with his accomplishments as a
Christian while retaining the general scheme (Or.
18.5-40),[2] and a consolation addressed to his mother,
the widowed Nonna (Or. 18.42-3).[3] Even the oration
on Basil, while reflecting a certain independence of
style, was shown by F. Boulenger to incorporate all
items requisite for an epitaph of its kind.[4] It is

---

[1]M. Guignet, Saint Grégoire de Nazianze, p. 310,
speaks of Gregory's "splendid emancipation" from the
tyranny of rhetorical practices and rules of the era.
This is quoted in Funeral Orations, ed. and trans.
Martin R.P. McGuire, Fathers of the Church, Vol. 22
(New York: Fathers of the Church, Inc., 1953), p.
xix.

[2]Gr. Naz. Or. 18.5.

[3]Justin Mossay, La Mort et l'Au-Delà dans Saint
Grégoire de Nazianze, Recueil de Travaux d'Histoire
et de Philologie, 4e Série, Fascicle 34 (Louvain:
n.p., 1966), p. 52: "Les éloges de Césaire et de
Grégoire le père se conforment au schéma régulier
et developpent donc les consolations traditionnelles;
ils nous donnent ainsi l'occasion de mesurer avec
quelle aisance Grégoire traite les topiques de genre."

[4]F. Boulenger, Grégoire de Nazianze: Discours

established, we can conclude, that both Gregories
turned, in the composition of their consolatory homilies, to the tradition of consolation formalized (and
very nearly codified) by rhetorical practice. The
point is not registered, of course, as a criticism.
That the rhetorical craftsmanship of the Cappadocians
compels respect is conceded,[1] and more importantly,
nothing could have been more natural for educated
churchmen (especially those in the Origenist tradition) than to arm themselves with the best weapons
of the ancient and contemporary wise and turn them
to Christian purposes. Reticence about "borrowing"
of this kind had vanished among Christian authors
with the Apologists (if not Paul!); so also, in many
cases, had the practice of crediting sources! More
is at stake here than a judgment, pro or con, about
the literary creativity of the Cappadocians. We are
intent upon underlining the fact that these writings
of Basil and the Gregories cannot be seen for what
they are unless the inherited tradition of consolatio
is perceived and taken seriously. Only a clear
appreciation of the forms and the ideas which constitute the literature allows any assessment of what
might be distinctive in the consolations of the
Cappadocians.[2]

Funebres (Paris: n.p., 1908), pp. xxix-xxxi.

[1]J. Bauer remarks of Nyssa's Oration for Meletius: "Vom Standpunkte der Rhetorik der Zeit aus
wird über die Rede nur ein günstiges Urteil gefällt
werden können" (Trostreden, p. 56). Many other fa-
vorable judgments are available of the literary talents of the Cappadocians -- see, e.g., the description of Gregory of Nazianzus as an "oratorical vir-
tuoso" in Hans Von Campenhausen, The Fathers of the
Greek Church (New York: Pantheon Books, Inc., 1959),
p. 97.

[2]See above, note 1, p. 71.

Our examination of the structure of the παραμυθητικὸς λόγος provokes a few last questions and ob-
servations about the form of Basil's epistles. How
do we account for the fact that many of his letters
appear to be more complex, to have more going on in
them, than other letters of condolence of equal
length? A re-reading of the letters, with the
funeral orations in mind, helps to bring things into
focus. We see that by the fourth century two initially different kinds of consolation literature co-
exist and in fact melt into one another. The letter,
even when it tended to expand into a disputation, was
originally the vehicle of the philosophers. As such,
it occupied itself primarily with arguments directed
to therapy of the distraught soul. The consolatory
oration represented incorporation by the rhetoricians
of elements of earlier panegyric and monody, as well
as the time-tested philosophical solacia. Sentiments and utterances which had their origins in
ancient burial practices and grave-side rites had
by this time become literary, and were prefixed to
the body of solacia which were products of sages
whose ponderings about the lot of mortals had become
common philosophy, the possession of the entire culture.

In light of this development, it is understand-
able that Basil's letters (and indeed, some of the
letters of his precursors) frequently contain a more
elaborate structure than one might have anticipated
in an informal or private letter of condolence. He
is dependent upon the models of consolatory epistles,
as we have seen, and upon the elaborated tradition
of funeral oratory as well. Basil's letters of consolation are, as a result, miniature λόγοι παραμυθητικοί. As such, they conform not only to the canons
of epistolary art, but also preserve certain features
known to us from the orations. Among these we may
cite the combination of eulogy and lament (Basil's
Eps. 5, 6, 300, and noted also in the non-Christian
Greek and Latin examples), which no doubt stems ultimately from funerary rites, and the reproach of the

"evil daemon" (Eps. 5, 6).[1] The impression that Basil
draws upon the developed oratorical consolations is
further confirmed, no doubt, by the character of his
more "official" missives of condolence -- those, for
example, sent to churches whose leaders have died.
His letters expressing sympathies to the churches of
Neocaesarea and Ancyra (Eps. 28, 29), we notice, are
marked by much fuller eulogies than are found in his
usual consolations, and the epistles strike the reader as being much more in the idiom of public address.

As a point of further interest, what appeared
to be an unstylistic disjointedness at a critical
point in Basil's consolatory letter becomes explica-
ble when one has in mind the structure of the παραμυθητικὸς λόγος. Repeatedly the transition from
eulogy and lamentation to the consolation is seen to
be awkward, even jarring.[2] The change of mood from
despair to hopefulness, and the shift in ideas from
the pains of separation and loss to arguments urging
confidence that death is a good -- these transitions
appear to have strained even the ingenuity of a proponent of the New Sophistic! The sharp break which
one notices at just this point in consolation writings is not a lapse to be charged to the author, but

---

[1]The complaint against the offering of fate, and
the cursing of the daemons were suggested as effective ideas with which to begin the monody. See
Menander De demons., in Spengel, Rhetores III, 434-5.
This suggestion is followed by Libanius in the monody and the epitaph composed for the Emperor Julian,
by Himerius in the lament for his son, and by the
Cappadocians repeatedly, both in the letters and in
the consolatory sermons. See the references to the
maledictions of Envy in Gregory of Nyssa's Oration
for Meletius (pp. 443, 445, 446 in Opera, IX, Jaeger
ed.).

[2]Note the transitions in Basil Eps. 28 (LCL, I,
167), 6 (LCL, I, 40-1), 300 (LCL, IV, 221).

a "seam" which marks the juncture of two bodies of
materials which have distinct origins and purposes.
When we sense that the correspondent or orator has
failed to move gracefully from lamentation to his
string of consolatory teachings, we are in fact being
confronted by one of the structural liabilities of
a genre which is an amalgam of originally separate
crafts. There are "conflicting interests" at work
within the παραμυθητικὸς λόγος , as J. Bauer perceived,[1] and it is just this uneasy juxtaposition
which is so noticeable in Basil's letters (as also
in the letters and orations of Libanius, Gregory of
Nyssa, Gregory of Nazianzus and, for that matter,
the proposed scheme of Menander). One must suppose
that the problem goes back to the initial purposes
of the elements which came to comprise the consolatory speech. The lamentatio was meant to evoke and
intensify the sorrow of the mourners. Indeed, the
eulogy and the exclamations of woe were designed to
effect a catharsis of grief, and no great imagination
is needed to envision their use in funeral ceremonies
in the ancient world.[2] In our literature, however,

---

[1]Bauer, Trostreden, pp. 24-6.

[2]Plutarch De cohib. ira 5 (trans. W.C. Helmbold,
LCL, Vol. VI, 1962, p. 107) writes: "...the surrender of mourners to weeping and wailing carries away
much of their grief together with their tears."
Cumont, After Life, p. 47, suggests other purposes
for the lament: "The funeral cult, celebrated at the
tomb...proceeds from fear as much as from piety, for
the dead are prone to resentment and quick in ven-
geance. The unknown force which inhabits them, the
mysterious power which causes them to act, inspired
great awe...The wrath of those who had thus been
torn from their homes and their wonted way of life
was to be dreaded. Loud outbursts of grief followed
by prolonged manifestations of mourning must prove
to them, in the first place, that they were truly

77

the lamentation or monody, with its particular intentions and ideas, is made merely the initial segment
of a new kind of writing. Consequently, it becomes
little more than the preparatio for the consolatory
section, in which the whole store of philosophical
medicines is brought to bear upon the situation of
the mourner. It is no overstatement to say that the
philosophical solacia have a raison d'etre which
stands in absolute contradiction to the lament. They
are designed to suppress, not to excite, sorrow. For
this reason, virtually all of the strictly paramythetic arguments are marshalled in order to convince
readers and listeners that death is not an evil, not
an occurrence which calls for tears, and that grief
is, at best, a vain enterprise. Put in harsher
light, as it frequently is, grief is reprehensible as
an emotion beneath human dignity -- it is irrational
and therefore morally indefensible.

Our examination of the structures and devices
of consolatory letters and orations has made manifest the extent to which the Cappadocian fathers sub-
scribed to the canons which prevailed among rhetoricians of the day. The components of the consolatory
oration were seen to have "rubbed off" on the epistolary form, with the result that although we have
no orations, as such, from Basil, his consolation
letters reveal at certain points a thorough familiarity with oratorical practice -- so much so that one
feels justified in describing his epistles, on the
basis of structure and constitutive elements, as
consolatory orations in miniature.

Perusal of the formal characteristics of this
literature has produced another dividend. We have
uncovered a tension within the genre παραμυθητικὸς
λόγος which the rhetorical polish of the sophists

---

lamented and that no attempt had been made to get
rid of them."

was unable to camouflage. It has been treated here
as tension of a structural kind: the contrasting purposes of the ἐπιτάφιος λόγος - μονῳδία and the παραμυθητικός made the union of the two an uneasy marriage. It is possible, however, and I think inevitable, to see behind the development of these two
responses to death and its sorrowful aftermath a
more basic tension of ideas and attitudes. We noted
its presence as a point of division among the philosophers in the last chapter, where reference was made
to the question of whether grief was an unavoidable
or an inexcusable reaction to misfortune. We have
now encountered the structural counterpart of the
same kind of issue: is grief to be indulged, or is
it to be quelled as something injurious to the soul?

It is necessary, before commencing our study
of Cappadocian theology and philosophy of consolation,
to return for a more careful look at the debate which
occupied early "physicians of the soul", men like
Crantor and Chrysippus and their successors. From
the beginnings of this literature, the question of
the permissibility of grief was a subject of genuine
dispute. As we shall presently discover, it was a
question which could not be detached from fundamental
considerations about the nature of the soul, definition of the good, and estimates of human nature -
just those points of doctrine which separated one
philosophical tradition from another.

CHAPTER 3:
THE PROBLEM OF "APPROPRIATE GRIEF":
Ἀπάθεια AND Μετριοπάθεια

A philosopher of antiquity who set about the
task of consolation found ready to hand a vast number of argumenta of an ideologically neutral sort.
These could be used at random and were, by their very
nature, incapable of coming into conflict with this
or that doctrinal position. We have already noted,
however, that all topoi were by no means neutral in
this sense. We observed, for example, that when the
classical consolers described the state of the
deceased person, they went to some lengths to give
expression to particular notions of afterlife and
eschatology. Lucretius and Plutarch were unable to
employ similar language or imagery. It remains true,
however, that a composer of consolations had access
to numerous tested pieces of wisdom which were virtually all-purpose (and as a result, sometimes relatively innocuous). Such an author, whether Epicurean, Platonist, Stoic or Neo-Pythagorean, could
employ the topos arguing that death is no evil --
indeed, Cicero expends considerable energy at the
opening of the Tusculans proving that the proposition holds firm regardless of one's philosophical
stance. Similarly, our hypothetical consoler found
himself free to remind his reader, without at all
jeopardizing whatever creed he favored, that mortals
have no right to consider death a surprise or an
injustice. He might argue that a fate common to all
mankind cannot legitimately be regarded as a particular tragedy, or again, that death signals, at the
very least, deliverance from the toils and hardships
which fill earthly existence. He might have urged
that death be counted only the repayment of a loan.
Clearly many commonplaces like these travelled
easily and did not impinge upon the tenets of individual schools of thought.

Precisely because so much consolation thought could be appropriated by thinkers of diverse persuasions, it is striking to discover a cluster of ideas intrinsic to consolation which had sufficient edge to mark out the lines of an ongoing dispute. From the earliest time that philosophers addressed that aspect of the consoling art touching upon the definition and valuation of grief, however, a rift appeared, and a reader of the literature quickly is alerted to the fact that issues and principles more pivotal and philosophically prior to "methods of therapy" hang in the balance. Nor was the question settled in early confrontations, for traces of the battle over the propriety or impropriety of mourning run like a thread through our letters and treatises of consolation.

The briefest preview of the energies which came into play during this discussion can best be expressed in a series of questions: What is the nature of grief? Is it an involuntary or voluntary emotion? Natural or unnatural? Is mourning an expression of concern for the deceased or for the mourner himself? Is compassion a sign of an individual's strength or weakness? His wisdom or foolishness? Is it the duty of one who has learned his philosophy well to control or to extinguish his sentiments? Can one speak of "appropriate" grief? Can a person who has dedicated himself to pursuit of the good, and that alone, be affected by those events over which the general run of mankind laments?

It seems wise to state with some clarity what this portion of our study purports to do, and not to do. The beckonings to venture forth from consideration of the single πάθος of grief into the huge set of problems posed for Greek thought by the passions and their relation to the mind or soul have a Siren-like quality, and will be resisted. Our subject is the affect, the emotion, or the "state of mind" which went by the terms λύπη and aegritudo in Greek and Latin writings of condolence. We are

interested in defining the outer limits of the conflict which centered upon the human experience of
grief and its causes. Beyond that, it is our concern to take note of the meanings and philosophical
assumptions which attached to words like ἀπάθεια
and μετριοπάθεια both in early consolations and in
those Hellenistic writings upon which the Cappadocians drew for many of their consolatory teachings.

Though it is impossible to say with any certitude who precipitated the recurring arguments over
the morality of grieving (for it was decidedly a
question of ethics), it is a good guess that initia-
tors of these squabbles were advocates of what É.
Bréhier has called (somewhat prejudicially) "savage
impassivity."[1] The acknowledged master of the consolatio, Crantor of Soli, appears, at any rate, to
have had an enemy (or enemies) in view when he composed his widely-acclaimed περὶ πένθους. The pertinent passage is found in Cicero's Tusculan Disputations:

> And it is not ridiculous of the famous Cran-
> tor, who held the foremost place of distinc-
> tion in our Academy, to say, 'I do not in
> the least agree with those who are so loud
> in their praise of that sort of insensibility
> which neither can nor ought to exist. Let
> me escape illness: should I be ill, let me
> have the capacity for feeling I previously
> possessed, whether it be knife or forceps
> that are to be applied to my body. For
> this state of apathy is not attained except
> at the cost of brutishness in the soul
> and callousness in the body.'[2]

---

[1]Émile Bréhier, The Hellenic Age, trans. Joseph
Thomas (Chicago: University of Chicago Press,
Phoenix Books, 1965), p. 50.

[2]Cicero Tusc. 3.6.12-3 (trans. J.E. King, LCL,

The author of the <u>Consolatio ad Apollonium</u> attributes only the remark about the retention of sensibility in illness to Crantor, but surrounds the quotation with teachings generally considered to have come from the same source.[1] Here the term μετριοπάθεια is used with reference to mourning, and receives rather full definition:

> ...I, for my part, cannot concur with those who extol that harsh and callous indiffer- ence, which is both impossible and unpro- fitable. For this will rob us of the kindly feeling which comes from mutual affection and which above all else we must conserve. But to be carried beyond all bounds and to help in exaggerating our griefs I say is contrary to nature, and results from our depraved ideas. Therefore this also must be dismissed as injurious and depraved and most unbecoming to right-minded men, but a moderate indulgence (μετριοπάθειαν) in grief is not to be disapproved.[2]

Two leading consolers of a later era, then, under- stand Crantor to be the consolation tradition's cele- brated proponent of moderation in grief, one who calls for the tempering of an emotion which human beings possess because they are not "sprung from

---

1966, pp. 238-41).

[1]So contend Zeller, <u>Plato</u>, p. 620, n. 74, and de Vogel, <u>Greek Philosophy</u>, II, 299. The frag- ments of Crantor's writings are gathered in Guil. Mullachius, <u>Fragmenta Philosophorum Graecorum</u> III (Paris: Firmin-Didot, 1881), 139-52.

[2]Plutarch <u>Cons. ad Apoll.</u> 102C (trans. F.C. Babbitt, LCL, Vol. II, 1962, pp. 110-3).

rock."[1] Crantor was intent upon branding the counsel of indifference (Ps. Plutarch employs the term
ἀπάθεια) not only the urging of the impossible
(ἔξω...τοῦ δυνατοῦ   ), but the advocacy of an attitude which renders the body and the soul callous. A
notion of the "mean" is in view, for Crantor apparently was careful to warn that exaggerated grief was
also contrary to nature -- παρὰ φύσιν . "Moderate
indulgence" was not to become an errant concession
to the frailty of human nature. It signified, rather,
the striking of a balance between cold-bloodedness
and excessive sorrowing.[2] In another Ciceronian
work we find further evidence of Crantor's estimate
of the πάθος of grief, and of passions generally.
His name is linked with a contention of the Academy
to the effect that emotions "were bestowed upon our
minds for actually useful purposes -- fear for the
sake of mercy; anger itself ... [as] a sort of whet-

---

[1]Cicero Tusc. 3.6.12: Non enim silice nati
sumus, sed est natura in animis tenerum quidam atque
molle, quod aegritudine quasi tempestate quatiatur.

[2]See Plutarch Cons. ad Apoll. 102D. Zeller,
Plato, p. 620, writes: "We...read that he denounced
the Stoical indifference to pain as the murder of
natural feelings, and advocated moderation in grief,
which is also Platonic." Johann von Arnim, in "Krantor," P-W, Vol. XI.2, col. 1587), remarks: "Bezeich-
nend für die akademische im Gegensatz zur stoischen
Trostwiese ist, dass sich Krantor nicht Ausrottung
des Affekts (ἀπάθεια), sondern nur Mässigung
(μετριοπάθεια) als Ziel setzt. So wenig bei lei-
blichen Krankheiten und Verletzungen können wir bei
seelischen Schädigungen ganz unempfindlich und
schmerzfrei zu bleiben wünschen. Die Unempfindlich-
keit gegen den Schmerz würde allgemeine Unempfind-
lichkeit und somit eine tierische Verrohung der
menschlichen Natur voraussetzen und damit zu teuer
bezahlt werden."

stone for courage."[1] We meet here a view of the
affects which assumes them to be intrinsic to human
nature, understanding these emotions as being unnatural or "passions" in some dangerous sense only
when they become extreme. In the case of one subject to grief, impassivity and moroseness are equally
reprehensible. Familiarity with other extant fragments of Crantor's writings makes it obvious that
his remarks about the permissibility of controlled
grief do not represent an isolated opinion -- certainly not a casual precept standing in no real relation to the overall thrust of his philosophy. It
issues directly from those principles and fundamental
assumptions the endorsement of which identified him
unmistakably as a teacher of the Academy. Additional
evidence of this fact, if it is needed, can be re-
trieved from the delightful segment of Crantor's
ethics preserved in Sextus Epiricus' Against Ethicists.[2] Before a theatre audience consisting of
the entire Greek world, the philosopher parades the
dramatic personages Virtue (ἀνδρία), Health (ὑγεία),
Pleasure (ἡδονή) and Wealth (πλοῦτος), each making
a poetic bid for chief place among the goods. They
are ranked in the expected order, and Sextus remarks
about the illustration that it shows how the Academics and Peripatetics contended that "health is
indeed a good, but not the prime good...they held
that one ought to assign each of the goods its own
proper rank."[3] One is justified in perceiving a
correlation between this concept of the ordering and
graduation of multiple goods and Crantor's estimate
of μετριοπάθεια , which is distinctly "relativist"

---

[1]Cicero Acad. Post. 2.44.132 (trans. H. Rack-
ham, LCL, 1933, pp. 642-3). See von Arnim's comment, P-W, XI.2, col. 1587.

[2]Sext. Emp. Math. 51-8.

[3]Ibid., 51 (trans. R.G. Bury, LCL, Vol. III,

rather than "absolutist." In Crantor's understanding of the πάθη , that is to say, elimination of the affects is considered neither desirable nor possible. We are met, rather, with a theory of the emotions which admits of shadings and movements in relation to a "mean" (μεσότης), which discriminates, for example, between "levels" of grief. The πάθος itself, far from being an extraneous or unnatural intrusion, is seen to have been bestowed by nature. If a mourner tends to the deficiency of impassivity or the excess of unmodulated distress, his error is one which necessitates language about disharmony and disproportion. The flaw is not traced to the fact that a creature is possessed of πάθη , but that he is one who has not controlled his affective endowments. If we may anticipate for a moment what will emerge in clearer detail among Stoic consolation teachings, these aspects of Crantor's doctrine of goods and his notion of moderation point directly to a likely opposition party. Well known to us are the Cynic insistence upon virtue as the sole good[1] and the related ideals of self-sufficiency (αὐτάρκεια) and indifference (ἀπάθεια).[2] Prominent

---

1936, p. 410). In <u>Math</u>. 59, Sextus notes that "Crantor put health in the second place, adopting the order of the philosophers previously mentioned [i.e., the Academics and Peripatetics]."

[1]Diog. Laert. <u>Vitae phil</u>. 6.11 (trans. R.D. Hicks, LCL, Vol. II, 1931, pp. 12-3): "And he [Antisthenes] held virtue to be sufficient in itself to ensure happiness (αὐτάρκη δὲ τὴν ἀρετὴν πρὸς εὐδαιμονίον) since it needed nothing else except the strength of a Socrates." See the discussion in A.H. Armstrong, <u>An Introduction to Ancient Philosophy</u> (4th ed., London: Methuen & Co., 1965), pp. 117ff.

[2]Diog. Laert. <u>Vitae phil</u>. 6.15 (trans. Hicks, II, 14-5): "Antisthenes gave the impulse to the

emphases in Cynicism, both became important features
of Stoic dogma, and they present a sharp contrast to
the values held dear by our Academician.

Is it fruitful to inquire more specifically
into the origins of Crantor's μετριοπάθεια -doctrine?
The presence of the oracular byword of Greece, μηδὲν
ἄγαν , in the Consolation for Apollonius is thought
to stem from the περὶ πένθους [1], and though it is
intriguing to realize that Crantor might have utilized the saying from Delphi[2] as a proof text, the
slogan is so ubiquitous in Greek literature that our
author's mention of it can hardly be accorded great
significance.[3] More to the point, it would seem, is
a passage written by Crantor's master which relates
precisely to the question of the control of grief.
In the tenth book of his Republic, Plato discusses
the plight of a virtuous man who suffers the misfortune of losing a son.[4] The dialogue takes up several
themes which are interesting in themselves. It is
observed that a person in the throes of grief might
permit himself utterances in private which would be
shameful in public, and that grief prevents one from

---

indifference (ἀπαθείας) of Diogenes, the continence
of Crates, and the hardihood of Zeno..." Also 6.2,
which refers to Antisthenes: [from Socrates] καὶ τὸ
καρτερικὸν λαβὼν καὶ τὸ ἀπαθὲς ζηλώσας κατῆρξε
πρῶτος τοῦ κυνισμοῦ . See the remarks of J.M. Rist,
Stoic Philosophy (Cambridge: University Press, 1969),
pp. 62ff.

[1]Buresch, Consolationum, p. 50

[2]H.W. Parke, A History of the Delphic Oracle
(Oxford: Basil Blackwell, 1939), pp. 395ff.

[3]See, for example, Plato Menex. 248D, Prt. 343B.

[4]Plato Resp. 10.603E ff.

doing what crises most demand: reflecting or deli-
berating (βουλεύεσθαι) upon what has occurred ἐν
πτώσει κύβων -- "in the fall of the dice." Our attention is arrested, however, by two points in particular. The first has to do with the language used
by Plato to describe the manner in which a reasonable man will cope with sorrow: "Will he feel no
pain, or since that is impossible (τοῦτο ... ἀδύν-
ατον), shall we say that he will in some sort be
moderate in his grief (μετριάσει δέ πως πρὸς λύπην)?"[1]
The appearance of the verb μετριάζω is noteworthy in
this context. It has suggested to more than one
commentator that Plato is waging war upon the kind
of "savage impassivity" which became a banner for
men like Antisthenes and Diogenes.[2] Whether or not
a polemic tone is to be detected in the passage,
there is no room for doubt about Plato's approach
to the problem of assuaging grief. The affect of λύπη
is incapable of being eradicated -- the rational person will temper his sorrow, refusing to give way to
"bare feeling itself" (ἀυτὸ τὸ πάθος).[3] From this
latter suggestion of an inner tug-of-war emerges the

---

[1]Ibid., (trans. Paul Shorey, LCL, Vol. II, 1935,
p. 452.

[2]Ibid., n. f. Zeller, Plato, p. 444, writes:
"We cannot fail to perceive the moderation, the respect for all that is in human nature, the striving
for the harmonious culture of the whole man by which
the Platonic Ethics prove themselves such genuine
fruits of the Greek national mind. Plato is far removed from the apathy of the Cynics...: all that can
...be expected of a man is moderation and control of
his grief." We note that Diogenes Laertius, in Math.
5.31 reports Aristotle's notion of moderation of the
passions: ἔφη δέ τὸν σοφὸν ἀπαθῆ μὲν μὴ εἶναι, μετριο-
παθῆ δέ.

[3]Plato Resp. 10.604B.

second provocative issue, for the consideration of grief has led Plato into a brief account of psychology. A grief-stricken person, he says, experiences an internal conflict in which he is beset by "two opposite impulses": reason and law (λόγος and νόμος) exhort him to resist, while "bare feeling itself" impels him to capitulate to grief. Because the opposing impulses are "things" within man, it is possible to speak of his "best part" (τὸ ἀλόγιστον ... καὶ ἀργὸν).[1] It is not difficult to recognize, both from preceding references to the "better" and "inferior" parts of the soul[2], and from the passage in question, a partitive psychology -- a definition of the soul which envisions its parts (μέρη) standing in a dynamic relation of cooperation and tension. Nor are the ramifications of such a view of the ψυχή insignificant for a dispute over the relative merits of μετριοπάθεια and ἀπάθεια , for it is obvious that a definition of the soul which incorporates the seat of the passions is logically bound to an ethical strategy of moderation rather than extirpation. The πάθη , far from being removable from the ψυχή , issue from an integral part of the soul itself. They are not alien intruders into the precinct of pure rationality, even when seen to be in tension with the λογιστικόν part, τὸ βέλτιστον of the soul. The manner in which the basic bipartition of the soul leads to a tripartite scheme is evident in several Platonic works. Book Four of The Republic contains an account of the movement from an initial delineation of λογιστικόν (rational) and ἀλόγιστικον (irrational) parts to a further division of the irrational element into θυμικόν (irascible or high-spirited) and ἐπιθυμητικόν (appetitive).[3] The

---

[1]Ibid., 10.604B-D.

[2]Ibid., 10.603.

[3]Ibid., 4.439.

"high spirited" element is a "helper of reason by
nature unless it is corrupted by evil nurture,"[1]
and Plato portrays an alliance of "the rational part"
(which rules, "being wise and exercising forethought
on behalf of the entire soul") and "the principle of
high-spirit," enabling the duo to "preside over the
appetitive part which is the mass of the soul in
each of us."[2] Striving to underline the analogy
between the three classes in the state and the soul's
structure, Plato ends with a conception of the ψυχή
which emphasizes a harmony of the three principles.[3]
In the optimal situation, a "natural relation of controlling and being controlled by one another" is
maintained.[4] The three-fold character of the soul
is likened in the Phaedrus to a charioteer and a
team, "the two horses driven by reason, one of which
strives upwards to the realm of ideas, while the
other endeavors to pull the team into the realm of
the earthly."[5] And in a striking passage in the

---

[1]Ibid., 4.441A (trans. Shorey, LCL, Vol. I,
1930, pp. 404-5).

[2]Ibid., 4.441E-442A (trans. Shorey, I, 410).

[3]Ibid., 4.444D. T.M. Robinson, Plato's Psychology, Phoenix: Classical Association of Canada, Suppl.
Volume VIII (Toronto: University of Toronto Press,
1970), p. 43: "Whatever reservation Plato may have
about his new doctrine, elements of it are an un-
doubted advance on the psychology of the Phaedo. Conflict of motives -- a conflict within the soul itself
-- is now fully recognized, and a psychology is out-
lined which to a large degree caters for it. No
longer is the conflict between body and soul, as in
the Phaedo; the conflict lies rather within the
soul itself, as in the Gorgias."

[4]Plato Resp. 4.443D ff.

[5]Eduard Zeller, Outlines of the History of Greek
Philosophy (13th Ed., New York: The World Publishing Company, Meridian Books, 1931), p. 153. The

<u>Timaeus</u>, in keeping with the physiological interests
of the work, Plato locates the parts of the soul
within the human frame. The immortal principle
(ἀθάνατον) of the soul resides in the head, separated by the neck from the mortal kind (θνητόν),
which is placed in the chest ("between the midriff
and the neck in order that it might hearken to the
reason").[1] This part of the soul, characterized by
courage (ἀνδρία) and spirit (θυμός) is depicted as
a "buffer zone" between the rational, counselling
part and the ἐπιθυμητικόν, that seat of the appe-
tites found in the lower abdomen.[2]

As is well known, the tripartite psychology
does not represent the only "formula" within Platonic writings -- indeed, its incompatibility with the
uncompounded (αξύνθετος) soul of <u>Phaedo</u> 78c has
been noted repeatedly. It is impossible for us to
enter the controversy about Platonic psychology,
except to acknowledge, first, the judgment of P.
Merlan to the effect that "Plato's statements concerning the nature of the soul are inconsistent,"[3]
and to point to the fine recent study by T.M. Robinson, which prompted him to conclude:

> As far as the doctrine of 'personal' <u>psyche</u>
> is concerned, the dialogues...suggest no
> particular development on Plato's part. On
> the contrary, he appears to use particular
> 'models' of <u>psyche</u> (uniform, bipartite,
> tripartite, etc.) to suit particular con-
> texts, and seems to be peculiarly unbound
> by dogmatism in this regard till the end

---

passage to which reference is made is the <u>Phaedrus</u>
246A ff. Cf. Robinson, <u>Plato's Psychology</u>, pp. 122-3.

[1]Plato <u>Tim</u>. 70A (trans. R.G. Bury, LCL, Vol.
VII, 1952, pp. 180-1).

[2]<u>Ibid</u>., 69ff.

[3]A. H. Armstrong, ed., <u>The Cambridge History of</u>

of his life.[1]

We have undertaken this brief foray into Plato's treatment of the problem of grief and the doctrine of the soul which informs it in Republic 10 because it sheds light on the teaching of μετριοπάθεια found in Crantor's περὶ πένθους. The digression had another purpose as well. We shall see that as things unfold in the Hellenistic philosophical tradition, the partitive definition of the soul becomes identified as "Platonist," and especially so, as it is counterposed to Stoic psychology.[2] Consequently, when we have occasion to note changes in consolers' attitudes towards ἀπάθεια and μετριοπάθεια (for example, departures from the doctrines of their own traditions), we shall need to be sensitive to concurrent important shifts in school principles -- shifts which are indicative of major reorientations in ethical and psychological theory and practice. The arguments revolving around the proper therapy for grief, especially as they appear beginning in the second century B.C., must be scrutinized, as suggested above, not as random and "neutral" topoi, but as evidences of philosophical realignments and new oppositions which distinguish the Hellenistic period, and form

---

Later Greek and Early Medieval Philosophy (Cambridge: University Press, 1967), p. 28 (Hereafter, Armstrong, Later Greek and Early Medieval Philosophy).

[1]Robinson, Plato's Psychology, p. vii.

[2]Diog. Laert. Vitae phil. 3.90 is representative of what later commentators considered Plato's psychological model to be: ἡ ψυχὴ διαιρεῖται εἰς τρία τὸ μὲν γὰρ αὐτῆς ἐστι λογιστικόν, τὸ δὲ ἐπιθυμητικόν, τὸ δὲ θυμικόν. The last, says Diogenes αἴτιόν ἐστι τοῦ θαρρεῖν καὶ ἤδεσθαι καὶ λυπεῖσθαι καὶ ὀργίζεσθαι. See also Plutarch De virt. mor. 442A, and Cicero Tusc. 2.20.47-8; 4.4.10-1.

the boundaries of the intellectual world into which Christian consolers necessarily stride.

Crantor's notion of μετριοπάθεια revealed a sturdy confidence in reason's ability to control and modulate the emotions (themselves part of the soul, according to the Platonic conception of ψυχή). To his way of thinking the affect of grief, while admittedly liable to excesses of callousness or exaggerated mourning, was, from a more positive angle, seen to be the source of mercy -- a natural endowment with a potential for creating virtuous attitude and action. Grief, in itself, he regarded as an involuntary πάθος, a given potentiality in the human make-up. Sorrow was not able to be eliminated, only checked. The wise man was the temperate man, and a wise man suffering misfortune was able to keep a sense of proportion. He was one in whom "a moderate indulgence in grief [was] not to be disapproved."[1]

There prevailed among the Stoics of the fourth and third centuries a radically different assessment of the πάθη , and therefore a different therapeutic strategy for the particular πάθος of grief. Zeno of Citium, the founder of the school (and a teacher whose career overlapped that of Crantor)[2] studied with the Cynic Crates, and later with the Megarian Stilpo who, Stobaeus tells us, counted the impassive soul the highest good.[3] The position of the older

---

[1]Plutarch Cons. ad Apoll. 102E:... τὴν δὲ μετριο-πάθειαν οὐκ ἀποδοκιμαστέον.

[2]Crantor and Zeno died within a few years of each other, the former in 262/1 B.C., the latter in 264 B.C.

[3]Stobaeus Flor. 108.33. Cited in Émile Bréhier, The Hellenistic and Roman Age, trans. Wade Baskin (Chicago: University of Chicago Press, Phoenix Books, 1965), p. 31.

Stoics with respect to the general and particular
issues in question is captured in two statements which
fall close together in Diogenes Laertius' account of
Zeno:

> Now they say that the wise man is passionless
> (ἀπαθῆ εἶναι τὸν σοφόν), because he is not
> prone to fall into...infirmity.[1]

> Nor indeed will the wise man ever feel grief
> (οὐδὲ μὴν λυπηθήσεται τὸν σοφόν), seeing
> that grief is an irrational contraction of
> the soul (τὸ τὴν λύπην ἄλογον εἶναι συστολὴν
> τῆς ψυχῆς)...[2]

It is instructive that Diogenes reports a Stoic clarification of the first of these comments. It is possible, they assert, to attribute the term ἀπάθεια
also to a bad man, in which case it connotes callousness and obstinacy. No endorsement, certainly, of
that brand of "apathy" is intended.[3]

How then did the older Stoics understand ἀπάθεια?
What are the underpinnings of their philosophical
ideal of freedom from affects? It is necessary to
sketch in broad strokes the rudiments central to the
ethics of the Stoa.

The entire moral theory is grounded in the
assumption of a cosmos permeated by λόγος , a cosmos
in which "everthing that happens is determined by

---

[1]Diog. Laert. Vitae phil. 7.117 [Johann von
Arnim, Stoicorum Veterum Fragmenta III (4 vols.,
Stuttgart: B.G. Teubner, 1968), #448 (Hereafter,
SVF)]

[2]Ibid., 7.118 (SVF III, #412).

[3]Ibid., 7.117. See Rist, Stoic Philosophy, pp.
51ff.

sovereign Reason."[1] The human being is positioned in
this universe as pre-eminent among creatures because
he is endowed with reason. The ruling principle
(ἡγεμονικόν) in man is pure reason, a fragment (ἀπό-
σπασμα) of that Logos which sustains and directs all
things. Because his soul has the property of reason
itself, man is uniquely able to understand and give
conscious assent to the laws by which the universe
operates. When Zeno took as his motto "life (or
living) in agreement with nature" (τὸ ὁμολογουμένως
τῇ φύσει ζῆν),[2] it was an expression capable of
restatement as "life in accordance with reason."
When the Stoic asserted that virtue was the only
good, and that it was the only permissible end (τέλος),
his claim issued from these precepts. This comes
clear in a passage from Diogenes Laertius:

> Virtue [is] the goal towards which life
> guides us ...living virtuously is equiva-
> lent to living in accordance with the ex-
> perience of the actual course of nature...
> for our individual natures are parts of
> the nature of the whole universe...[3]

And, a few lines later:

> ...virtue...is a harmonious disposition,
> choice-worthy for its own sake and not
> from hope or fear or any external motive.[4]

Establishing virtue as the sole, not the chief good

---

[1]Edwyn Bevan, Stoics and Sceptics (Oxford:
Clarendon Press, 1913), p. 30.

[2]Diog. Laert. Vitae phil. 7.87.

[3]Ibid.

[4]Ibid., 7.89.

-- as the τέλος which "is in a category by itself,"
as J. Rist has put it, the Stoics proceed to argue
that none other of the things men count as goods has
positive moral value. Virtue alone is good, vice the
only evil.

The wise man's only legitimate concern, then, is
the condition of his soul (ἡγεμονικόν), which is all
reason. He is to maintain that virtue as a fixed
disposition (διάθεσις)[1] of the soul, enjoying the
stability resulting from unconcern for external
things and eventualities. Tranquility of this kind
is the sage's _natural_ state, as E. Bevan's words
illustrate:

> ...the attitude of the Wise Man to the inner
> good -- the good which consisted in a cer-
> tain direction of the will -- really was
> other than his attitude to any outside thing.
> His attitude towards every outside thing
> was emptied of desire -- that is why they
> were all alike _indifferent_ (ἀδιάφορα) in
> respect of good.[2]

Consonant with this close definition of the good,[3]
but under the pressure of providing guidance for
some practical decisions to be made by everyman
(the Stoics were embarrassed by the scarcity of
sages!), these moralists divided external things
into three classifications: προηγμένα or "preferred" (beauty, health, wealth and the like),
ἀποπροηγμένα or "unpreferred"(poverty, pain, etc.)

---

[1]Plutarch De virt. mor. 441C (SVF I, #202).

[2]Bevan, Stoics and Sceptics, p. 58.

[3]See Eduard Zeller, The Stoics, Epicureans and
Sceptics, trans. Oswald Reichel (New York: Russell
& Russell, 1962), pp. 230-3.

and the ἀδιάφορα or "indifferent" in the strict
sense.[1] Though the "preferred" and "deprecated"
classes represented things and conditions of "appre-
ciable positive or negative value,"[2] they were neither goods nor evils -- thus not ultimately important
to the wise man. Since they did not pertain to the
good of the ἡγεμονικόν , and had no real bearing
upon that virtue which suffices in itself for human
happiness, they were not to be desired or feared.
For the sage, health or loss of health, plenty or
poverty were matters of indifference.

It is not unfair, even after making allowance
for the fact that much of our information about the
Stoics comes from critics, to characterize their
ethics as absolutist. Impatience with ethical "means"
and genuine animosity towards relativism are the
foundation of the system. Stoic moralists might
well have raised a banner reading "all or nothing
at all." There is no sharper signal of the school's
intolerance of "middle ground" than the notion of
ἀπάθεια . It is the inevitable consequence of views
of the πάθη as well as a notion of the "personality"
or "true self" (as one modern commentator chooses to
translate ἡγεμονικόν)[3] intent upon removing ambi-
guity from moral life. Although we cannot discuss
here the intricacies and variations which distinguish
the theories of Zeno, Cleanthes and Chrysippus,[4]

---

[1]Diog. Laert. Vitae phil. 7.102ff.; Stobaeus Ecl.
2.142; Cicero Acad. Post. 1.10, 36.

[2]Zeller, Stoics, Epicureans and Sceptics, p. 283.

[3]Rist, Stoic Philosophy, p. 25.

[4]Max Pohlenz, Die Stoa: Geschichte einer geistigen Bewegung II (3rd ed., 2 vols., Göttingen: Vandenhoeck & Ruprecht, 1959) 143ff. Also, Rist, Stoic
Philosophy, pp. 22-36.

we must at least observe with É. Bréhier, that the
"existence of passion poses one of the most difficult
problems in Stoic psychology: if the soul consists
of pure reason, how can there be in it anything irrational?"[1] The initial phrase in Bréhier's remark
reflects the Stoic unwillingness to admit an irrational faculty or portion within the soul itself.
Such a concession was unthinkable in terms of their
paramount commitment to the λόγος which determines
cosmic and personal order. More specifically, these
thinkers refused to surrender the insight that inclinations and capitulations to πάθος involve the assent
of a rational being, and cannot be separated from
the ἡγεμονικόν . The presupposition of a monistic
psychology led Zeno to define πάθος "as an irrational and unnatural movement in the soul" (ἡ ἄλογος καὶ
παρὰ φύσιν ψυχῆς κίνησις   )[2] or an "excitement of
the soul" (πτοία ψυχῆς)[3] -- the irrational emotion
which disturbed the quiet and tranquility intrinsic
to the wise man. Apparently sniffing an assumption
by Zeno that an immoral decision consists of a purely
mental act resulting in emotional turbulence (movement), Chrysippus produced a more "psychosomatic"
definition which tied the emotional effects to the
judgment itself: the πάθη are "certain judgments
of the reason" (κρίσεις τινὰς ... τοῦ λογιστικοῦ).[4]

---

[1]Bréhier, Hellenistic and Roman Age, p. 58.

[2]Diog. Laert. Vitae phil. 7.110 (SVF I, #205).

[3]Stobaeus Ecl. 2.7.1 (SVF I, #206).

[4]I am indebted to the analysis of J.M. Rist in
Stoic Philosophy, pp. 22-36. Cf. Helen North, Sophrosyne, Cornell Studies in Classical Philology, Vol.
XXV (Ithaca, N.Y.: Cornell University Press, 1966),
p. 214, where it is argued that Chrysippus' scheme is
"even more rationalistic" than that of Zeno. Again,
Pohlenz, Die Stoa, I, p. 143.

The "emotions" are, by either accounting, irrational and thus destructive of the equilibrium of the rational soul. Plutarch's summary is admirable:

> [The soul, according to the Stoics] contains nothing irrational within itself, but is called irrational whenever, by the overmastering power of our impulses, which have become strong and prevail, it is hurried on to something outrageous which contravenes the convictions of reason.[1]

Only he who lives according to nature (i.e., reason) avoids the "overmastering power of impulses." The sage's life entails conscious and voluntary choices of things in conformity with nature, things consistent with his disposition of virtue. (It is equally true that the fool errs through conscious and voluntary choices -- choices of things not pertaining to good, hence irrational and unnatural things). Emotions, or πάθη, are irrational, and as such, destructive of virtue. It is just here that the familiar extremist phrases of the Stoa come into play. One is either virtuous or wicked. If he is nearly wise, he is a fool. One drowns as thoroughly in a foot of water as in a sea. And the wise man is either absolutely free from πάθη, or he is not wise. "Apathy" is at one and the same time the ideal and the minimal requirement for the sage.

There is, however, an angle of vision from which Stoic treatment of the πάθη presents a less forbid-

---

[1]Plutarch De virt. mor. 3. See the argument of Phillip H. De Lacy, "The Stoic Categories as Methodological Principles," American Philological Association, Transactions and Proceedings, Vol. 76, 1945, pp. 246-63, and particularly his remarks concerning the relationship of impulse and reasoning in Stoic ethical theory, on p. 260.

ding and severe appearance. On more than one occasion, Cicero comments that the term πάθος might be translated most precisely as <u>morbus</u>, disease.[1] When the passions are estimated to be not merely emotions, but irrational impulses of a pathological sort, so that they may fairly be called diseases, the Stoic remedy is perfectly intelligible. Nothing other than ἀπάθεια could reasonably be prescribed, for one who is ill does not hope for a moderate recovery. Restored health is understood as the elimination of illness. Similarly, the Stoic ethical system is not designed to promote a moderately wise man, nor a relatively rational soul. It is a case of all or nothing at all.[2]

Our sketch of ἀπάθεια requires, as did our consideration of μετριοπάθεια, some mention of its supporting psychology. The ruling principle, the soul of man, is simplex. It has no irrational part with which it is locked in some manner of tussle.[3] The older Stoics, even when elaborating the functions of the ἡγεμονικόν, view them as "derivative powers"

---

[1] Cicero <u>Tusc.</u> 3.4.7; 3.10.23; <u>De fin.</u> 3.35.

[2] "It would be rather stupid to argue that the effects of a disease should be moderated when it would seem to be possible to banish the disease altogether with much more desirable results. The Stoics, many of whom regarded their school as a kind of hospital, would have been very peculiar doctors if they had not fought for the total suppression of what they held to be serious mental illness (νοσήματα). After all, who wants to be a partial neurotic?" So writes Rist, <u>Stoic Philosophy</u>, p. 27. Pertinent texts are found in Diog. Laert. <u>Vitae phil.</u> 115; Cicero <u>Tusc.</u> 4.10.23; Galen <u>De plac. Hipp. et Plat.</u> 5.2; Seneca <u>Ep.</u> 75.11.

[3] Plutarch <u>De virt. mor.</u> 3.

of the soul, not separate faculties.[1] In this regard
they stand in direct opposition to Plato and Aristotle. As J. Rist remarks, "...Zeno, like Chrysippus,
believed that the unitary personality can be either
well or ill affected, but that neither of these
states depends upon an emotional 'root' in the soul
apart from the ἡγεμονικόν ."[2] The soul, then, is a
rational principle requiring the expulsion of πάθη
in order to be what it truly is. Or to say it another way, only the extirpation of passions, the eradication of all irrational impulses and disturbances
renders the wise man wise. Because the soul is <u>one</u>,
and rational <u>only</u>, it must not have a disposition
other than that of ἀπάθεια . For the Stoic, the
problem is not that πάθη , natural to the psychic
make-up of man, drift from a perfect median into
excesses and deficiencies. Rather the very presence
of πάθη in the soul makes "life in agreement with
nature" an impossibility. Vulnerability to a single
πάθος is, to this way of reckoning, as deadly as
capitulation to all, for (if we may revert to the
shop-worn metaphor), though it may be a shallow
drowning, it is a drowning nonetheless. We are now
in a position to discuss grief, which presented an
especially knotty problem to the philosophers of the
Porch. Sensitive to the fact that a single πάθος
had the power to undermine a virtuous man, they believed grief to pose the most formidable threat,
calling it "the most poignant form of distress."[3]

---

[1]See the remarks of Zeller, <u>Stoics, Epicureans,
and Sceptics</u>, pp. 214-5. Also, J.H. Waszink, <u>Ter-
tullian's De Anima</u> (Amsterdam: J.M. Meulenhoff,
1947), pp. 209ff.

[2]Rist, <u>Stoic Philosophy</u>, p. 32.

[3]Cicero <u>Tusc.</u> 3.33.81.

Therefore it is not surprising to find the guests at
Cicero's villa in Tusculum devoting a day's disputation to this proposition: "the wise man...is susceptible of distress (aegritudo):" The stakes are clearly high, since the wise man is, by Stoic definition,
"free from all disturbance (perturbatione omni
vacuum)."[1] And that freedom from "all disturbance"
necessarily means freedom from any one πάθος comes
clear from several syllogistic comments typical of
Stoic argumentation:

> If the wise man could be capable of feeling
> distress, he could be also of feeling com-
> passion (misericordiam), he could feel
> envy...as compassion is distress due to a
> neighbor's misfortunes, so envy is dis-
> tress due to a neighbor's prosperity.
> Therefore the man who comes to feel com-
> passion comes also to feel envy. The wise
> man, however, does not come to feel envy;
> therefore he does not come to feel com-
> passion either...distress keeps away from
> the wise man.[2]

It is an argument which points to the fact that if
a person admits any πάθος , he stands to be impli-

---

[1]Cicero Tusc. 3.8.18. The broader context in
which the πάθη are discussed by the Stoics appears
in Tusc. 4.6.11-2 (among other places): "They hold
furthermore that there are divisions of disorder originating in two kinds of expected good and two of
expected evil, with the result that there are four
in all: lust and delight, in the sense of delight
in present good and lust of future good, originate
in what is good; fear and distress, they consider,
originate in what is evil, fear in future and distress in present evil " (trans. King, pp. 338-9).

[2]Ibid., 3.9.20.

cated in them all.

Chrysippus emphatically favored one remedy above all others for the grieving, and this θεραπεία tells us a great deal about the manner in which Stoic consolation was articulated in theory and presumably in practice as well.[1] Believing, predictably, that λύπη was capable of being utterly removed,[2] Chrysippus looked upon grief as an indulgence which was voluntary -- the person in distress was thought to be in that state as a result of his own act of will and conviction.[3] On the basis of a misguided decision that mourning the dead is an obligation, a duty, one

---

[1]Kassel, Konsolationsliteratur, pp. 23ff., contests Pohlenz' theory that Chrysippus composed his θεραπευτικός as a competitor to Crantor's περὶ πένθους , designing it for a philosophical audience. On page 24, he writes: "Unser Ergebnis ist, dass der θεραπευτικός nicht ein propagandistisches Werk für das philosophisch interessierte Publikum war, sondern Schulschrift, ein Leitfaden für die Jünger der Stoa, die sich an ihren Mitmenschen als ἰατροὶ τῆς ψυχῆς bewahren sollten. Nur weil für diese Zielsetzung das Prinzip der Adiaphorie, das noch Kleanthes zur Grundlage auch der consolatio machen wollte, nicht ausreichte, gab Chrysipp, bei strenger Bestreitung der peripatetischen Metriopathie (vgl. Tusc. IV 34-7), Anweisungen für die Affektentherapie, die auch die Behandlung akuter Fälle ermöglichten."

[2]Cicero Tusc. 3.25.61 (trans. King, pp. 296-9): "Chrysippus thinks that distress gets its own name λύπη as being a dissolution of the whole man, and it can be entirely rooted out (quae tota poterit evelli) when we have disentangled its cause..." For the example of philosophic minds who do not become overwhelmed by λύπη , see Tusc. 3.28.68-71.

[3]Cicero Tusc. 3.26.62-3.

falls subject to great distress. This misconceived
sense of obligation is the source of the many shameful displays of sorrow which the philosopher found
abhorrent. A surely Chrysippean proof that grief
stems from a notion of duty, rather than from any
irrepressible or natural instinct, takes this penetrating form: "if any of those who think they should
be sorrowful chance to act more humanly or speak more
cheerfully, they resume a gloomy demeanor and accuse
themselves of misconduct because of this interruption
to their grief." Our Ciceronian text continues, not-
ing that children are rebuked if their deportment
does not reflect "family sorrow."[1] A consolatory
argument attributed to Cleanthes proceeds from the
same assumption that grief is a voluntary decision,
badly made, the product of a belief: since nothing
is evil except "baseness," one should not mourn over
a misfortune, which is morally neutral. What needs
curing is folly, not sorrow.[2] The thrust of these
therapies is Stoic throughout, cutting against the
μετριοπάθεια - argument at every important point.
The act of grieving is a voluntary action, and as
such is by no means inevitable. Because it is an
impulse, "an irrational mental contraction."[3] it
can in no way, given the identity of reasoning with
"life according to nature," be considered natural.
Indeed, as we have seen, the πάθη, conceived both as
irrational judgments and as diseases, have no legitimate place in the soul of the wise man. Grief, an
especially insidious passion, must be completely an-
nihilated for the soul to remain healthy. Diogenes'
comment serves the point: "It is a tenet of theirs
that between virtue and vice there is nothing inter-

---

[1]Ibid., 3.27.64

[2]Ibid., 3.31.76. The same line of reasoning is
attributed to Zeno in Tusc. 2.12.29.

[3]Diog. Laert. Vitae phil. 7.111.

mediate, whereas according to the Peripatetics there is, namely the state of moral improvement."[1]

We had reason earlier to mention the Stoics' own qualification or clarification of the idea of "apathy": the good man is not ἀπαθής in a callous or utterly unfeeling way. Even though our portrait of the Stoic sage thus far has a decidedly austere quality, it is certainly arguable that Zeno and Chrysippus sought to build into their ethics some means of moderating the harsher form of the ἀπάθεια - doctrine as it was delivered to them by the Cynics.[2] Though the Stoic wise man is without πάθη , which are illnesses, he is by no means impassive, regardless of the charges so frequently laid at his door by opposing philosophers. There are, as we learn from Diogenes Laertius and others, "rational states of emotion" or "right feelings" which are called εὐπάθειαι .[3] The doctrine of the "emotional states which are good" goes back at least as far as Chrysippus, and perhaps to Zeno as well.[4] Three εὐπάθειαι are designated: joy

---

[1]Ibid., 7.127. There was, however, a concession made by the Stoa to those whose attention to the virtuous life, while not establishing them as sages, marked them as "ones advancing" (προκόπτοντες). See Seneca Ep. 75, and Zeller, Stoics, Epicureans and Sceptics, pp. 293-6.

[2]Rist, Stoic Philosophy, pp. 54-80. Zeller, Stoics, Epicureans and Sceptics, p. 278, heads a chapter dealing with categories of "preferred" and "deprecated" things with the title, "The Stoic Theory of Morals as Modified by Practical Needs."

[3]Diog. Laert. Vitae phil. 7.116; Cicero Tusc. 4.6.12ff; Lactantius Inst. 6.14-5. Rist, Stoic Philosophy, p. 72, translates εὐπάθειαι as "rational states of emotion."

[4]Diog. Laert. Vitae phil. 7.115. See Rist, Stoic Philosophy, pp. 72ff.

(χαρά), caution (εὐλάβεια) and willing (βούλησις),
representing <u>rational</u> counterparts of pleasure, fear
and desire. Like the πάθη , each εὐπάθεια has sub-
sidiary aspects. Under willing, for example, one
finds listed benevolence, respect, affection and the
like. This category of "good emotional states" has
the effect of distinguishing between ἀπάθεια and
"savage impassivity." The Stoic wise man is free of
those passions which pervert reason (this is his
definition of πάθος), but he is not insensible. He
is subject to pleasure and pain, but he does not give
assent to the notion that they are good or evil --
that is, he does not "register" them as πάθη . The
point is clear: Zeno and Chrysippus are not nearly
so vulnerable to Crantor's dictum about retaining
sensibilities in illness as certain Cynics might
have been.[1]

There is something missing, however, in the

---

[1]The Cynic abhorrence of pleasure and indifference to pain is seen in numerous colorful examples
in Diog. Laert. <u>Vitae phil.</u> 6. A difference in attitude towards pleasure and pain has been argued for
the older Stoics, for whom the issue turned not on
whether pleasure and pain were experienced, but whether the sage would give assent to the notion that
these were good or evil. (See Rist, <u>Stoic Philoso-</u>
<u>phy</u>, pp. 37-53). The remark in Stobaeus <u>Flor.</u> 7.21
(SVF III, #574) bears on this point: ἔλεγεν δέ, ὁ
χρύσιππος ἀλγεῖν μὲν τὸν σοφόν, μὴ βασανίζεσθαι δὲ
μὴ γὰρ ἐνδιδόναι τῇ ψυχῇ.
Even the account of Posidonius, whose approach to the
problem of the passions is quite different from his
predecessors, retains this distinction between experi-
encing and "assenting" to πάθος , for he is said to
have met attacks of pain with the words, "It is no
use, pain! for all the distress you cause I shall
never admit that you are an evil" (Cicero <u>Tusc.</u> 2.
15.6, trans. King, p. 217).

107

doctrine of the εὐπάθεια -- something which propels
us back to the question of grief. The rational states
of emotion are counterparts, according to Stoic
theory, of the passions. How has it come to pass that
of the four great πάθη which Zeno designated in his
work, περὶ παθῶν , there are "matches" for only three
---φόβος , ἐπιθυμία , and ἡδονή ?[1] We find no corresponding "rational state of emotion" or εὐπάθεια
for λύπη . It appears that Stoic ethics has been able
to devise no rational version of distress or grief. It
is just this dilemma concerning the peculiar character
of grief which prompts the following remark by Cicero:

> Lust (libido, which translates ἐπιθυμία)
> involves passions...but distress involves
> worse things, it means decay, torture,
> agony, hideousness; it rends and corrodes
> the soul and brings it to absolute ruin.
> Unless we strip it off (exuimus) and
> manage to fling it away we cannot be free
> from wretchedness.[2]

Cicero advances the Stoic argument in the fourth book
of the Tusculan Disputations: although there are

---

[1]Diog. Laert. Vitae phil. 7.110-1.

[2]Cicero Tusc. 3.13.27. Kassel, Konsolationsliteratur, p. 18: "In einem Punkte ist bei Cicero
die Sonderstellung der λύπη deutlich aus dem Zusam-
menhang des stoischen Systems entwickelt, bei der
Besprechung der εὐπάθειαι [Tusc.] IV 12ff. Sie werden als vernunftgemässe und daher zulässige Seelenre-
gungen mit den πάθη zu Gegensatzpaaren zusammen-
gestellt, ἐπιθυμία: βούλησις, ἡδονη: χαρά, φόβος:
εὐλάβεια -- praesentis autem mali sapientis affectio
nulla est, stultorum aegritudo est (14); eine vernunftgemässe Betrübnis ist nach den Voraussetzungen der
orthodoxen Schuldoktrin in der Tat nicht denkbar."

four perturbationes (disorders) there are but three constantiae (which translates εὐπάθειαι), "since there is no equable state in opposition to distress (aegritudo)."[1] The fourth century Latin Christian Lactantius registers his disapproval of this flaw in the Stoic theory of εὐπάθειαι in no uncertain terms. Complaining that the grief and sadness which follow upon personal misfortune and national calamities cannot be eradicated, he labels the doctrine of three rational dispositions a "defective and weak discussion [which] ought to have been completed; that is," he says, "something ought to have been substituted in the place of grief, since the former ones having been so arranged, this naturally followed."[2] The attempt to mark out permitted feelings or emotions which were not πάθη , a project of definition which these thinkers undertook with some seriousness, stumbles on the phenomenon of grief, which can be seen to have no redeeming features. Grieving, it would appear, focuses with especial intensity an aspect of human experience which is not convertible to usefulness in the wise man's exercise of virtue. Of course the classification of death among the ἀδιάφορα compelled the Stoics to count grief irrational. But beyond that, one suspects that the difficulty can be traced to the indispensable idea behind ἀπάθεια, that firm donation of the Cynics, αὐτάρκεια or self-sufficiency. The many expressions of distress, and the obvious enfeeblement brought by sorrow simply could not be considered compatible with the residual core of this ideal. Was it thinkable that one whose attention to virtue entailed detachment from the external things of the world, including death, might fall victim to grief? This potential disturbance of

---

[1] Cicero Tusc. 4.6.14.

[2] Lactantius Inst. 6.5 (SVF III, #437). (Trans. from Alexander Roberts and James Donaldson, eds., The Ante-Nicene Fathers, Vol. VII, p. 180).

the soul's calm has no permissible form.

As we have argued throughout the chapter, ἀπ-άθεια and μετριοπάθεια, the important therapeutic options articulated in consolation literature, were summary battle cries of two quite different philosophical lines of thought. And the problem of grief makes the contrast between the Academic-Peripatetic and Stoic traditions unmistakably sharp. For the former, grief, when it is moderated and controlled, remains a natural and reasonable emotion. It is viewed as a healthy and balanced concomitant of affection and friendship, to which it stands in a sure relationship. Even if it can tend to unnatural extremes, grief's "status" as an emotion in itself natural and laudable is not obscured.

For the Stoa, grief is beyond the pale. Even in the context of a scheme to modify (and soften) certain connotations attaching to the school's doctrine of the πάθη, and to qualify the harshness of the ideal of ἀπάθεια, grief (with its accompanying attributes of compassion, pity and mourning) cannot be tolerated. There is no way, apparently, to fashion a suitable or permissible disposition out of λύπη . It is from the beginning an erroneous judgment about what is central to "life according to nature," and so it is the possession of a fool, a state of disturbance which leaves souls "downcast and shrunken together in disobedience to reason."[1]

A further word about the teaching of ἀπάθεια among the older Stoics: although there is abundant evidence (both in the notion of "preferred" and "unpreferred" things, and in the elaboration of a scheme of rational states of emotion) that their ethics represented a modification, and in important respects, a moderation of austere energies inherited from the

---

[1] Cicero Tusc. 4.6.14.

Cynic tradition, this was not the impression which lodged in the public mind. Subtleties and nuances which they brought to moral theory and specifically to the concept of ἀπάθεια were missed by friends and foes alike. As far as the general populace was concerned (including readers and writers of consolations), the picture (nearly a caricature) of the unfeeling Stoic sage and his uncompromising behavior prevailed, and much of what was ingenious and admirable in the philosophy went unnoticed. One can even say that this grim figure had more endurance and wider audience than the thought which produced him. So ἀπάθεια became a code-word for a brand of austerity and denial of natural affections which, regardless of its accuracy in terms of Stoic thinking itself, was eminently attackable from any of several viewpoints -- learned or unlearned. In a word, ἀπάθεια (understood, to be sure, along lines the Stoics themselves would have wished to protest) became a commonplace, along with its (problematically rare) personification, the wise man.[1]

It may be that in the course of time the figure of the apathetic sage, frequently drawn so simply as to invite ridicule from the urbane, became an embarrassment even to those philosophers who proclaimed Zeno and Chrysippus their masters. This can have been only one of many factors, however, leading to a series of important rearrangements of the intellectual landscape in the centuries surrounding the beginning of the Christian era -- among them a rethinking in virtually all quarters of those issues bearing upon man and his passions, and upon the unresolved tension between the ideals of ἀπάθεια and μετριοπάθεια . This more proximate background to the thought and writing of the Cappadocian fathers

---

[1]Seneca Ep. 42.1: Scis quem nunc virum bonum dicam? Huius secundae notae. Nam ille alter fortasse tamquam phoenix semel anno quingentesimo nascitur.

requires brief attention, for we shall see them to be, in their consolations as well as in their more explicitly theological productions, both debtors and contributors to the continuing discussion of just these ideas.

It is obviously beyond the scope of this study to undertake an examination of the range of opinions concerning "apathy" and "metriopathy" for which there were so many spokesmen in the Hellenistic forum. We must be content here to consider briefly the ideas of two figures, Posidonius and Plutarch. Although these men were by no means the only (or even the chief) philosophical influences upon the early Church, the tendencies of their thought form a backdrop against which later developments are seen with greater clarity. Specifically, it is our intention in these few pages to gain a glimpse of the ways in which long-standing differences regarding the πάθη began to fade, either as positions converged, or as one was co-opted by the other. Posidonius merits our attention for having changed the sense of the word "Stoicism," and Plutarch compels notice as a representative of that somewhat aggressive (at the very least, accomodating) Platonism which loomed large on the intellectual horizon in late antiquity. The following samplings of ideas about the passions from a professed Stoic and a Platonist, we contend, reveal a congruence which needs to be seen clearly if the mixture of notions of ἀπάθεια and μετριοπάθεια to be met later is to be understood. For when we discover that these ideas have become thoroughly intermingled and combined in the Alexandrian tradition, both non-Christian and Christian (i.e., in Philo, Plotinus, Clement and Origen), and in the theology of that favored nephew of the Alexandrian Church, the Christian community in Cappadocia, we shall need to see this as a consequence of the convergence of thought exemplified in the texts to which we now turn.

The philosophy of the "middle Stoic" Posidonius

(130-46 B.C.), like that of his predecessor Panaetius,[1] affords an insight into what has been described variously as the "humanization" of Stoicism and the emergence of a new Platonism.[2] A significant portion of the innovations which are traceable to the name of this popular teacher have to do directly with our subject. By what avenues, we wish to know, did Posidonius and his colleague before him (both firmly identified with the lore and teaching of the Porch) come to jettison several basic doctrines of the older Stoics concerning the πάθη and their treatment? The doctrine of ἀπάθεια was rejected -- presumably on the grounds that it was too harsh.[3] But the reason

---

[1]Panaetius abandoned several of the mainstays of Stoic dogma -- most notably the doctrines of ἐκπύρωσις and παλιγγενεσία (advocating instead ἡ ἀφθαρσία, according to Philo De aetern. mundi 76), the practice of mantic, and the proposition that virtue alone is sufficient for happiness. Pertinent texts are gathered in de Vogel, Greek Philosophy, II, 234-6.

[2]For the former estimate, see Armstrong, Introduction, p. 141. The latter (not uncontested) view of Posidonius is advanced by Werner Jaeger, Numesios von Emesa: Quellenforschungen zum Neuplatonismus und seinen Anfängen bei Poseidonius (Berlin: Weidman, 1914), pp. 24ff. Philip Merlan, From Platonism to Neoplatonism (The Hague: Martinus Nijhoff, 1968), pp. 34-58, concurs with Jaeger. Compare Rist, Stoic Philosophy, pp. 201-18, who considers the designation of Posidonius as "the virtual founder of Neoplatonism" inadequate and "discredited."

[3]Gellius N.A. 12.5: "'Ἀναλγησία enim atque ἀπάθεια non meo tantum' inquit, 'sed quorundam etiam ex eadem porticu prudentiorum hominum, sicuti iudicio Panaetii, gravis atque docti viri, improbata abiectaque est.'"

for departure from this Stoic standard apparently
derives from the replacement of one of the school's
foundation stones. Here we encounter only one of
the major doctrinal revisions stemming from the epoch's
renewed interest in Platonic writings.[1] As we have
seen, the doctrine of ἀπάθεια presumed a particular
view of the rational faculty of man, a view which
denied the co-existence in a single ruling-principle
of rational and irrational components. Posidonius,
however, threw over the unitary ἡγεμονικόν of the
Stoics in favor of the Platonic psychology -- that
is, the partitive definition of the soul familiar
to us from the Republic, Phaedrus and Timaeus.[2] A
celebrated passage from his work περὶ παθῶν (written against Chrysippus!) shows that the fundamental
duality of the λογιστικόν and ἀλογιστικόν is determinative for Posidonius:

> The cause of the passions -- the cause, that
> is, of disharmony and the unhappy life, is
> that men do not follow absolutely the daimon

---

[1]See the remarks of Philip Merlan in Armstrong,
Later Greek and Medieval Philosophy, p. 126.

[2]Galen De plac. Hipp. et Plat. 5.459-61. See the
analysis of Posidonian psychology in Rist, Stoic Philosophy, pp. 212ff., where he writes: "We know from
many sources, but in particular from Galen, that Posidonius, presumably to give an account of moral conflict, rejected the psychological theories of Chrysippus and based his own views on the Platonic tripartition of the soul. Posidonius held that, since children and animals can display anger and desire without
reason, the rational faculty must be distinct. This
illustration also shows that for Posidonius, as for
Plato, although there is a tripartition between reason, spirit and passion, yet the basic distinction is
between reason and the other two together, between
the rational and the nonrational."

that is in them, which is akin to, and has
a like nature with, the Power governing the
whole kosmos, but turn aside after the lower
animal principle and let it run away with
them. Those who fail to see this...do not
perceive that the first point in happiness
is to be led in nothing by the irrational,
unhappy, godless element in the soul (τοῦ
ἀλόγου τε καὶ κακοδαίμονος καὶ ἀθέου τῆς
ψυχῆς).[1]

The existence of an irrational element which belongs
to the soul obviates the counsel to become absolutely
free of πάθη. Indeed, Posidonius claims that vice
has its roots in the soul itself (... τὴν κακίαν ...
ἔχουσαν ... ῥίζαν <ἐν> ταῖς ψυχαῖς ἡμῶν).[2] The
Posidonian scheme makes it inevitable that the issue
of virtue be settled in a continuing struggle in the
arena within man, and here we are confronted once
again by the idea of controlling the passions, of
subjugating the irrational to the rational part of
the soul. We are definitely not in the presence of
an anthropology which makes extirpation of πάθη either
an option or a desideratum.

We may comment upon two additional ingredients
in Posidonius' thought which can be regarded as other
ramifications of his adoption of the Platonic psycho-

---

[1]Galen De plac. Hipp. et Plat. 5.469 (trans. E.
Bevan, Stoics and Sceptics, p. 103).

[2]Galen Quod animi mor. corp. temp. seq., Scr.
min. 2, p. 78, 8ff. Müller. Text appears in de
Vogel, Greek Philosophy, III, 262. The passage continues, as translated by Bevan (Stoics and Sceptics,
p. 104): "The germ of badness is in ourselves, and
what we all need is not so much to run away from the
wicked as to follow after those who may make us
clean and hinder the badness from growing in us."

logy. Although fragments of his writings do not indicate Posidonius' abandonment of the cardinal precept
that virtue was sufficient in itself for the wise man,
it may be argued that a passage from Diogenes bears
some testimony to a loosening of the time-honored
Cynic and Stoic definition of the good. It is of a
piece with a psychology which upholds discriminate
moderation as the proper treatment of the passions to
take cognizance of a multiplicity of goods capable of
being ranked, or conceived as standing in some graded
relation to each other. Some such departure from
the traditional absolutism of the early Stoics seems,
at least, to be known to Diogenes Laertius. He specifically notes the similarity of the teaching of
our two "middle Stoics" to the doctrine of the Peripatetics (and Crantor's little dramatic scene will
be recalled to us): "Panaetius, however, and Posidonius [contra Zeno, Chrysippus and Hecato] deny that
virtue is self-sufficing: on the contrary, health
is necessary, and some means of living and strength."[1]

Secondly, the dualistic psychology of Posidonius,
even if he maintained the materiality of the soul
(as we suppose) and whether he had any such thing in
mind or not,[2] links him with that philosophical-religious crux which was to be so important to the Neo-
Platonists. Eroded by the new, Platonically-inspired
doctrine of Posidonius was the bedrock of Stoic
psychology and ethics -- the hard assertion of the
unity of personality which served persistently to call
people back to the truth that "it was one self which
reasoned and desired, one self which ultimately chose
this or that sort of consciousness."[3] Future Stoics

---

[1]Diog. Laert. Vitae phil. 7.128-9.

[2]See the cautionary remarks of Rist, Stoic
Philosophy, pp. 215-8.

[3]Bevan, Stoics and Sceptics, p. 101.

and Platonists, especially those who were more popular than precise, found themselves the possessors of
a "working misunderstanding," for the dichotomies of
rational and irrational parts of the soul and the
bifurcated soul and body were capable of confusion --
capable, in fact, of coalescence, in the service of
various sorts of philosophic and religious dualism.[1]

How differently from Posidonius (whom he surely
read) does Plutarch, an avowed Platonist, address the
same issues? Although we know that he chided "fol-

---

[1]Bevan remarks in Stoics and Sceptics, p. 100:
"A characteristic running through the mystical doctrines -- popular, Pythagorean, Platonic -- was the
strongly marked dualism of body and soul. 'The body
a tomb' (soma - sema) was everywhere its keynote...
But Stoicism in its original form had strictly ruled
out this dualism. The body was of the same substance,
in a depotentiated state, as the soul. The antithe-
sis for the orthodox Stoics was not between body and
soul, but between emotion (pathos) and tranquility."
Cicero's Tusculans reveal the hand of a popu-
larizer of current philosophical trends. The work
provides a full study of a pot-pourri of philosophical tendencies which, though they pretend to be distinguished along school-lines, are by no means consistent for the writer himself. With respect to the
passions, for example (and the problem of λύπη
in particular), Cicero inclines to Stoic definitions,
but retains the Platonic psychology, which would
point in the direction of the doctrine of metriopathy. But this latter notion is attacked repeatedly
by him. Here as elsewhere, the borrowing principle
of the New Academy -- "probability" -- is responsible for as much mingling of ideas as it is for
clarification and discrimination.

lowers of Posidonius" for their notion of soul-mat-ter,[1] it is clear that in their enunciations of the make-up of the soul and their renunciations of ἀπά-θεια they speak very much the same language. A Plutarchian essay designed to obliterate Stoic psychology established this fact. A single theme pervades De Virtute morali: virtue consists not in the "abolition of the irrational in the soul, but [in] an ordering and regulation thereof."[2] The dogma of "apathy" is the clear target of Plutarch's exposition:

> ...reason does not wish to eradicate passion completely (for that would be neither possible nor expedient), but puts upon it some limitation of order and implants the ethical virtues, which are not the absence of passion but, a due proportion and measure therein (οὐκ ἀπαθείας οὔσας ἀλλὰ συμετρίας παθῶν καὶ μεσότητας).[3]

Not only are the passions able to "intensify the virtues"[4] (an argument we encountered in Crantor), the man stripped of them becomes lifeless and inert, "like a [ship's] pilot when the wind dies down."[5]

---

[1]Plutarch De an. procr. 22. See the discussion by Philip Merlan in Armstrong, Later Greek and Early Medieval Philosophy, pp. 58-64.

[2]Plutarch De Virt. mor. 444D: ... τοῦ ἀλόγου τῆς ψυχῆς οὐδ᾽ ἀναίρεσις ἀλλὰ τάξις καὶ διακόσμησις ...

[3]Ibid., 443CD. As this and surrounding passages demonstrate, Plutarch's argument makes extensive use of language and ideas from Aristotle's Nicomachean Ethics.

[4]Ibid., 451D.

[5]Ibid., 452B.

Plutarch leaves little doubt that the question of the soul's constitution is central to his contentions. He insists upon the distinctness of the rational and irrational parts of the ψυχή , making clear reference to the scheme known to us from Republic and Phaedrus,[1] and strains to demonstrate how the operating principles of the older Stoics themselves demand an admission of the existence of these two entities within the soul.[2]

The problem of grief is addressed directly in the work, and Plutarch complains that his opponents call every πάθος an error (ἁμαρτία), accusing everyone who grieves of "sin" (πᾶς ὁ λυπούμενος ... ἁμαρτάνει).[3] He sees an opening for his counter-argument in what we have called the absolutism of the Stoa. The fact is, he argues, that different intensities of grief are experienced and observed among men, depending upon circumstances and the bonds between the people involved.[4] By pointing to the gradations of λύπη , Plutarch ties the problem of grief to his general thesis: virtue consists in reason's guidance and control of the passions which emanate from the irrational part of the soul. Grief needs management and modulation, not abolition.

---

[1]Ibid., 442AB and 445C.

[2]Ibid., 450B ff.

[3]Ibid., 449D.

[4]Ibid., 449EF. Seneca is able to relate the same fact to a more Stoic definition of grief: People are affected differently because "their minds are coloured by habit, and a false presumption, which arouses a fear of things that are not to be feared makes a man weak and unresisting" -- Seneca Marc. 7.3 (trans. Basore, II, 25).

Brief mention must be made of another thread
which runs through Plutarch's treatise on virtue. It
is legitimately labelled Platonic in derivation, even
if our attention to distinctions between ἀπάθεια
and μετριοπάθεια may not make it seem so. Plutarch
wants to hold up the possibility of "reasoning where
passion is absent."[1] There are states of mind, he
means to say, in which the emotions are not involved,
"because passion has set up no opposition to the
contemplative and scientific part of the soul and
the irrational part remains quiet."[2] Plutarch envisions a kind of intellectual activity in which reason
contests reason without struggle -- to be distinguished from the warlike tension which exists between
the rational and irrational segments of the soul.
This intralogical activity presupposes, it needs to
be emphasized, Plutarch's notion of the composite
soul. When he speaks of the tranquility (εὐθυμία)
of the wise man, accent falls upon the calm which
reason can bring to the πάθη through the exercise
of self-control, moderation and temperance.[3]

In several important respects, then, Posidonius
and Plutarch agree about the nature and origin of
the passions. Their accord, though they declare
themselves to be proponents of antithetical schools
of thought, is a signal of the revived Platonism
which was able to influence and incorporate so many

---

[1]Plutarch De virt. mor. 447D ff.

[2]Ibid., 448A. Plutarch points to the fact that
philosophers change their opinions repeatedly, but
without "dismay or pain." This is unlike lovers,
who must deal with forces at variance: reason and
passion.

[3]Plutarch De tranq. an. 476A.

intellectual energies of the period.[1] The thorough
interweaving of ideas and ideals from once distinct
and even combative philosophies is a striking feature
of the world of thought into which the Christian movement was born. In this connection, we would want
simply to mention Philo and Plotinus, to whose writings we shall return in connection with ideas found
in the literature of the Cappadocians. Both thinkers
made use of the concept of ἀπάθεια, preserving the
Stoic term and much of its heritage. In this they
are important for our later considerations of Cappadocian consolation argumentation. Though the
assumptions upon which this idea is based differ in
the two writers, both adopt the idea in a shape which
our consideration of Posidonian and Plutarchian
thought illuminates. Ἀπάθεια appears in a trans-
muted form, and there are as many marks of Platonic
theology in it as there are traces of that notion of
life free from passions so carefully framed by the
older Stoics. In the case of Philo, ἀπάθεια appears
as the zenith of a virtuous soul's successful progress through a life of moderation of the πάθη.[2]

---

[1]The word "eclecticism" is capable of being used
carelessly here. As Armstrong has remarked in his
Introduction, p. 142, the "undenominationalism" of the
period is more typical of the populace than of working
philosophers. Philip Merlan's quip about Plutarch is
to the point: "In a number of writings Plutarch criticized not only the Epicureans but also the Stoics.
In other words, he certainly did nothing to promote
syncretism (eclecticism) consciously." Armstrong,
Later Greek and Early Medieval Philosophy, p. 63.

[2]A few of the relevant texts are: Leg. alleg.
2.102 (Exodus 15.1 is exegeted as a teaching of God's
intent to drown the passions and the mind which is
"astride" them), Leg. alleg. 3.129-34 (where the
μετριοπάθεια of Aaron and the ἀπάθεια of Moses are
juxtaposed) and Leg. alleg. 3.143-144 (in which Levi-
tical injunctions to wash are allegorized to high-

And for Plotinus, anthropological considerations and indeed the shape of his entire system make the notion of ἀπάθεια something new. It does not aim to extirpate the passions from the "lower self," but has to do with the establishment of a condition in the "higher self" unimpaired by the illusions and distractions which threaten to intrude upon the life of the mind from below.[1] But to these ideas Basil and the two Gregories will bring us again.

We have isolated in this chapter a single cluster of ideas which play a significant role in consolation literature from its beginnings, and have attempted to show in what ways the notions of ἀπάθεια and μετριοπάθεια can be seen to describe the boundaries of substantially different philosophical assumptions. We discover that the two notions are, in essence, contrary answers to the question, "Does the wise man mourn?" As such they include distinctive valuations of the passions, of the goal of the virtuous life and man's means for attaining it, and of the ways in which humans may respond to suffering and misfortune. The issues revolving around the πάθη and their therapy are not, of course, the only issues addressed in consolation writings, as we shall promptly observe. But it makes sense to reiterate the point with which we began the chapter. Though there are numerous consolatory topoi which do not call into question those central precepts and dogmas which define and contrast philosophies, it is also true that certain arguments and teachings do give particular identity and profile to the case a

---

light the difference between the man who renounces passions and he who merely moderates them). See also Philo, De plant. 98; De migr. Ab. 44.

[1] So argues Armstrong, Later Greek and Early Medieval Philosophy, p. 229. See Plotinus Enneads 1.2.3, 1.2.5, 4.3.32.

consoler pleads. The skein of attitudes and assertions which we have seen to be attached to the dispute about ἀπάθεια and μετριοπάθεια belong to these,
and in fact provide a helpful context in which to
examine other arguments -- especially those thought
by their propounders to matter, to count for more
than the familiar offerings of a genre in which the
banal saying endures.

As we turn to the consolatory writings of Basil
(and of his confreres, Gregory of Nazianzus and Gregory of Nyssa), both kinds of items will need to be
held up to scrutiny -- the commonplaces which come
from the Greek tradition and Christian scripture and
lore, and those argumenta in which the author appears
to have more than the usual investment. In the process we shall see the convergence of two streams
larger and more diverse than those which have occupied us in the foregoing pages. Plainly before our
eyes in the Cappadocian writings is the encounter of
two cultures, a meeting of the enduring Hellenic
energies and the still-developing vitalities of the
Christian movement, each with its ample supply of
values, authorities, hallowed writings, and yearnings
for the fulfillment of humankind. In an important
sense the meeting was inevitable. It was a merger
demanding that spirited assertions and convictions
be shared and reforged and adapted, for both Greek
culture and the Christian faith laid adamant claim
to universal truth about the workings of the universe
and its richest riddle, the nature and goal of the
human journey.[1]

---

[1]Werner Jaeger, Early Christianity and Greek
Paideia (Cambridge, Mass.: The Belknap Press of Harvard University Press, 1961), pp. 40-1.

CHAPTER 4:
BASIL THE CONSOLER:
THE CONVERGENCE OF HELLENIC
AND CHRISTIAN TRADITIONS IN THE CONSOLATIO

The Cappadocian Fathers belong to that company
of early Christians in the East who refused, however ascetic their practice of the faith, to disavow
the world to which they preached, and who refused,
despite the strictures of their fellow believers,[1] to
renounce their loyalty to the very culture they
labored to convert and reform. The result was a posture which might seem to moderns paradoxical: advocates of detachment from the world are unwilling to
surrender their attachments to the cultural heritage
of the Hellenists. In this the Cappadocians, like
the Alexandrians before them, were simply advancing
and elaborating the thesis of the early Apologists:
their Christ revealed -- was in fact himself the
ultimate revelation of -- that wisdom and virtue
towards which the entire pilgrimage of Greek poets
and philosophers had been straining through the
centuries. One does not find in the Cappadocian
church and its leadership a strategy of world-renun-
ciation which does not fully intend to carry into
retreat the best of Greece's insights into things
human and divine. As W. Jaeger wrote, the Cappadocians produce "a kind of Christian neoclassicism
...Christianity through them now emerges as the heir
to everything in the Greek tradition that seemed
worthy of survival."[2]

---

[1] Jaeger, <u>Early Christianity and Greek Paideia</u>,
p. 81, and n.1, p. 138.

[2] <u>Ibid.</u>, 83.

Seen from this perspective, it is not at all inconsistent with Basil's reputation as the formulator of rules for monastic life that he also enjoyed great acclaim for a work in which he approved the reading of pagan writings by Christians, the treatise "To Young Men (On How They Might Benefit from Pagan Literature)."[1] Acknowledging quickly that such reading must be selective -- since the tradition is filled with unsavory episodes involving "deities" and men, and the deceits propagated by orators -- Basil affirms an affinity (οἰκειότης) between Hellenic and Christian teachings, because both extoll virtue and point up the treacheries of vice. He proceeds to draw parallels between Greek and Christian precepts and values. Among them, to provide a typical example, is his reflection that Plato and Paul alike view the body as serviceable only for the pursuit of virtue.[2] Following the apologetic lead of Philo and his Christian mentors in Alexandria, Basil takes it for granted that the learning available from "the outside" is, like Moses' training in Egyptian wisdom, a beneficial preparation or propaideia to "the contemplation of Him who is."[3] So he likens alert Christians' use of pagan lore to the shrewd industry of bees, who penetrate beyond the color and fragrance of flowers to obtain the sweet substance, not visiting all the blossoms equally nor taking from them anything which does not advance their work.[4] The similitude is self-evidently faithful to Basil's own practices as a Christian writer, for the image itself is a Hellenistic commonplace.

---

[1] Basil Leg. lib. gent.

[2] Ibid., 12.

[3] Ibid., 3.

[4] Ibid., 8.

It would be a critical error to underestimate
the care and sensitivity with which Basil expresses
the relationship of Greek and Christian bodies of
teaching -- it is a precise and delicate bond.[1] In
considering his letters and the writings of the other
Cappadocians, we take in hand a literature which is
at every point cognizant of antique culture's frail-
ties and residual powers, its fissured and its unspoiled monuments to the efforts of the mind. Far
from envisioning a fundamental opposition at the
cores of Hellenic παιδεία and the παιδεία τοῦ χρισ-

---

[1]We have an instructive sample of Gregory of
Nazianzus' opinions of the same subject in his Panegyric on Saint Basil, 11: "I take it as admitted by
men of good sense that the first of our advantages
is education; and not only this our more noble form
of it, which disregards rhetorical ornaments and
glory, and holds to salvation, and beauty in the objects of our contemplation: but even that external
culture which many Christians ill-judgingly abhor, as
treacherous and dangerous, and keeping us afar from
God. For as we ought not to neglect the heavens, and
earth, and air, and all such things, because some
have wrongly seized upon them, and honour God's works
instead of God: but to reap what advantage we can
from them for our life and enjoyment, while we avoid
their dangers...so from secular literature we have
received principles of enquiry and speculation, while
we have rejected their idolatry, terror, and pit of
destruction. Nay, even these have aided us in our
religion, by our perception of the contrast between
what is worse and what is better, and by gaining
strength for our doctrine from the weakness of theirs.
We must not then dishonour education, because some
men are pleased to do so...[who desire] to escape
the detection of their want of culture." Translation
is from Philip Schaff and Henry Wace, eds., Nicene
and Post-Nicene Fathers, Second Series (Grand Rapids,
Michigan: Wm. B. Eerdmans Publishing Co., 1886-90),
vol. 7, pp. 398-9.

τοῦ (especially as they systematically excised Greek religion from the cultural tradition to which they paid homage), Basil and the Gregories evince on every page the confidence that certain ideas and truths have been the common possession of the best Greek and Christian minds. Turning a Stoic concept to their own purposes, they regard the existence and the connectedness of these κοιναὶ ἔννοιαι as sure evidence of the providential operation of the Reason of God, a cross-cultural foundation-laying preparatory to the ingathering of a creation which has lost sight of its center and source. Similarly the intellectual journey of the Hellenes is for them but a long-planned piece of the strategy of the Logos, whose incarnation has signalled, as they preach, the consummation of a redeemed catholic culture. For Basil, then, Greek culture is the cooperative and foundational prepara-tio for Christian truth. The Christian παιδεία supersedes Hellenic wisdom but does not supplant it -- fulfills but does not abandon it. Culture, no less than the "old man," is being made new. There is at the heart of his theology an assumption which makes transparent his indebtedness to the Alexandrian school: the heritage of ancient Greece in which Basil was steeped as a student in Athens and as a rhetor, because it speaks of the good life, the natural life, in images of the ascent of the human mind and spirit, is both in the service of, and answered by Christ, the divine pedagogue.

If this estimate of the relationship of the Greek and Christian παιδεῖαι in Cappadocian thought is accurate, as this entire study presumes, certain criteria by which their writings have frequently been evaluated need to be questioned, if not abandoned. Specifically, it would seem to be wrong-headed to conduct an investigation of Basil's consolatory epis-tles with a view to determining whether Greek or Christian ideas predominate, especially if some judg-ment of their worth or "legitimacy" is thought to hang in the balance. We are not dealing with authors whose works will yield to an assumed competition between profane and holy wisdom, at least if what is presumed is a conflict between Hellenic philosophy and the Christian faith. The two do not confront one another as adversaries. One has exposed no Achilles' heel, that is, when he discovers the eager appropriation of a classical image, genre or idea in the theologizing of the Cappadocians,[1] who I suspect would have had equal difficulty comprehending Tertullian's trepidations about Athens, or Adolph von Harnack's about Hellenismus.[2]

Conversely, it can only be a misperception of the operating assumptions and the purpose of the literary offerings of Basil and the Gregories to count them successful only to the extent that they seem to have transcended the Hellenic modes of conveyance and displaced the ideas of the Greeks with Christian dogma.[3] To the view that Christianity

---

[1]Bauer, Trostreden, throughout. Bauer concludes that the clear derivation of the Christian oration from ancient rhetoric, as it is examined carefully, establishes the "Herrschaft" of the latter. His comments about the relationship of Christian teachings to the received Hellenic topoi are judicious, though his concern to isolate the marks of the rhetorical tradition frequently lead him to pass over other materials which are not so tidily categorized, as for example in the paramythetic section of Nyssa's oration for Meletius (about which we remarked above, p. 71, n.1).

[2]See the opening comments in Henry Chadwick, Early Christian Thought and the Classical Tradition (New York: Oxford University Press, 1966), about the Alexandrian theologians' supposed response to Tertullian's famous query.

[3]This is a clear concern in Martin McGuire's remarks about early Christian funeral orations:

infused "the sclerotic arteries of Hellenistic tradition with fresh blood" not all commentators add so
judiciously as W. Jaeger the correlate truth that
the early church required the language and thought of
Greek civilization as the instruments by which it
understood itself and found a voice for its proclamation.

What, then, are our objectives as we turn to the

"Christian consolation, whatever the literary vehicle
of its expression, is based on the central doctrines
of the Christian religion." Besides the fact that
McGuire's enumeration of these doctrines is somewhat
over-elaborate, at least in comparison with the explicitly Christian solacia which we shall meet in our
letters and orations, the assumption that Christian
consolers use the Greek tradition to obtain "literary
vehicles," that is, for form rather than content, is
misleading. Martin R.P. McGuire, Funeral Orations,
p. xiii. The attempt to cut too-neat distinctions
between Greek and Christian arguments is hazardous.
The difficulties to which this tendency leads are
seen in M.M. Wagner's treatment of Theodoret's consolation, some aspects of which evoke words of apology: "One feels distinctly the presence of an alien
note amid all of Theodoret's eager emphasis of the
Christian viewpoint in his insistence upon philosophical reasoning as a corrective of sorrow in bereave-
ment...Surprisingly, the reading of the Scriptures
is explicitly urged in only two letters and even
there as a source of consolation auxiliary to philosophy." Wagner, "Byzantine Epistolography," DOP IV,
p. 160. The contrast being highlighted here, between
scripture and φιλοσοφία, would surely not have
struck the Cappadocians with the same sharpness, if
indeed they could have seen any incompatibility at
all. Cf. Jaeger, Early Christianity and Greek
Paideia, pp. 28-33, 86-93.

consolatory arguments which are employed by Basil
(and, supplementarily, by Gregory of Nazianzus and
Gregory of Nyssa)? In simplest terms, we want to
determine the shape of consolation philosophy among
the Cappadocians. If we may speak of a first stage
of our investigation, there are two distinct aims:
we shall trace and identify the major solacia employed
by Basil and the Gregories which can be shown to
derive from the genre's already developed collection
of topoi. We hope in the process to spy out notable
philosophical preferences among the Christian consolers -- their tendencies, for example, in respect to
particular definitions of the passions, or favored
therapeutic measures among those familiar to us from
the classical argumenta. Because of the peculiar
relationship of the two παιδεῖαι we have been discussing, our second line of questioning can only be
carried out concurrently with the first: when does
Cappadocian consolation take on the appearance of
Christian teaching in ways distinguishable from the
Hellenic therapies? Are there recognizable lines
of demarcation, or do the themes interlock in a
manner which results in a melding of elements from
the two traditions? What specifically Christian
ideas, and what biblical texts and figures recur,
and do these have pre-histories in other Patristic
writings which are able to illuminate our documents?

    In a second phase (Chapter 5) of the study, our
objective is to discover whether, or to what extent,
our consolers departed from the conventions of the
genre, both Greek and somewhat standardized Christian topoi, in order to invest their consolatory
works with the particular brand of Christian θεωρία
for which these thinkers are famous. In this connection, we shall want to resume our consideration of
the problem of the πάθη and the several issues which
we have seen to belong properly to the discussion of
ἀπάθεια and μετριοπάθεια -- this time in reference
to the Cappadocian philosophy and theology of consolation. We are, in effect, conducting a case
study, through the genre of the consolatio, of the

interpenetration of Greek and Christian paideias in fourth-century Cappadocian thought.

Our study of Cappadocian consolation philosophy concentrates upon nineteen of Basil's epistles, each of which has as its stated purpose the offering of sympathy and paramythetic counsel to persons and communities who have fallen prey to misfortunes of one kind or another. Nine of these letters are addressed to individuals, and are occasioned by the deaths of spouses or relatives (Eps. 5, 6, 101, 184, 206, 269, 300, 301, 302).[1] Four of the letters are written to entire Christian communities, offering condolences because their bishops have been taken from their midst, either by death (Eps. 28, 29, 62) or by reappointment to another post (Ep. 227, to the clergy of Colonia). These letters, though clearly framed as consolations, reveal other interests of the author, as we shall see -- Basil lived at a time when successions to episcopates were critically important to the power struggle which for so long occupied the leaders of the orthodox and Arian Christians. Another six epistles are precipitated by news of harrassment or persecution being suffered in various churches or monastic centers at the hands of the Arians (Eps. 139, 140, 238, 247, 256, 257), and these letters qualify as consolationes on the grounds of both structure and argumentation; as the Greek philosophical schools had developed consolatory arguments capable of application to a wide range of eventualities, from sickness and financial set-back to exile and death, so these letters represent a turning of solacia to a particular kind of crisis in the early life of the church.

In the interests of highlighting the more important among the several hundred arguments and topoi

---

[1]Basil, St. Basil, trans. Roy J. Deferrari (4 vols.; Cambridge, Mass.: Harvard University Press, 1961-1962).

scattered through these letters, and to avoid the
repetition which would come from discussing them
individually and seriatim, it seems best to organize
the consolatory ideas according to the design which
we saw to be basic to the consolatio itself, gathering in turn those features which most usually are
located in the proem, the section devoted to eulogy
and lamentation, the consolation proper, and the
epilogue. Along the way, parallel and additional
solacia which appear in the epistolary and oratorical
writings of Basil's best known correspondents, Gregory of Nazianzus and Gregory of Nyssa will be cited.
It is hoped that these additional references will
put us in a position to appreciate both the texture
of an identifiably Cappadocian philosophy of consolation (one which weaves an uncommon παραμυθία out
of commonplaces selected and adapted from the Hellenic and Christian literatures), and those particular consolatory emphases or recurring motifs which
seem to distinguish the three theologians from each
other.

τὸ προοίμιον

The introduction of a consolatio, so often or-
nate and exaggerated, conceals in fact a quite simple goal. The author is bringing himself "on the
scene" at the same time that he constructs a greet-
ing appropriate to the grave circumstances which
have prompted his letter. In a situation involving
a death, the need exists to declare that the news
is known, to confront the terrible and to communicate
to the bereaved that his sorrow is shared. Standard
techniques for opening letters of this type involved
letting the reader know how the author learned of
the unhappy tidings, or bemoaning the fact that a
letter, rather than a visitation, must be the mode of
consolation.

We need not devote a great deal of space to this
aspect of Basil's letters, since the expressions

which characterize the proems of his consolatory epistles are, for the most part, unremarkable. They
speak, usually, of the reception of the news, its
impact upon Basil, and then proceed to an expression
of sympathy. All three items are handled in a few
lines in a letter sent by Basil to a widow:

> Why should we even mention how deeply we
> lamented at the tidings of the misfortune
> which has come upon the best of men,
> Briso? For surely no one has a heart so
> stony that he, having had experience of
> that man, and then having heard of his
> being suddenly snatched from among men,
> did not consider the removal of the man
> to be a common loss to life. But
> straightway our grief was succeeded by
> solicitude for you...your soul has most
> likely been deeply affected by the
> calamity...[1]

Basil's proem is a model of gracious statement, pay-
ing homage to the man and acknowledging his widow's
sense of loss. In its essentials, though addressed
to a man whose son's long illness has ended in death,
Plutarch's letter to Apollonius corresponds almost
exactly.[2] Both adhere to the conventions of the
epistolary type. Virtually all of Basil's consolations contain one or more of these introductory
requisites; even the letters occasioned by persecution unfold in the same manner. It is not unusual
for our author to insert a biblical reference in
order to underscore or enliven his point, as in Ep.
140, where a line from Psalm 54 expresses his desire
to be with the Antiochene church in its mourning:
"'Who will give me wings like a dove, and I will fly'

---

[1]Basil Ep. 301 (trans. Deferrari, IV, 231).

[2]Plutarch Cons. ad Apoll. 101F-102A. See the
introduction of Basil Ep. 247.

to you...?"[1] Elsewhere, in a letter consoling the
community at Ancyra over the death of Bp. Athanasius,
Basil remarks that he needs, in order to give full
vent to his distress, "the lamentations of Jeremiah
(τῶν Ἰερεμίου θρήνων) or of some other blessed man
who has passionately (ἐμπαθῶς) bewailed a great misfortune."[2] In these and similar instances, the writer is seen to be marshalling images familiar to his
Christian readers (with polished ease, as it seems)
to emphasize quite standardized topics.

Though we must take up Basil's treatment of the
question whether grief is to be moderated or completely suppressed in its proper place -- that is, in
connection with the consolatory arguments which pertain to the problem -- it is necessary to insert a
parenthetical remark at this juncture: the rules
of the epistolary type, dictating as they do the
expression of συμπάθεια , make it impossible for the
author to maintain or advocate a posture or disposition of "apathy." Indeed, as we shall see in treating the lamentative portion of the letter, one who
composes a consolatio is obliged to begin, in the
nature of the case, by sharing the distraught mood
of his correspondent, and even enough composure to
warrant the appellation μετριοπάθεια is something
which must be attained in the course of the letter.[3]

---

[1]Basil Ep. 140 (trans. Deferrari, II, 333). Cf.
also Ep. 47.

[2]Basil Ep. 29 (trans. Deferrari, I, 171).

[3]When Gregory of Nazianzus denies this starting-
place in his consolatio to Amphilochius of Iconium,
the effect is striking: Ἀλγεῖς; Ἐγὼ δὲ τρυφῶ δηλονότι.
Δακρύεις; Ἐγὼ δέ, ὡς ὁρᾷς, πανηγυρίζω καὶ τοῖς παροῦσι
καλλωπίζομαι.   Gr. Naz. Ep. 63. Text is
taken from Gregor von Nazianz: Briefe, ed. Paul
Gallay, Die Griechischen Christlichen Schrift-

This progression of mood is compelled at least as much by the evolved structures of the ἐπιτάφιος λόγος (recall our conclusions in Chapter 2) as by any inner logic of human temperament or experience. In an important sense, the initial outbursts of a consoler cannot be "held against him" when at a later point he argues for a particular view of the passions and their therapy, because the argumenta selected for παραμυθία proper reveal his philosophical orientation more clearly.

We meet in the proem of the Plutarchian Consolation to Apollonius an interesting explanation for his delay in writing. Just as the best doctors do not treat fresh wounds immediately, but allow the pain to subside and the injury to begin to repair itself before applying medicines, so, according to the author, was it more suitable for him to withhold his consolation until a time when it might be a beneficial φάρμακον .[1] This topos had a lengthy history and enjoyed wide popularity. We are not surprised that Basil employed a form of it in his παραμυθητική to the wife of Nectarius on the death of her son (Ep. 6). Knowing that the most well-intentioned expressions of condolence can disturb a soul "in the very moment of anguish," like even the gentlest applications to an inflamed eye, he determined to delay his letter, but changed his mind in view of the fact that he would be "speaking to a Christian, long since instructed in the ways of God."[2] The

---

steller Der Ersten Jahrhunderte (Berlin: Akademie-Verlag, 1969). (Hereafter, Gregor von Nazianz: Briefe, GCS).

[1]Plutarch Cons. ad Apoll. 102A.

[2]Basil Ep. 6 (trans. Deferrari, I, 39). In Cicero Tusc. 4.37.81, the inflammation of the eye is used to illustrate another kind of problem: as

image reminds us of Stoic enthusiasm for analogies
between illnesses of the body and the soul, and perhaps, in the present context, Zeno's description of
grief as a "fresh opinion" (δόξα πρόσφατος) is relevant.[1] At any rate, both Basil and the author of the
letter to Apollonius are drawing upon a well-known
teaching of Chrysippus, who is reputed to have for-
bidden "the application [of remedies] to fresh fer-
ments as it were of the soul."[2] He apparently argued that an ἰατρός τῶν ψυχῶν must be alert to the
opportune moment for therapy, because the passions
(which not only resemble, but are illnesses, according to Stoic psychology) are more susceptible to
treatment just after the initial feverish excitement
(Cicero speaks of fervor concitatioque animi tristitia) and before the injury becomes chronic and stub-
born, settling in venis medullisque.[3]

---

chronic infection is harder to cure than a sudden
swelling, so also vice of long standing is most difficult to expel.

[1]Galen De plac. Hipp. et Plat. 4.7 (SVF I, #212).

[2]Cicero Tusc. 4.29.63. The theme is prevalent
in the literature. See Plutarch Cons. ad uxorem 610C,
and Pliny Ep. 6.16 (trans. Radice, I, 381): "Passage
of time will make [our mutual friend, Fundanus]
readier to accept this: a raw wound shrinks from a
healing hand but later permits and even seeks help,
and so the mind rejects any consolation in its first
pangs of grief, then feels the need of comfort and
is calmed if this is kindly offered." Seneca Marc. 2
contains the same topos, linked in a somewhat affected
way with the author's own wound (his exile), which he
says he covers with his hand as he creeps forward by
letter to bind Marcia's injury.

[3]Cicero Tusc. 4.10.23-24. Under discussion is
the unhealthy fruit of corrupt beliefs, according to

The topos was not ignored by Gregory of Nazianzus,[1] and at the outset of the funeral sermon on
the Empress Flacilla, Gregory of Nyssa remarks that
silence is an excellent medicine for the bereaved.
Speech, if it comes while the soul's pain is still
easily inflamed, will cause the wound of grief (τὸ
τῆς λύπης τραῦμα), forced to recall its misfortune,
to become inveterate, as happens when one is scratched

Stoic theory: νοσήματα and ἀρρωστήματα -- the
soul's diseases and sicknesses. We see the topos
directed graphically against the possibility of
treatment too long delayed in Seneca Marc. 1.8 (trans.
Basore, II, 9): "...I should have liked to approach
your cure in the first stages of your sorrow. While
it was young, a gentler remedy might have been used
to check its violence; against inveterate evils the
fight must be more vehement. This is likewise true
of wounds -- they are easy to heal while they are
still fresh and bloody. When they have festered and
turned into a wicked sore, then they must be cauter-
ized and, opened up to the very bottom, must submit
to probing fingers. As it is, I cannot possibly be
a match for such hardened grief by being considerate
and gentle; it must be crushed." For a good discussion of this topic, see Johann, Trauer und Trost,
sections 54-68. I am not convinced by Bauer's contention that the advice of immediate attention to
wounds is an opposing prescription from Crantor
himself (Bauer, Trostreden, pp. 79-80). Its presence in Plutarch Cons. ad Apoll. 112C does not
lead inevitably to this conclusion.

[1]Gr. Naz. Ep. 78: οἴδαμεν ὅτι χαλεπόν ἐστι,
προσφάτου τῆς ἀδικίας οὔσης καὶ τοῦ θυμοῦ ζεόντος
ἔτι, παραδεχθῆναι τοὺς λογισμούς· τυφλὸν γὰρ
ὁ θυμὸς καὶ ἡ λύπη, καὶ μάλιστα ὅταν τὸ δικαίως
ἀγανακτεῖν παρῇ.

by "certain poisonous thistles."[1]

We see that the Cappadocians utilize the introductory themes and devices naturally, and insert no
substantial innovations. Indeed, even Basil's re-
traction of his consolatory caution with Nectarius'
wife on the grounds that she is a Christian may not
be particularly striking, for in classical letters it
is not unusual to flatter the person to be consoled
that he or she is so wise that the consoler may dis-
pense with certain therapeutic procedures and _argu-
menta_. It is, however, a prevalent notion in our
letters and orations that the Christian is exempt
from grief's onslaught, or ought to be, and we shall
want to examine the bases for this contention as
we proceed.[2]

τὰ ἐγκώμια - θρῆνος

We spoke earlier of the combination of eulogistic and lamentative elements which carried over from

---

[1]Gr. Nyss. _Placill_. 880M (_Opera_, Jaeger ed., IX,
475-6). Cf. Gr. Nys. _Pulch_. 865M (_Opera_, IX, 461-2).
The Cappadocians were not the only Christian authors
who used the _topos_. Cyprian uses the image in _Ep_.
36.3.

[2]Basil _Ep_. 6, and also _Ep_. 206 (trans. Deferrari,
III, 179): "I have learned that the death of a
little child has afflicted you, whose loss, for you
as a grandfather, is naturally grievous, but for a
man who has already attained to such a degree of good-
ness, and who knows human nature both from daily
experience and from spiritual training, it is fitting
that the separation from near relatives be not in
all respects hard to endure. For the Lord does not
exact the same due both from us and from ordinary
men."

the monody into the παραμυθητικὸς λόγος . This pair-
ing of commendation of the deceased and what can only
be called ritual outburst of woe harks back to ancient
grave-side practices and stubbornly holds its place
throughout the literary development of consolatory
epistles and orations.

Before turning to Basil's letters, it is useful
to call to mind once again those components which
made up the classical eulogy. Menander's "rulebook"
suggested that in a proper tribute to the deceased,
remarks were to be fashioned ἀπὸ πάντων τῶν τόπων
τῶν ἐγκωμιαστικῶν . Among the things typically recounted were the person's nationality, family and
birth, rearing, education, the pursuits and accomplishments of his career, and those physical attributes and qualities of the soul most worthy of
praise.[1]

As might be anticipated, Basil's letters reveal
an awareness of these encomiastic categories. He
mentions Briso's military triumphs and the impact of
his death through the Empire, and the exploits of
the general, Arinthaeus, which, when they had been
narrated by the historians, took on the grand pro-
portions of myth![2] The son of Nectarius is extolled

---

[1]Menander De demons., Spengel, Rhetores, 420-1.
See chapter 2, page 63, n.3. It is not at all necessary to resort to epideictic handbooks for these
encomiastic categories. They are seen practiced in
numerous letters. See the consolations of Pliny, in
which one frequently learns of the various changes
of fortunes of the deceased under different political
regimes (e.g. Pliny Ep. 3.7, concerning the Latin
poet Silius Italicus), and Libanius Or. 18, which
contains a panegyric amounting to a miniature bio-
graphy of the Emperor Julian.

[2]Basil Eps. 302, 269.

in Ep. 5 as "the heir of an illustrious house, the bulwark of his race, the hope of his fatherland, the offspring of pious parents, a lad nurtured amid countless prayers." Basil's letters, no doubt because they are letters rather than full-scale orations, do not systematically run through the panegyric topoi. More careful attention to both the topics and the customary format for encomia is evident in the Cappadocian funeral speeches. By a series of colorful metaphors in the Oration for Pulcheria (the young girl, now gone, was a dove in the royal nest, a newly blossoming flower standing under the protection of her father, the "lofty scion, the palm with its towering foliage...which overshadows with virtues...all the world and controls all things"), Gregory of Nyssa pays profuse tribute to the imperial house.[1] Similarly, Gregory of Nazianzus' Panegyric for Basil makes use of most of the expected categories, referring to his friend's distinguished parents, education (he went to school in Caesarea, "that he might not be surpassed by the busy bee, which gathers what is most useful from every flower!"), and his many accomplishments as rhetor, then as a leader in the church. One is struck by a series of remarks in this oration by which Gregory strives to indicate that the standards used by the world to measure fame and the well-spent life are inadequate for eulogizing a Christian, especially one of Basil's qualities. Birth and birthrights, physical beauty and strength, "those infinitely little objects of those whose eyes are on the ground," were not sources of pride to Basil, who, with his family, was distinguished most of all by piety.[2] Here we can see a shift of emphasis in the eulogies which appear in Christian consolations. It cannot be said that the classical criteria for com-

---

[1] Gr. Nyss. Pulch. 867M (Opera, IX, 463). Trans. by author.

[2] Gr. Naz. Or. 7.3,4,10 (trans. from NPNF, VII).

mending the lives of the dead are put aside by these writers. For Gregory of Nazianzus they are a platform for the qualifications he wants to make, and Basil nowhere displays reticence about the traditional topics of the encomium. It is undeniable, however, that the things singled out for praise in Basil's epistles as well as in the orations of the Gregories often bear the stamp of their religion, and make the basis for commendation those attributes and deeds which cannot be understood apart from the values and practices of the Christian community in fourth-century Cappadocia.[1] The most unambiguous evidence of this adaptation of time-honored ἐγκωμιαστικά to the Christian context is seen in the several consolations addressed by Basil to entire churches, of which the eulogy for the deceased bishop of Neocaesarea (probably Musonius) is a good example:

> A man has passed away who was quite manifestly superior to his contemporaries in the sum total of human virtues; a bulwark of his native land, an ornament of the churches, a pillar and foundation of the truth, a firm support of the faith of Christ, a steadfast helper for his friends, a most formidable foe for his enemies, a guardian of the ordinances of the Fathers, an enemy of innovation; in his own person he showed forth the ancient character of the Church...[those who knew him] seemed to live in the society of those who shone like stars two hundred years and more ago.[2]

---

[1]See, e.g., Gr. Naz. Or. 7.2-16; Or. 8.3-20; Or. 18. 4-50, where the panegyric elements speak in detail of acts of piety, wondrous healings, virtues comparable with those of biblical heroes, etc.

[2]Basil Ep. 28 (trans. Deferrari, I, 161).

The εὐλογία , as constructed in this and other of
Basil's letters, and more uniformly in the orations
of his colleagues, is consciously in the debt of and
yet different from its classical model. As a result,
even though the traditional encomiastic topics have
not vanished from sight, the profiles of honored men
and women are painted in a different, Christianized,
style. The model for the well-spent life, for all
that it has in common with the Hellenic τύπος of
the virtuous and wise soul, is the saint, the church-
man. A career is deemed praiseworthy insofar as it is
demonstrative of loyalty to the Nicene faith, of
adherence to the disciplines of the community, and
of qualities which are found in a good shepherd of
the sheep.[1]

It is not being suggested here that Basil's
letters are intent upon "redeeming" a genre or legi-
timizing, from a Christian standpoint, Hellenistic
rhetorical practices. These missives have concrete
purposes of their own, of which the shifts of emphasis and redefinitions of topoi we have been discussing are by-products. In Basil's letters to disconsolate churches this fact is particularly obvious,
for his eulogies of the deceased bishops patently
serve to do more than meet a rhetorical requirement.
To his already abundant praise of Bishop Musonius (?),
quoted above, Basil adds that he kept his church
sheltered from the "blasts of heresy," led his people in the tradition of the church's founder, Gregory Thaumaturgus, and won respect in ecclesiastical
councils as one who "produced nothing of his own,"
no εὕρημα νεωτεράς φρενὸς , but drew upon "the oldest
of the old store" (Lev. 26.10). The late bishop of
Neocaesarea, Basil wants to say in the most emphatic
way possible, was orthodox, and this was chief among

---

[1]Basil insists, in his letter of encouragement
to the beleaguered church in Antioch (Ep. 140), that
the creed of Nicaea (which he recites in full) be
defended in the midst of adversity. See Eps. 29, 62.

τὰ τοῦ ἀνδρος θαύματα .[1] And in the unlikely event
that his primary motive in writing was not clear
from the eulogy, he invokes toward the letter's end
St. Paul's warnings against dogs and evil-workers
(Phil. 3.2): because Arian infidelity threatens,
care must be taken in the appointment of a successor.
So Basil charges each member of the community "by
the Fathers, by the true faith, and by this one who
has now gone to his rest" to make the filling of the
episcopal vacancy his own business. In this and
similar letters the components of the εὐλογία , we
must assume, far from being casually strung together,
actually cast before the readers' eyes Basil's version of a job description, and the profile of a
worthy successor. He declares by his selection of
ἐγκωμιαστικά for the departed bishop just what characteristics should be found in the next occupant of
the episcopal chair. More than a commendation of a
leader now gone, the eulogy constitutes an important
part of Basil's advice (perhaps "directive" is a more
accurate term) to elect an orthodox leader. Both the
panegyric and the remaining body of the letter, written ostensibly for consolatory purposes, are turned
to the service of one of the Bishop of Caesarea's
most urgent political-ecclesiastical tasks: the provision, in every church which he can influence, of
"a shepherd who will tend wisely."[2]

---

[1]Basil Ep. 28 (trans. Deferrari, I, 159-71).

[2]Basil Ep. 62. These remarks hold true for each
of the three letters written to congregations upon
the demise of their bishops: Eps. 28, 29, 62. Ep.
227 is a different matter, since Basil's intention
there is to smooth ruffled feathers in the church in
Colonia -- their popular bishop, Euphronius, was sent
to Nicopolis after the death of Bp. Theodotus in 375.
Basil writes to the miffed clergy of Colonia in Ep.
227 (trans. Deferrari, III, 345): "Do not consider
this a human arrangement...but be convinced that it

It must be assumed that traditions and their
literary expressions endure, when they do, by virtue
of having captured something fundamental to experience. They survive because they give voice to feelings and reactions shared by human beings across
ages and cultures. The use of lamentation as contra-
puntal to eulogy rests, no doubt, upon a basic dynamic of grief; the recollection of the most sorely
missed attributes of the person now dead makes more
acute the sense of loss, and results in outbursts of
unhappy questions and exclamations. In the oratorical
tradition (reflecting ancient Mediterranean funeral
practices), the combined effect of the εὐλογία and
θρῆνος was intended to be cathartic, to provide an
occasion for the audience to "break down" in a stream
òf dolorous outcries. Hellenistic consolations are
sufficiently stylized to make genuinely fresh forms
of lamentation nearly impossible. It is more usual
for the rhetor to betray an attachment to a very few
lamentative formulas, which he employs again and
again. The sentences which fall at the beginnings
of letters (properly part of the proem, but setting
the tone for the lament which is soon to follow) are
seen to be standard for their authors: Julian is
fond of remarking that he could not read through
the letter informing him of the misfortune tearless
(ἀδακρυτί)[1], and Basil on several occasions wonders
aloud how anyone could receive grim tidings unfeelingly (ἀπαθῶς).[2] Basil has no qualms about admit-

---

is through union with the Spirit that those who are
committed with the care of the churches have done
this, and impress this source of their action upon
your minds." He adds in a definite tone that he who
will not accede to such decisions "resisteth the
ordinance of God."

[1]Julian Ep. 69.

[2]Basil Ep. 5.

ting his own tears and distress.[1] Who is so "stony
of heart," so "adamantine," he asks repeatedly, that
he can endure the blows of fortune without pain?[2]
The queries are, in effect, invitations to indulge
grief, and they attune the reader to what will follow quickly upon the eulogy -- a series of unhappy
exclamations. One cannot doubt that panegyric was
capable, on occasion, of straining the credulity of
those who knew the deceased well, but there was at
least this control of acquaintance and memory upon
the extravagance of eulogy. Hyperbole is unrestrained
in the lament: a bishop's death is the severest
affliction the city has ever known; the sun itself

---

[1]Basil Eps. 29, 301, 302. See especially Basil's
apparently credible claim to feel a father's grief at
the death of a young student, since the Lord had set
him "in the second rank of fathers to Christians."
This, he says, puts him in a strong position to know
the depth of the natural father's grief (Ep. 300).

[2]Basil Eps. 5, 140. The same language is found
in the orations of his brother and his friend. See
Gr. Nyss. Pulch. 864-5M (Opera, 461, 1.9; 462, 11.
7ff.). It is interesting that Basil does not encour-
age lamentation in those letters in which he harbors
doubts about his correspondent's ability to cope with
his misfortune. Ep. 206 to Bp. Elpidius, who is un-
strung by his grandson's death, provides a good
illustration. Seneca also expressly denies gentle
treatment of those who display weakness, and tells of
departing from the usual consolatory form in this
situation: Seneca Ep. 99 (trans. Gummere, III, 131):
"Is it solace that you look for? Let me give you a
scolding instead! You are like a woman in the way
you take your son's death; what would you do if you
had lost an intimate friend? A son, a little child
of unknown promise is dead; a fragment of time has
been lost."

must have shuddered at the horror of a youth's extinction; the transformation of waterways into tears
would not be adequate to the public grief.[1] Such
grandiose language is not, of course, peculiar to
Basil's consolations. One sample of this brand of
exaggeration is found in a literary epitaph for Julian
"the Apostate": "Not without reason...has the cry of
lamentation re-echoed over land and sea, and after
his death men have been either glad to die or sorry
to be alive."[2] Frequently the laments are given more
personal expression, as the consoler confesses his
own sorrow at being robbed of a particularly close
friend, teacher, or confidant. Pliny asserts that
he fears for his own conduct after the inconsolable
suicide of Corellius Rufus -- he has "lost the
guardian and mentor who watched over [his] life."[3]
In a similar vein Basil mourns the demise of Athanasius of Ancyra ("Whom now shall I take as a part-
ner for my sorrow? Whom as a sharer of my joy? Alas
for my loneliness, truly wretched and sad!"), and
Gregory of Nazianzus commiserates in language of the
same kind with Gregory of Nyssa, when he writes to
console him over the death of Basil.[4]

More colorful than these descriptions of the
abject despair of mourners is another feature of the

---

[1]Basil Eps. 28, 6, 5. On more than one occasion Basil mentions a chorus of mourners, once urging
that the indiscriminate wailings be orchestrated by
the selection of a leader for the dirge (Ep. 28).

[2]Libanius Or. 18.283 (trans. A.F. Norman, LCL,
Vol. I, 1969, p. 471).

[3]Pliny Ep. 1.12 (trans. Radice, I, 39). See
also Libanius Or. 17.36.

[4]Basil Ep. 29; Gr. Naz. Ep. 76.

lament, the intermittent cursings and angry accusations against fortune, or against malevolent gods and
spirits. Spurred by a sense of the injustice of
death, especially when visited upon the young, and
alert to fate's unaccountable pursuit of the heroic
and virtuous, these outcries (however stylized they
later became) issued from the depths of the Greek
spirit, spilling forth like resented confessions of
mortality and the folly of mortals. There is in
Seneca's Consolation to Polybius a fine indictment of
the goddess Fortune, whom the author blames for the
death of Polybius' brother. In his reproaches he
accuses her of being "by the verdict of all men most
unjust," picking her targets with cruel precision,
"for the better a man is, the more often is he wont
to endure your assaults." The passage concludes:

> O unbridled Fortune, clearly what you
> aimed at was this -- to show that no one
> can be protected against you -- no, not
> even by Caesar...We can go on blaming
> Fate much longer, change it we cannot.
> It stands harsh and inexorable; no one
> can move it by reproaches, no one by tears,
> no one by his cause; it never lets any-
> one off nor shows mercy.[1]

Libanius, the contemporary of the Cappadocians, likewise holds the deities accountable for the death of
their most devoted advocate and sponsor, Julian.
Asserting that this architect of the pagan revival
played no favorites among the gods, the rhetor
decries the injustice aloud:

> Which of the gods can be blamed for this?
> Have they all alike abandoned the guard

---

[1]Seneca Polyb. 2-4 (trans. Basore, II, 358-
65).

they should have stood around his noble
person in return for the many sacrifices,
the many prayers, the countless offerings of incense and the blood of sacrifice that flowed day and night?[1]

Elsewhere, in a reference to Julian's fateful Persian
campaign, Libanius writes that "a band of envious spirits" (χορὸς φθονερῶν δαιμόνων) dashed the Empire's
hopes, returning its champion in a coffin.[2]

One might expect that the Cappadocians' theological scruples would have caused them to steer clear
of these kinds of utterances. It is legitimate to
suppose, for example, that they found in the men-
tality which produced these reproaches a notion of
history intolerably graceless (in both senses of the
word), and an elevation of mere demons to a status
and potency philosophic Christians could not allow.[3]
The consolationes of Basil and the Gregories are
peppered, nevertheless, with complaints couched in
precisely the terminology we have been examining.
"Oh, plague of an evil demon, how great a calamity
it has had the power to wreak!", Basil exclaims about
a child's death, and complains in another place that
"by the jealousy of a demon" (βασκανίᾳ δαίμονος) the
happiness of a household has been destroyed.[4] In a

---

[1]Libanius Or. 17.4 (trans. Norman, I, 254-5).

[2]Libanius Or. 18.283.

[3]This had been a major point of dispute between
their mentor Origen and the pagan philosopher Celsus.

[4]Basil Eps. 6, 5 (trans. Deferrari, I, 41, 35).
Deferrari's attempt to relate the phrase βασκανία
δαίμονος to Luke 13.16 and 2 Cor. 12.7 is open to
question on linguistic grounds. We might just as
readily point to the employment of βασκανία in Plato
Phaedo 95B.

number of the orations we meet with an hypostatized
φθόνος , who bears the brunt of the accusations. Gregory of Nyssa's reference to the death of Meletius of
Antioch is typical:

> Envy, that has an eye for all things fair,
> cast a bitter glance upon our blessedness;
> and one who stalks up and down the world
> also stalked in our midst, and broadly
> stamped the foot-mark of affliction on
> our happy state.[1]

The same image of life-snatching Envy appears in his
orations on Pulcheria and Flacilla, and in Gregory
of Nazianzus' orations for his brother, Caesarius,
and for Basil. The presence of these "heathen expressions" in Cappadocian writings has been the subject
of various judgments, some condemnatory and some
(more accurately, in my opinion) recognizing that
the retention of this long-popular rhetorical device
is not indicative of a compromise of theological
acuteness on the part of these church fathers.[2] To
see the issue as a clear-cut one of pagan versus
Christian theology is to lose sight of the proximity
of the thought worlds of the two, even (perhaps especially) while they were opponents. It cannot be considered surprising that the Cappadocians, like Seneca,
Libanius, Himerius and so many others, made use of
these reproaches of the demons in their consolations
-- this attests more to the power of the genre's

---

[1]Gr. Nyss. _Melet_. (trans. from NPNF, 2nd series,
V. 514).

[2]See _Gregory of Nyssa_, NPNF, 2nd series, V, 513-
4, n. 3. Bauer, _Trostreden_, p. 47, n. 1: "Den Vor-
würfen gegen die Dämonen begegnen wir auch in den
Trostbriefen der Kirchenväter; sie werden bei der Untersuchung über den Stoff und den Zweck der Totenlo-
breden einer eingehenden Prüfung unterzogen."

conventions than it does to an intellectual lapse on the part of our writers.[1] No threat to their religious identity was perceived, and it is not the case that the employment of these figures of speech locked Basil and the Gregories into particular estimates of fate or conceptions of theodicy. We shall observe in a moment that the same authors are free later in the same works to construct _argumenta_ concerning the design of history and the causes of human travail which have little in common with the fatalist theology implied in accusations of demons. It is difficult not to think, after all, that these time-worn, ritualized interjections had become common pieces of dramatic expression, like market-place oaths, rather than statements with serious religious intent. But it may be an ironic truth that Christians were in the fourth century peculiarly able to make such denunciations seriously, for we need to be sensitive to the "collapsibility" of Greek and Jewish-Christian demonologies into one another. Satanic powers were lively realities to the patristic church, and it was no difficult work for Christian thinkers to re-costume the likes of ὁ φθόνος for their own cosmological dramas. Specifically, the cursings of an envious spirit or a malicious demon would have a clear authenticity in the thought of those responsive to the biblical tradition, even if their utterances retained a distinct Hellenic flavor. And we know that for the Cappadocians, reference to Envy cannot be counted as a literary nod in the direction of Greek education. Basil had addressed himself to the place of jealousy in Satan's deceptions, and Gregory of Nyssa gave Envy a prominent role in his account of the origin of vice, incorporating this "bias towards evil" into his theological system.[2]

---

[1] Bauer, _Trostreden_, p. 46.

[2] Gr. Nyss. _Or. catech_ 6. See also Basil's Hom. 11 (_De Invidia_).

We have seen that in conformity with the design
of the early portion of the consolatory treatise,
which was patterned after the monody, the Cappadocians
combine elements of eulogy and lamentation. The
desired effect is a heightened sense of tragedy,
brought about by the artful juxtaposition of a panegyric which magnifies the loss and spontaneous (?!)
exclamations of woe. The structure of the genre
determines not only the sequence of the elements, but
to a significant degree, the emotional tone of the
consolation. To these prescribed ingredients our
authors managed to add, as any rhetoricians worthy
of the title might, their particular emphases, and
we noted that neither the εὐλογία nor the θρῆνος
were intolerant of the kinds of shadings inevitably
placed upon them by Christian authors addressing
other Christians. Generally speaking, however, the
requirements of the eulogy and the lament are seen
to control the selection of language and theme, both
of which are in the service of the rhetorician's
goal of exciting the passions of the audience.

τὸ παραμυθητικὸν μέρος

The main body of the consolatio, the παραμυθητικός proper, aspires to undo the work of the eulogy
and lament, to check and subdue grief by showing it
to be vain, thankless or in some other way ill-
advised. The paramythetic section is taken up with
all manner of arguments by which philosophers sought
to obliterate the grounds for lamentation, to prove
grief manageable, and to sing the beatitude of the
departed. As a consequence, we shall meet here those
ideas and motifs most attractive to Basil and the
Gregories in their capacity as consolers, the particular solacia they found most to their liking and most
flexible to their own purposes.

In a conscientiously constructed funeral oration
or letter of condolence, it is not a difficult matter to locate the beginning of the specifically

consolatory section (τὸ παραμυθητικὸν μέρος). Bringing his own and his audience's lamentation to an
abrupt halt with a reproof, or some kind of chastise-
ment for unmanly behavior, the work takes an entirely
different turn. The business now at hand is reasoning rather than emoting, and the author sets about
the presentation of a string of λογισμοί which will
in time reveal the mourners, rather than the deceased,
to be the unlucky ones. Some transitional device is
customarily provided -- the imagined voices of the
gods giving assurances about the now happy state of
the departed, or the paraphrase of a well-known quotation, or the recounting of a disaster which dwarfs
the present unhappiness. This new point of departure
paves the way for the consoler's musings about human
nature, the problem of death, and such topoi as he
believes will relieve the distress of those who
mourn.[1]

Although celebrated sayings from Homer or Euripides do not decorate Basil's consolations (there are
in fact no explicit allusions to non-Christian writers in the nineteen letters), one line, familiar at
least to members of the church, crops up again and
again. Significantly, it is usually quoted loosely
or paraphrased, and we cannot doubt that Basil, when
he adhered to this method of initiating the παραμυθητικός , was in the habit of using this text, I Thessalonians 4.13, as the citation which marked the
starting point for his consolation. In place of a
line of poetry from one of the Greek authors, he uses
a line from St. Paul's assurance to a church troubled
by the condition and eschatological prospects of
"those who had fallen asleep": Christians are "not
to grieve after the manner of those who have no hope."
Basil does not place the text with unfailing consistency where the canons controlling a full oration

---

[1]Bauer, Trostreden, pp. 23-9. Menander De
demons., Spengel Rhetores, III, 413, 1. 22).

would dictate (the epistolary form is apparently not
subject to the same degree of regimentation), but in
several of the letters (Eps. 5, 28, 62, 101, 302) the
appearance of the passage in paraphrase and/or in a
position marking the end of a lament makes clear its
function as an answer to rhetorical practice. In
the latter two instances (Eps. 101 and 302) the reference seems to operate additionally as part of more
expanded arguments concerning hope. Although we
shall want to take up at a later point the implied
and articulated theology introduced by this Pauline
statement (one which is inseparable in our literature,
as in I Thessalonians itself, from resurrection teaching), our concern at this juncture is the utilization
of the text to displace the expected quotation of a
Greek playwright or historian. For the Cappadocians,
this was a natural, rather than a combative practice,
for however highly they prized classical literature,
they chose to leave no doubt about what body of writings was authoritative for the Christian. The same
element of choice, even if it was not exercised in
practice, was not present for the preacher of a consolatory or funeral sermon, who was obliged, presumably, to address himself to the scripture specified
for the occasion. Is is interesting to notice, however, that these scriptural passages do not undergo
exegesis or exposition of the kind known to us from
other homilies. They are not "preached upon," and
in fact are not sermon texts at all. They function
instead as citations of the sort called for in the
rhetorically complete παραμυθητικὸς λόγος , and thus
receive no elaboration. In the homily prepared for
the daughter of Theodosius and Flacilla, Gregory is
seen to turn to the passage from I Thessalonians
(the day's lection), but it is introduced in a manner
(just after an extended lamentative section) which
reveals how completely Hellenistic rhetorical practices dominated at least this kind of preaching in
the Eastern church:

> Therefore, seeing that the reason has been
> conquered so thoroughly by the suffering,

it would be a propitious time for the
weariness of the understanding to be
strengthened afresh, as much as is possible, by the counsel of arguments. For
it is no small risk that those who disobey
in this matter the voice of the Apostle
be condemned along with those having no
hope. For he says, as we heard just now
from the reader, that one must not grieve
over those who have fallen asleep; for
this is the feeling of those alone who
have no hope.[1]

This particular New Testament dictum appears in a
number of places in Greek Christian consolations --
in Gregory of Nyssa's Oration for Meletius and at the
beginning of his treatise On the Soul and Resurrection, as the stated text for a consolatory sermon
falsely attributed to Basil, and in writings of
Chrysostom and Theodoret.[2] The reason for its popularity as a citation among Christian rhetors/prea-
chers is not hard to discover. To those members of
the church who possessed knowledge of classical
genres, Paul's letter to the Thessalonians must

---

[1]Gr. Nyss. Pulch. (Opera IX, 464, ll., 15-6),
trans. author. This is the first of the λογισμοί in
the "consolatory portion," and it is repeated at the
sermon's conclusion.

[2]I Thess. 4.12-3 appears in Basil Eps. 5, 28, 62,
101, 302, in his De grat. act. 6, in pseudo-Basil
Cons. ad aegrotum, in Nyssa's Anim. et res., Melet.,
in Chrysostom's De Lazaro, and in Theodoret Ep. 14.
Max Pohlenz argues that Christian consolers invoked
the passage in a superior and polemical spirit in
his article, "Philosophische Nachklänge in altchristlichen Predigten," Zeitschrift für wissenschaftliche
Theologie, 48 (1904), pp. 72-96. (Hereinafter,
Pohlenz, "Nachklange").

surely have appeared to be the closest approximation within their own literature to a consolatory epistle, and the verse which enjoyed such wide application must similarly have suggested itself as the basis, in a nutshell, of Christian consolation. The assertion that Christians, unlike the rest of mankind, have a solid basis for hope in the face of death was both the starting point and, as we shall see, the concluding argument for these consolers.

Nor were the Cappadocian theologians the first to use Paul's word to soften the burden of misfortunes suffered in Christian communities. A century and a half earlier, in his treatise De patientia, Tertullian had fastened upon the passage from Thessalonians as one showing that "not even that species of impatience under the loss of our dear ones is excused, where some assertion of a right to grief acts the patron to it."[1] And shortly thereafter Cyprian had exhorted his followers, victims of the great plague which hit the Roman Empire in the mid-third century, to recall the Apostle's assurance, not letting their grief give "the Gentiles" grounds for ridiculing them, or becoming "prevaricators of [their] hope and faith."[2]

Although clearly one of the most popular biblical passages to place at the head of τὸ παραμυθητικὸν μέρος in the Christian consolation, I Thessalonians 4.13 was not the only possibility (we see, for instance, that Basil curtails the lamentation over Nectarius' son by citing the gospel logion about God's

---

[1]Tertullian De patientia 9 (trans. from ANF, III, 713).

[2]Cyprian De mort. 20 (trans. from ANF, V, 474). See the informative study of this treatise by Hannan, Thasci Caecili Cypriani: De Mortalitate.

oversight of falling sparrows),[1] and it is only one
of many scriptural quotations and allusions encountered in the letters and orations. But we shall postpone, for the time being, our examination of these in
order to register the more immediate point: Basil
and the Gregories, heeding the rules of the literary
type in an unselfconscious way, supplied from the
Bible, which was their own store of wisdom and the
source of their παιδεία as Christians, the sayings
which were to set the tone for the deliberations
necessary to a consolatio. There are no grounds for
supposing that they harbored reservations about using
the best literary models available, non-Christian
inventions though they were, nor that they displaced
the expected classical texts in a pugnacious spirit,
as if to lodge a protest. Their use of the tools
provided to them by their school training, no less
than their commitment to the writings deemed holy by
the proud religious history in which their families
figured prominently can only be considered natural.

We have come to the point at which we may discuss
the consolation arguments employed by Basil -- ideas
and images which represent an interesting mixture of
Greek and Christian influences. He and the two Gregories drank deeply and often from the fountain of
tested Hellenic solacia, and we shall want to note
parallels -- other places and contexts in which some
of their favored topoi are found. As for the arguments which owe their existence to biblical lore and
the teachings of the church, it will be appropriate
for us to inquire into the impact of these newer
pieces of παραμυθία upon the shape and tone of the
literature.

It is usual for consolation thought to be portrayed as weary or hackneyed, and it is undeniable
that many of the topoi have become smooth stones. We

---

[1]Basil Ep. 6.

might, however, before embarking upon an investigation of some ideas and themes with long histories,
propose a different estimate. The durability of the
stream of consolation ideas invites an alternate
judgment just as surely, one which the introduction
of Christian thought and imagery might affect less
drastically than we imagined: consolation has as
its basic material, as the essential stuff of its
commonplaces, some irreducible insights about death
and life. It knows of everything that can harm the
human being, and it knows, quietly, of those few
things one can use to arm himself against tragedy
and meaninglessness. Like an aged man who has gar-
nered from travels and time and unnumbered people all
worth saving of the things to experience and perceive,
this literature frustrates the proposition that there
might be something new under the sun.

It is intriguing that so many consolationes,
confronted by the problems raised by death, take as
their point of departure the manifold problems presented by life -- by the frustrations and limitations
of existence. Like their Greek precursors, the Cappadocians more often than not commence their argumentation with topics centering on the inescapable
fact of human finitude, the bedrock of ancient solacia. In his letter to Briso's wife, Basil asks (and
answers):

> ...what consolation is there for what has
> happened? First, the legislation of our
> God which has prevailed from the begin-
> ning, that whoever comes to birth must
> surely at the proper time depart from
> life. If, then, man's lot from Adam to
> ourselves has been so ordered, let us
> not be vexed with the common laws of
> nature.[1]

---

[1]Basil Ep. 302. Also, Gr. Naz. Or. 7.18 (trans.

158

This is an idea which is prevalent in the Cappadocian consolationes, and Basil's Ep. 301 and Gregory of Nazianzus' Ep. 197 even employ identical language (ἀλλὰ τί χρῆ παθεῖν πρὸς νόμον θεοῦ πάλαι κεκρατη-κότα;). Counting death the other half of life's bargain, and, like Basil, understanding it to be the decree of God or Nature, the Latin and Greek consolers who precede him give voice to the same principle. Seneca lays down the formula in a letter in which he dispenses advice on the composition of a letter of condolence: "Every one is bound by the same terms: he who is privileged to be born, is destined to die."[1] He does not express the view any more gently when he writes to Marcia: "If you grieve for the death of your son, the blame must go back to the time when he was born; for his death was proclaimed at his birth; into this condition was he begotten, this fate attended him straightway from the womb.[2] Cicero, in the epilogue to his discussion of death in the Tusculans speaks of departure from life as "a sentence delivered from God," urging his friends to consider nothing evil "which is due to the appointment of the immortal gods or of nature, the mother of all things."[3] The author of the Consolation to Apollonius has among his passages touching upon the subject Hector's words of comfort to Andromache:

---

from NPNF, 2nd series, VII, 235): "We must discharge the common and inexorable tribute to the law of nature (λειτουργῆσαι τῷ τῆς φύσεως νόμῳ τὴν κοινὴν εἰσφορὰν καὶ ἀσάλευτον), by following some, preceding others, to the tomb, mourning these, being lamented by those, and receiving from some that meed of tears which we ourselves had paid to others."

[1]Seneca Ep. 99.8 (trans. Gummere, III, 135).

[2]Seneca Marc. 10.5-6 (trans. Basore, II, 31).

[3]Cicero Tusc. 1.49.118 (trans. King, p. 143).

For not a man among mortals, I say, has
    escaped what is destined,
Neither the base nor the noble, when
    once he has entered life's
    pathway.[1]

There are several topoi which are closely related
thematically. Basil's frequent rhetorical question --
"You knew that you, a mortal, had given birth to mortal offspring. How then is it strange if this mortal
has died?" -- has an ancient pedigree.[2] It harkens
back to a tale Crantor reputedly told in his famous
consolation about Anaxagoras, who, upon receiving
word of the death of his son "stopped for a moment
and then said to those present, 'I knew that I had
begotten a son who was mortal.'"[3] Equally popular was
the argument which urged upon the bereaved the acknow-
ledgement that life was a loan, and death simply the
repayment which should be made in an ungrudging spirit. When Basil writes to a grieving father,

---

[1]Plutarch Cons. ad Apoll. 118A, quoting Homer
Iliad 6.486 (trans. Babbitt, II, 191).

[2]The topos appears in only slightly different
forms in Basil Eps. 6, 206, 300, his treatises De
grat. act. 7, Hom. in mart. Julittam 4, De morte 9.

[3]Plutarch Cons. ad Apoll. 118E: ἤδειν ὅτι
θνητὸν ἐγέννησα υἱόν.   The story appears in many
places -- e.g., Cicero Tusc. 3.14.30; 3.24.58; Aelian
VH 3.2; Jerome Ep. 60.5; Plutarch De tran. 463D, 474D.
The topos is given in characteristically harsh form
by Seneca Marc. 11.2-3 (trans. Basore, II, 33):
"Mortal have you been born, to mortals have you given
birth...Your son is dead...Toward this, at different
paces, moves all this throng that now squabbles in the
forum, that looks on at the theatres, that prays in
the temples; both those whom you love and revere and
those whom you despise one heap of ashes will make

"We have not been bereft of the boy, but we have given him back to the lender,"[1] he invokes an argument which is paralleled in countless other places -- in inscriptions ("Father, if you long for me, I pray you put away your grief; for this was an acknowledged loan, the daylight that I looked on"),[2] in consolations ("We hold our life, as it were, on deposit from the gods, who have compelled us to accept the account, and there is no fixed time for its return..."),[3] and in the starkest language in the Encheiridion of Epictetus, who writes:

> Never say about anything, 'I have lost it,'
> but only - 'I have given it back.' Is
> your child dead? It has been given back.
> **Is your** wife dead? She has been given

---

equal. This, clearly, is the meaning of that famous utterance ascribed to the Pythian oracle: Know thyself."

[1]Basil Ep. 5 (trans. Deferrari, I, 37). See also Hom. in mart. Julittam 4.

[2]Richard Lattimore, Themes in Greek and Latin Epitaphs (Urbana, Ill.: University of Illinois Press, 1962), p. 170: Ὦ πάτερ, ἔι με ποθεῖς μεταθοῦ τῆς λύπης, ἱκετεύω. ῥητὸν γὰρ δάνος ἦν τοῦθ᾽ ὅπερ εἶδα φάος.

[3]Plutarch Cons. ad Apoll. 116B (trans. Babbitt, II, 181-3). Ibid., 107, quoting Euripides Alc. 780:
> By all mankind is owed a debt to death,
> And not a single man can be assured
> If he shall live throughout the coming day.
Cf. also Seneca Marc. 10.1; Lucretius De rer. nat. 3.971, Horace Ep. 2.2.171ff., Horace Cons. ad Liviam 369ff., Ambrose Or. 4, Apollonius Ep. 93, Boethius De cons. phil. 2.1

back.[1]

In its shortest form, as when Seneca remarks of Fortune, "abstulit sed dedit," the topos did not tax Christian consolers who sought some scriptural authority for the theme. Again and again, Basil and the other Cappadocian fathers insert in their consolations Job's words: ὁ κύριος ἔδωκεν, ὁ κύριος ἀφείλατο· ὡς τῷ κυρίῳ ἔδοξεν, οὕτω καὶ ἐγένετο .[2]

When Basil urges a mother whose son has died not to consider her suffering in isolation, but to compare it "with all things human," assuring her that this will bring consolation, he is marching out a version of the familiar idea that a misfortune common to all cannot be a particular tragedy.[3] "Nature," says Seneca,"has made universal what she had made hardest to bear in order that the uniformity of fate might console men for its cruelty."[4] For Basil it is not only men who share a common fate, but the entire created order. He argues that a glance upward at the sky, the sun and stars, all of which will be dissolved, and a look about at the earth's beauties, πάντα φθαρτά, cannot fail to provide consolation to one who has been deprived of a child.[5] The background of the argument, for a Christian, was the

---

[1] Epictetus Ench. 11 (trans. W.A. Oldfather, LCL, Vol. II, 1966, p. 491).

[2] Basil Ep. 5 (Cf. Job 1.21). He quotes the passage also in Ep. 300, and in Quod mund. adhaer. non sit 10. See Gr. Nyss. Pulch. (Opera, IX, 470, l. 11 30-1).

[3] Basil Ep. 6. (trans. Deferrari, I, 43).

[4] Seneca Polyb. 1.4. (trans. Basore, II, 359).

[5] Basil Eps. 6, 139, 301, 302.

assertion that the creation was not co-eternal with
God, but the splendid product of his gracious activity. The cosmos, because it had a beginning in time,
would also have a terminus. A doctrine grounded in
the biblical record, it was compelling to our theologians because it assigned to God a clear superiority
over all else that exists. In his Hexaemeron Basil
chides pagan philosophers and physicists for their
inability to comprehend these truths, to speak the
simple words, "In the beginning God created."[1] The
idea of the earth's or the universe's dissolution,
even if proceeding from different cosmological suppositions, was used by other than Christian consolers,
and Stoic writers, invoking their dogma of the periodic conflagration which reduced the cosmos to its
prime elements, made particularly good use of the
theme.[2]

Was there, for the Cappadocian consolers, a particular view of the motive, the purposes behind those
events which took their relentless toll from humanity?
Many of their phrases about the fate of mortals (μοῖρα θνητῶν) have been seen to share in the common
Hellenic distress about the injustice of the lot of
man and the instability of all mortal life. It is
clear that cruel misfortunes and tragedies are held
by them to be the work of demonic forces, but the
cursing of envious spirits does not suffice to resolve

---

[1]Basil Hex. 1.2-3.

[2]Seneca Polyb. 1.2 (trans. Basore, II, 357-8):
"Some there are who threaten even the world with
destruction and...this universe, which contains all
the works of gods and men, will one day be scattered
and plunged into the ancient chaos and darkness. What
folly, then, for anyone to weep for the lives of individuals, to mourn over the ashes of Carthage and Nu-
mantia and Corinth...when this universe will perish
though it has no place into which it can fall..." Cf.
Seneca Marc. 24.

all the problems of theodicy. This is equally true
for Christians who speak of a loving God's paideutic
world and for pagan theologians, who posit Reason as
that which stands over or permeates all that is. The
consolations of Basil are manifestly concerned to
declare that no occurence which besets man, even
that which causes greatest pain, is random or blind.
"Nothing that befalls us," Basil proclaims, "is apart
from the guidance of Providence," and "whatever has
come to pass has come by the will of Him who made us."[1]
We do not find here references to the "workman's sha-
vings" theory of disaster, common to Stoic argumentation and useful to other Christian authors.[2] There
are, however, as we shall see, numerous signs of the
Platonic scheme which regards the world as a kind of
penitentiary, a testing place for souls in which ultimate rewards are being won (and lost).

Clearly, Basil and the Gregories share the convictions of that alliance of philosophical-religious
groups in the Hellenistic era which were emphatically
pro-πρόνοια , and judged its deniers, the Epicureans,
to be atheists. The consolationes, those penned by
Christians and non-Christians alike, provide their own
evidence of a widely shared confidence in a beneficent
purpose directing all τὰ ἀνθρώπινα , indeed, in a
"great friend behind the Universe,"[3] and one does not
perceive great differences, conceptual or terminolo-
gical, in the utterances which offer this solacium.
In virtually interchangeable pieces of argument Basil
and Plutarch assure readers of God's foresight and
care in setting for humans unequal life-spans, though
the cause (αἰτία) of every happenstance is not compre-

---

[1]Basil Ep. 6 (trans. Deferrari, I, 41).

[2]See Henry Chadwick, "Origen, Celsus, and the
Stoa," Journal of Theological Studies 48 (1947),
pp. 34-49.

[3]Bevan, Stoics and Sceptics, p. 152.

hensible to men.[1] Even if Gregory of Nazianzus has
reference to the triune God of the Christians, and
Seneca identifies "the God under whose guidance everything progresses" with the Zeus of Cleanthes' hymn,
both argue that suffering, distress and the various
evidences of life's fundamental instability have been
woven into human experience by the deity in order to
show man that God alone is reliable.[2] The topoi
respond to the need for an explanation of the calamity which has precipitated the consolatory letter,
and are bent upon giving assurance that there is some
rationale for the most horrible of events, "a method
in the madness." If there is a discernible difference
between Christian and non-Christian presentations of
the theme, it is the "submissiveness" of the former --
there is no inclination to challenge or interrogate
the intentions of God. This part of the Job tradition
has not found its way into the consolatory efforts
of Christians, who urge the mourners to examine their
own lives rather than the ways of the deity. But it

---

[1]Basil Ep. 5 (trans. Deferrari, I, 37): "For He
Himself knows how He dispenses to each that which is
best for him, and for what reason He sets for us
unequal terms of life. For there exists a reason,
incomprehensible to man, why some are sooner taken
hence, while others are left behind to persevere for
a longer time in this life of sorrows." (See also
Basil Ep. 101). Plutarch Cons. ad Apoll. 117D (trans.
Babbitt, II, 189): "For who knows but that God,
having a fatherly care for the human race, and fore-
seeing future events, early removes some persons from
life untimely? Wherefore we must believe that they
undergo nothing that should be avoided."

[2]Gr. Naz. Ep. 165.5: πλέκει γὰρ ταῦτα δἰ ἀλλήλων
ὁ θεός, ἐμοὶ δοκεῖν, ἵνα μήτε τὸ λυποῦν ἀθεράπευτον ᾖ,
μήτε τὸ εὐφραῖνον ἀπαιδαγώγητον καὶ ἵνα τὸ ἐν τούτοις
ἄστατον καὶ ἀνώμαλον θεωροῦντες πρὸς αὐτὸν μονον
βλέπωμεν.   Seneca Ep. 107: Optimum est

must be remembered that these topoi have a single aim:
to remove the suspicion that the occurrences of life
are absurd and random. As single arguments, however
dissimilar the conceptions of the deity or the assumed
ground of confidence in providence (saving historical
events, cosmic order, reason permeating matter and
men, etc.), they have this single and limited purpose
as solacia. One needs only to look at passages in
treatises like Gregory of Nyssa's Catechetical Oration
or Gregory of Nazianzus' Theological Orations to see
systematic statements about the God behind events
for which the Cappadocians were acclaimed as theologians.[1] But these ideas have been distilled to single sentences in the consolations.

We have, in making this observation, opened the
door upon an extremely problematic aspect of consolation literature -- one which, since it figures importantly in the methodology and the proposed conclusions
of our study, warrants a brief digression. Because
the consolatio is, by its very nature, more like a
basket than a chain of ideas, with the argumenta not
necessarily adding up to a sustained argument, the
philosophy of the consoler is only dimly perceived
unless we are able to turn from certain suggestive,
but truncated, topoi to more substantial treatments
of the same ideas and motifs in his other writings.
With respect to the topos under discussion, our knowledge of the particular thrust of Basil's denial that
things occur ἀπρονοήτος derives only partly from his
cursory statements in the consolatory epistles. We,
like those to whom he wrote, also know that Basil is
an Origenist, an exegete of Holy Scripture and one

---

pati, quod emendare non possis, et deum, quo auctore
cuncta proveniunt, sine murmuratione comitari; malus
miles est qui imperatorem gemens sequitur.

[1]See Gr. Nyss. Or. catech. 8, and Infant.,
throughout.

whose most direct experience of the deity who was to
be obeyed through all of life's shocks and woes
has been in the Christian church's survival in
an atmosphere which was, like the world itself,
threatening. Likewise, when he or his colleagues offer as a παραμυθία the assertion that our lives (and
deaths) unfold according to a God-directed 'economy'
(οἰκονομία), we are not ignorant of the other purposes to which this term has been put by these theologians of the incarnation.[1] A number of the paramythetic _topoi_ which the Cappadocians employ afford
us only hurried glances at larger theological tapes-
tries rich in design and detail, and it is in these,
if anywhere, that we are likely to discover what special nuances and skills they brought to their task
as consolers. Keeping in mind the possibility that
some of the _topoi_ are "freighted," or are less innocent than their modest dress suggests, let us return
to the consideration of _solacia_, and specifically
those urging that reason is the surest source of consolation.

The dispute between the Stoics and Platonists
about the permissibility of grief was possible because
of a shared assumption -- the belief, namely, that
reason was the key to the assuagement of sorrow. The
secret of a tranquil life was the equilibrium of the
rational faculty. On this point both traditions
agreed, even if, to put it in martial terms, one
argued that the warding off of the initial attack by
a slight and solitary πάθος was critical, while the
other approached the problem in terms of keeping the
rational forces in the majority on the battlefield.
Of the several _solacia_ bearing upon this subject in
the letters and orations of the Cappadocians we can

---

[1]Basil _Eps_. 101, 5, 300. For reference to the
incarnation in terms of the "economy" of God, see
Basil _Eps_. 210, 236, _Hom. in Ps._ 44; Gr. Naz. _Or._
29.18, _Or._ 41.11, _De fide ad Simplic._

discuss only the more pivotal -- those which describe
the effects of grief, and those which specify therapeutic measures. Basil and both Gregories speak of
the manner in which sorrow dims or clouds the reason,
and the supposition, essential to all consolations,
that philosophy and its reasonings bring relief, is of
course shared by all three of our writers.[1] Basil is
fond of saying that the recovery of sober reason (τὸν
λογισμὸν ... τὸν σώφρονα)[2] allows man to see once more
with "the eye of the soul" (τῷ τῆς ψυχῆς ὀφθαλμῷ)
what things make up the lot of humankind, what solace
is to be gained from the Bible and from the church's
teachings concerning hope.[3] We noted earlier that
Gregory of Nyssa breaks off the lamentation over the
child Pulcheria by proposing to strengthen the understanding διὰ τῆς τῶν λογισμῶν συμβολῆς .[4] We are
reminded of the same idea as it appears both in the
Consolation to Apollonius and in Cicero's Tusculans,
where the claim that argumenta can bring consolation
is shored up by reference to a line from Aeschylus:
"Words are physicians for an ailing mind...."[5]

---

[1] Basil Ep. 6, Hom. 15.2; Gr. Naz. Or. 7.18; Gr.
Nyss. Pulch. (Opera, IX, 464).

[2] Basil Ep. 5.

[3] Basil Ep. 300.

[4] Gr. Nyss. Pulch. (Opera, IX, 464). See above,
p. 152-3.

[5] Plutarch Cons. ad Apoll. 102B, Cicero Tusc. 3.
31.76. For the equally common topos that time heals
grief, but one need not wait, since reason accomplishes the same thing, see Cicero Att. 12.10, Fam.
4.5.6; 5.16.5; Tusc. 3.35. Gregory of Nazianzus frequently urges that "philosophy" (by which he means
the Christian faith) enables one to deal with all that
life holds in store. He writes to Gregory of Nyssa
upon Basil's death: "You two were a pattern of

How do the Cappadocians describe the restoration of clear-thinking to the grief-struck, and what therapy do they prescribe? Here we come upon familiar terrain, for their writings reveal an unwavering commitment to the doctrine of μετριοπάθεια. Basil's counsels on the subject speak of reason's capacity to keep us "within bounds." He knows, certainly, the traditional therapeutic options. In describing the pain caused by the death of Nectarius' son, he says such a blow cannot be endured ἀπαθῶς , nor even in μετρίῳ πάθει.[1] It is this latter prescription, however, to which Basil and the Gregories have recourse when the wailings have been hushed. Basil urges the members of the Neocaesarean church not to prove themselves similar "to those who have no hope" by unmoderated lamentation (θρήνων ἀμετρίᾳ), and urges that although the Christians of Parnassus cannot be unaffected by what has befallen them (ἀπαθῶς ... πρὸς τὸ συμβάν), nevertheless they should not collapse under the grief (ὑπὸ δὲ τῆς λύπης μὴ καταπίπτειν).[2]

---

philosophy to all, a kind of spiritual standard, both of discipline in prosperity and of endurance in adversity; for philosophy bears prosperity with moderation and adversity with dignity" (Ep. 76, author's translation). See Seneca Helv. 17.4, where the teachings of philosophy are said to be a protection against fortune.

[1]Basil Ep. 5.

[2]Basil Eps. 28 and 62. Basil Hom, in mart. Julittam 4, writes: "And when a share of the common destiny visited you, you bore it close-mouthed, not without passion nor unfeelingly (for what is the reward of insensibility?), but laboriously and with myriad pains" (author's translation). Basil's allegiance to the "Crantorian" position is not uniformly unwavering, if we may take all of his remarks equally seriously. He sometimes wishes that unpleasant situations could be subjected to the anaesthetic of

The statement of Gregory of Nazianzus in his epistle
to Stagirios is picture-perfect as a sample of the
Academic-Peripatetic formula which Crantor made a
mainstay of the consolatio:

> I approve neither of extreme insensibility,
> nor excess of emotion. (οὔτε τὸ λίαν ἀπαθὲς
> ἐπαινῶ, οὔτε τὸ ἄγαν περιπαθές) The one
> is inhuman, the other is unphilosophical.
> It is necessary to take the middle path,
> showing yourself more philosophical than
> those who are too unrestrained, but more
> human than those who philosophize inordi-
> nately.[1]

Μετριοπάθεια wins the firm endorsement of
Basil and the two Gregories as the proper means of
dealing with grief. It is explicitly sanctioned at
various points in the letters and orations, and ἀπάθεια is clearly held to be an impossible and unde-
sirable ideal to hold out to one who is mourning.
This is not to say that ἀπάθεια is an ideal which
these thinkers consider questionable in any context.
We note, for example, that Gregory of Nyssa's oration for Flacilla lists ἀπάθεια as one of the features of heavenly existence -- the Empress, having

---

physicians. The election of an Arian bishop to suc-
ceed Bp. Silvanus of Tarsus prompts such a remark in
Ep. 34!

[1]Gr. Naz. Ep. 165.2. Cf. Plutarch Cons. ad Apoll.
102E (trans. Babbitt, II, 113): "Reason therefore
requires that men of understanding should be neither
indifferent (ἀπαθεῖς) in such calamities nor extra-
vagantly affected (δυσπαθεῖς); for the one course
is unfeeling and brutal, the other lax and effeminate.
Sensible is he who keeps within appropriate bounds
and is able to bear judiciously both the agreeable
and grievous in his lot...."

been removed from a world beleaguered by such anti-
theses as pleasure and pain, fear and courage, enjoys
impassibility, bliss and separation from all evils.[1]
Ἀπάθεια is in Cappadocian thought the character of
man in the image of God, either before the image has
been sullied in the Fall, or after its purity has
been restored. About this use of the concept we
shall have more to say at a later point. What needs
to be underlined in the present discussion is that
the θεραπεία λύπης advocated by these Christian
consolers was the doctrine of μετριοπάθεια, and in
this they were able to claim the support of the Platonic tradition, and at least one face of Origen's
disciplinary and paideutic theory.[2] Although it is
impossible for us to enter into a discussion of the
views of the soul held by the Cappadocians (several
psychologies are operative, and more than one in the
works of a single author),[3] it may be said that they
are no strangers to that view of the ψυχή which
envisioned a struggle between rational and irrational
parts of the soul. Basil dresses the notion in language he deems suitable for God-fearers, speaking of
two faculties (διτταὶ δυνάμεις), one of which is
wicked, "that of the demons, drawing us along to their
own apostasy," and the other "more divine and good,
leading us up to the likeness of God."[4] Similarly,
Gregory of Nyssa asserts that the Bible provides

---

[1]Gr. Nyss. Placill. (Opera, IX, 486, 11. 4ff.).

[2]See Origen Ps. 2.12, where he speaks of education as the disciplined mode of life: παιδεία ἐστὶ
μετριοπάθεια παθῶν· ὅπερ συμβαίνειν πέφυκεν ἐκ τῆς
πρακτικῆς· ἥ γε πρακτική ἐστι διδασκαλία πνευματική,
το παθητικὸν μέρος τῆς ψυχῆς ἐκκαθαίρουσα.

[3]See Harold Fredrik Cherniss, The Platonism of
Gregory of Nyssa, University of California Publica-
tions in Classical Philology, XI (1930), pp. 12-25.
(Hereinafter, Cherniss, Platonism of Gregory).

[4]Basil Ep. 233 (trans. Deferrari, III, 367).

adequate materials for a tripartite psychology, but
his reference in the same work to Plato's image of
the three-fold soul as charioteer and team of winged-
horses is tell-tale.[1]

It is worth asking whether, beyond the prevalence
of the μετριοπάθεια doctrine in consolation writings
and in the philosophical tradition in which these
thinkers moved with such familiarity, there were other
factors in their choice of this therapy over the more
rigorous alternative of ἀπάθεια.   One important fac-
tor was the recorded life of their σοφός, Jesus.
It is undeniable that some aspects of his humanity,
an essential part of the preaching of God's saving
οἰκονομία , failed to suggest the ἀπάθεια of the
Stoic hero. The Christian savior was one who gave
vent to his feelings, who wept over Lazarus. Some
care must be taken in interpreting the Cappadocians
on this point. In their case, it would be mistaken
to read the statement that Jesus was subject to
πάθη as an incidental or grudging concession to the
gospel accounts. It was an assertion to which orthodox theologians attached positive significance, for
Jesus' possession of "passions" or emotions testi-
fied to a true humanity, and consequently made
untenable the docetism which had beguiled segments

The discussion relates the struggle of the soul's
parts to an opposition between idolatry and the appre-
hension of the divine, the latter activity being
thought "commensurate with its nature" (τῇ φύσει
σύμμετρον). The close coupling of this Platonic
psychological model with Stoic ethical categories
(virtue, vice, the indifferent) is not unusual in this
literature. The same juxtaposition is encountered
throughout the works of Philo and Origen.

[1]Gr. Nyss. Anim. et res. (M46), Hom. opif. 12,
14, 18. There is surely a strong echo of Plato
Phaedrus 246A in Basil's Leg. lib. gent. 9.

of the church from its very beginnings. The attribution of human emotions to Jesus also had clear implications for later Christological debates in which the
Cappadocians were willing participants, for the presence of πάθη in Jesus attested the existence and
function within him of a human soul, which in the
Apollinarian scheme had been replaced by the divine
Logos. In an epistle to the church in Sozopolis,
which apparently was attracted to the Apollinarian
Christology, Basil explains what kinds of πάθη Jesus
possessed:

> It is apparent that while the Lord took
> upon Himself the natural feelings (τὰ
> φυσικὰ πάθη) to the end of establishing
> the true and not the fantastic or seem-
> ing incarnation, yet as concerns the feel-
> ings that arise from wickedness (τὰ ... ἀπὸ
> κακίας πάθη), such as besmirch the purity
> of our lives, these He thrust aside as
> unworthy of His unsullied divinity. For
> this reason it has been said that He was
> 'made in the likeness of sinful flesh'
> ...Thus he assumed our flesh along with
> its natural feelings, but He 'did no sin.'[1]

It is not hard to imagine how our writers, given this
set of interests, made use of the consolation strategy of μετριοπάθεια , and portrayed Jesus as its
personification. With just such an argument, Basil
contests St. Paul's injunction to "rejoice always":
How can the apostle command uninterrupted rejoicing,
when he himself invites us to weep with those who
weep, and when Christ himself shed tears at the
grave of Lazarus?[2] His examination of Jesus' weeping

---

[1]Basil Ep. 261 (trans. Deferrari, IV, 81-3).

[2]Basil De grat. act. 3-5. This presentation of
Jesus as the archetype of μετριοπάθεια was first

173

concludes with the formula for which Lazarus' redeemer is presumably the model. It is very much like the teaching known to us from the consolations, arguing that "lack of sympathy is similar to the behavior of brutish animals; while fondness for sorrow and copious wailing smack of ill-bred begging."[1] Of the "mean," Jesus' deportment at Lazarus' tomb is a perfect example: he did not deny his affection, yet his grief was not uncontrolled. With the Cappadocians, we are in the company of philosophers for whom grief is neither a vice nor a virtue in itself, but permissible and even praiseworthy if one mourns nobly.[2]

We cannot conclude our discussion of the function of "reason" in consolation without pointing to an interesting topos of a slightly different kind. Gregory of Nazianzus, setting the theme of moderation over both the eulogy and the lament in the oration for his brother, and claiming that biblical justifications of praise and lament keep Christians ἴσον ἀναλγησίας ... καὶ ἀμετρίας , promises that his consolation will strive to recall to the hearers "the

---

noted by Pohlenz, who demonstrated that Basil utilized and in fact took much of the material for his De grat. act. from Plutarch's De tranq. anim. See Pohlenz, "Nachklänge," pp. 88ff.

[1]Basil De grat. act. 5 (trans. author). Sympathy is called a powerful remedy in several consolations (Gr. Naz. Or. 7.18, Gr. Nyss. Melet., and see also Aeschylus Prom. 378D) and the most effective sympathy is from one who has suffered similarly (Gr. Naz. Or. 7.18; POxy. 115).

[2]Gr. Nyss. Anim. et res. (see NPNF, V, 443). Like many of the consolers before them, our authors issue warnings that excessive sorrow or displays of mourning are irrational and only sharpen the λύπη : Basil Hom. in mart. Julittam 8, Plutarch Cons. ad uxorem 7, Epictetus Ench. 16.

dignity of the soul" and "transfer...grief from that
which concerns the flesh and temporal things to those
things which are spiritual and eternal."[1] In this we
see a turning of consolation in another direction,
and though, as will become evident, the Cappadocians'
vision of heaven is filled with landmarks and a community recognizable from the biblical and ecclesiastical tradition, this particular kind of solacium pre-
dates the Christian movement. It appears in Hellenistic consolation partly because of the period's zeal
in taking up one strain in Platonic thought -- what
E.R. Dodds has spoken of as the philosopher's "recog-
nition of human worthlessness...a denial of all value
to the activities and interests of this world in comparison with 'the things Yonder.'"[2] It is very much
in this spirit that Gregory advances the view that
reason enables man to transcend misfortunes, rushing
by them as if they were shadows, and to live "elsewhere" (ἀλλαχοῦ), fixing our gaze thither and knowing "that the only grief is evil and the only delight
is virtue and kinship with God."[3]

---

[1]Gr. Naz. Or. 7.1 (trans. from NPNF, VII, 230).
He cites Proverbs 10.7 and Ecclus. 38.16.

[2]E.R. Dodds, The Greeks and the Irrational (Boston: Beacon Press, 1957), pp. 215-6.

[3]Gr. Naz. Ep. 165.8 (trans. by author). Concluding words are: ἀρετὴν καὶ τὴν πρὸς θεὸν οἰκείωσιν.
The use of οἰκείωσις in this sense as familiarity or
fellowship with God appears in Origen, Comm. in Rom.
4.15ff., Origen Cels. 4.6, Clement Quis div. sal. 7,
Basil, Eun. 2.24, and Iamblichus VP 24.106, where
reference is made to οἰκείωσις εἰς τοὺς θεούς. Consolation which directs the thoughts of the dying or
bereaved heavenward belongs to our oldest writings.
Axiochus tells Socrates at the end of the latter's
arguments: "I have no longer a fear of death...for
a long time I have been thinking upon things on high,

This last theme provides a cue to turn our attention to a number of solacia which emphasize in various ways that death is no evil. Such a proposition required for its background those grim reminders of the transitoriness of human life which were the stock-in-trade of the consoler. The catalogue of life's ills is known to us from the Axiochus, where Prodicus argues that from the infant's wailing at birth to the return to childhood in the feebleness of limb and mind which accompany old age, existence is hard, oppressive, and best escaped.[1] The motif is used to good effect by Basil and the two Gregories, who were adept at making the argument work two ways: if the person being mourned died young, we are told how much he was spared; if older, how richly deserved was the deliverance from trials and hardships.[2] In place of the poets' "lamentations against living" (e.g. Iliad 17.446: "Of all that breathe and creep upon the earth there's nought than man more wretched from his birth")[3] the Christian consolers supplied words of Isaiah 40.6 ("All flesh is grass," etc.) or the Psalmist (LXX: 119.5 -- "Woe is me that my sojourn has been prolonged.")[4] Predictably, our authors

---

and I will go through the eternal and divine course" (Axiochus 370E).

[1]Plato Axiochus 366-367C.

[2]Basil Eps. 301, 101, Gr. Nyss. Pulch. (Opera, IX, 465ff.), Placill. (Opera, IX, 484ff.), Gr. Naz. Or. 7.20.

[3]Plato Axiochus 368A (trans. George Burges, Works of Plato, Vol VI, 1854, p. 46). Cf. the account of Hegesias' αὐτοκαρτερῶν in Cicero Tusc. 1.34.84.

[4]Basil De morte (M535), Gr. Nyss. Placill. (Opera, IX, 483-4). In a striking passage in Basil's Hex. 5.2, the image from Isaiah 40 precedes a graphic description of man in his vulnerability, sur-

connect with the worldly affairs of man the inevitability of temptation and the probability of sin, with
the result that their enumeration of the evils of
life takes the shape of a Lasterkatalogue, a list of
sins in the Pauline style: a young man, by his early
death, evaded "the iniquities of the marketplace...
compulsion of sins...falsehood...avarice...all those
passions of the flesh which are likely to be engen-
dered in dissolute souls."[1] Basil's notion of "the
wickedness which inheres in human life" is not peculiar to Christian consolations. Crantor himself is
credited with an explanation of the origin of wickedness and misfortune which many Christians would have
had no compunctions about making their own:

> ...even at our birth there is conjoined
> with us a portion of evil in everything.
> For the very seed of our life, since it
> is mortal, participates in this causation
> and from this there steals upon us de-
> fectiveness of soul, diseases of body,
> loss of friends by death, and the common
> portion of mortals.[2]

This sort of estimate of the evils of existence
pointed to two questions about departure from life:
when and how? We have already alluded to the first
issue, but mention should be made of the vast number of solacia which are directed at the problem of
untimely death. It is a topos which goes back to the

---

rounded by flatterers and disloyal kin, coming to
power, but able to die in an evening, "stripped in a
moment of all his stage accessories" (trans. from
NPNF, VIII, 76-7).

[1]Basil Ep. 300 (trans. adapted from Deferrari,
IV, 223).

[2]Plutarch Cons. ad Apoll. 104C. Cf. Gr. Naz. Or.
18. 42.

earliest paramythetic writings, and most variations on the theme are easily located within the works of the Cappadocians.[1] When Seneca writes to Marcia that "the souls that are quickly released from intercourse with men find the journey to the gods above most easy; for they carry less weight of earthly dross,"[2] he is utilizing a theme rarely missing from a consolatio for a child. Gregory of Nyssa's oration for the child of Theodosius I and Flacilla has as its closing portion a very elaborate Christian version of the idea (which places more emphasis upon escape from those grievous sins for which the baptized will have to answer at the judgment)[3] and his treatise On Infants' Early Deaths argues that these mortalities are not untimely at all, but the work of a "perfect Providence" bent upon forestalling evil choices before they have been made.[4]

When Gregory speaks in this last-mentioned work of those who need to be conducted from a banquet at mid-festivity because of drunkenness, and likens them to those who accuse God of injustice because of the deaths of the young, he is calling into play a well-tested consolatory image. Cicero quotes the rule of Greek feasts (ἢ πίθι ἢ ἄπιθι), urging that the one who is delivered from the revelry early does not risk violence in the banquet's later hours. He is utilizing an argument in favor of an early death which both Epicurus and Crantor turned to consolatory

---

[1]Plato Axiochus 367B, Seneca Ep. 99, Marc. 24.1, Polyb. 9.4, Fam. 4.5; 5.13; 5.16, Basil Ep. 300, Gr. Naz. Or. 2.27, Or. 7.18, Ep. 197.4.

[2]Seneca Marc. 23.1 (trans. Basore, II, 83).

[3]Gr. Nyss. Pulch. (Opera, IX, 465ff.).

[4]Gr. Nyss. Infant. (NPNF, V, 378-9).

purposes before him.[1] Although the import of the topos as it usually appears concerns advice to leave life with dignity, not with uncontrolled whining and resentments, Gregory has the question of theodicy in mind. God, he says, is like the president of the feast, intent upon having order prevail and considerately arranging for everyone present to conduct himself properly.

> Why does God, when fathers endeavor their utmost to preserve a successor to their line, often let the son and heir be snatched away?...We shall reply with the illustration of the banquet...to prevent one who has indulged in the carousals to an improper extent from lingering over so profusely furnished a table, he is early taken from the number of banqueters, and thereby secures an escape out of those evils which unmeasured indulgence procures for gluttons.[2]

Plato himself had provided the by-word for a "manly" departure from human existence by writing in the Phaedo that "those who pursue philosophy aright study nothing but dying and being dead,"[3] a remark which found favor with the Cappadocians, since it carried connotations not only of the teachings of immortality, but also of what Paul had referred to as "death to sin" (Romans 1.11). Further, the idea was linked in many consolations with the solacium for

---

[1]Cicero Tusc. 5.41.118, Lucretius De rer. nat. 3.938. See Buresch, Consolationum, p. 62. Also, Horace Ep. 2.2.213.

[2]Gr. Nyss. Infant. (trans. from NPNF, V, 379).

[3]Plato Phaedo 64A (trans. H.N. Fowler, LCL, Vol. I, 1917, p. 223). See Gr. Naz. Ep. 31.4, Or. 7.18.

which Aristippus and the Cyrenaics received credit --
their argument that grief could be avoided and misfortune robbed of its painfulness by consideration in
advance of the disasters which befall men. Only an
unexpected event was capable of causing distress, the
argument ran, and anyone boasting even moderate wisdom would surely heed the lines of Euripides: "...if
dread chance should bring calamity no sudden care
should rend me unprepared."[1] This ubiquitous argument for praemeditatio futurorum malorum was taken
over directly from Plutarch's treatise De tranquil-
itate by Basil, who wrote that men who had anticipated the worst were able to stave off "throbbings and
palpitations of the heart and lead their thoughts
toward tranquility and calm."[2] Another among the
items taken over "whole cloth" from the Hellenistic
tradition by the Cappadocians is the argument which
appears in Basil's Ep. 5:

> Let us abide a brief space, and we shall
> be with him whose loss we mourn. Nor will
> the period of separation be great, since
> in this life, as on a journey, we are all
> hastening to the same caravansary; and
> although one has already taken up his
> lodging there, and another has just ar-
> rived, and another is hastening thither,
> yet the same goal will receive us all.[3]

---

[1] Cicero Tusc. 3.14.29 (trans. King, p. 261).

[2] Basil De grat. act. 7. Cf. Plutarch De tranq.
474E. Pohlenz called attention to Basil's dependence
on this work in his homily on thanksgiving (see above,
p. 153, note 2). The topos appears in countless
places, e.g., Cicero Tusc. 3.22.54, Plutarch Cons.
ad Apoll. 112C, Seneca Polyb. 11, Marc. 9.5, Eps. 24;
15.5; 63.15; 107.4, Epictetus Disc. 3.24.83.

[3] Basil Ep. 5 and Hom. in mart. Julittam 4.

A common and presumably effective source of consolation which holds out the prospect of "translation" (rather than termination) and an ultimate reunion of those separated by death, the idea is used to good effect by Socrates at the end of Plato's Apology, and finds a firm place in the consolatory tradition.[1]

For those who remained behind, however, the pressing issue was endurance of the vicissitudes of life until relief, either in blessed insensibility or in heavenly community, was theirs. Out of this concern was born a number of topoi which attempted to invest human trials and afflictions with positive meaning, with a significance beyond the threadbare observation that good and happiness require their opposites in order to be defined and known. When the consoler exhorted the bereaved φέρειν τὰ ἀνθρώπινα ἀνθρωπίνως, he summoned forth all of his culture's hymning of the fortitude and courage of man the contestant, the battler against fortune, corruptions of spirit, and loss of self-control.[2] Ἀνδρεία, the prized virtue of the philosophical as well as the athletic arena, was known to be won only in adversity. As Seneca put it, "the only contestant who can confidently enter the lists is the man who has seen his own blood, who has felt his teeth rattle beneath his opponent's fist...who has been downed in body but not in spirit, one who as often as he falls, rises again in greater defiance than before...it is only in this way that the true spirit can be tested."[3] To these heroic images and to the ideal of courage our authors were no strangers, and the close coupling of these with

---

[1]Plato Ap. 40E. Also Plato Axiochus 365B. Seneca Marc. 19, Ep. 99, Plutarch Cons. ad Apoll. 113C.

[2]Plutarch Cons. ad Apoll. 118C.

[3]Seneca Ep. 13 (trans. adapted from Gummere, I, 73-5).

other more explicitly Christian notions is not difficult to find. Basil encourages Bishop Elpidius (Ep.
206) to "leave behind to the world an example of manliness (ὑπόδειγμα ἀνδρείας) and of the true attitude
based upon the things for which we hope" in his com-
portment at the death of his grandson. To this line
of argument that trials are not vain, but teach and
ennoble men, Basil and his colleagues added two
teachings which, though they had points of contact
with time-honored Greek ideas of human presumption or
hubris, and life either κατὰ φύσιν or pleasing to
the gods, were drawn from and directed towards the
historical experience of Christians. In the first
place, Christians needed reminding that they did not
stand in the world as innocents, wronged by hostile
events and circumstances. It was safe to assume that
most men, even those whose piety was celebrated, were
vulnerable to God-sent chastisements (those for whom
the law of retribution seemed inapplicable, like Job,
fell into a special category, as we shall see).
Basil writes to the Nicopolitan Christians (Ep. 247)
that human sufferings are the result of error and
sin. The second motif plays an important role in
consolationes, and particularly in those letters
addressed to communities undergoing persecution.
Like athletes of God and martyrs, Christians should
bear misfortune in full knowledge that their fidelity
is being tested, and that the rewards of life beyond
the world are being determined. So Basil reminds
Nectarius that μεγάλοι στέφανοι δόξης await those who
endure hardship, and advises another correspondent
"that these afflictions do not come in vain to God's
servants from the Lord who watches over us, but as a
test of their genuine love for the God who created
us."[1] In a passage which conveys a great deal about
the bitterness and complexity of hostilities within
the fourth-century church, he suggests that the times
are ripe for more courageous testimony than was seen
in the age of martyrs:

---

[1]Basil Ep. 101 (trans. Deferrari, II, 189).

I am convinced that a greater reward is laid
up by the just Judge for you than for the
martyrs of that time, since they not only
had the openly acknowledged approbation
that comes from men, but received also the
reward that comes from God, whereas for
you, on the strength of equally righteous
deeds, the honours that come from the
people are not at hand; hence it is reasonable to assume that the recompense
which is laid up in the next life for
your labours in defense of the true religion is many times greater.[1]

The extensive use of martyr language in the consolations of the Cappadocians, with the athletic imagery
interwoven, stems from the writings and experiences
of the Christian community, drawing liberally from
the models of church martyrologies, especially the
books portraying the noble intransigence of the
Maccabees.[2]

---

[1]Basil Ep. 257 (trans. Deferrari, IV, 33). Basil
is referring to the fact that the Arians, calling
themselves Christians, obscure the battle-lines. It
is, as he writes in Ep. 139, a strategem of Satan:
"...we took thought of the ingenuity of the devil's
warfare, -- how the devil, when he saw the Church
multiplying and flourishing still more amid the per-
secutions of its enemies, changed his plan and no
longer fights openly, but places hidden snares for
us, concealing his plot by means of the name which
his followers bear, that we may suffer as our fathers
did and yet not seem to suffer for Christ, because
of the fact that our persecutors also bear the name
of Christians" (trans. Deferrari, II, 327).

[2]Paul, of course, had already appropriated images
from the Hellenic contests into his descriptions of
life "in Christ." References to martyr's and ath-

We have reached a natural place to discuss a central feature of consolatory letters and orations: the example of those who bore adversities with dignity and despised death. Coming, as a rule, at the end of the solacia, and offered as proof that the consoler's strategies for resisting grief and meeting death were feasible, these ὑποδείγματα cast the deeds of others before the reader's eyes for encouragement. The classical paramythetic tradition multiplied its heroes (and its non-heroes: Niobe gained infamy for having weeped unremittingly until she was turned to stone),[1] adding men and women to an early list including Anaxagoras, Telamon, Pericles and Xenophon.[2] Seneca took pains to add figures known to the people he was writing, and to offer up names from the Latin-speaking world. In the consolation he composed for his mother, Helvia, he paid tribute to Aurelius Cotta's mother (who followed him into exile, and later, when he died, "let him go just as bravely as she had clung to him...no one saw her shed any tears") and to Cornelia (who lost ten of her twelve children, but "forbade [her friends] to make any indictment against Fortune").[3] We see also in one of his letters to Lucilius a similar inclination to provide from his own literature and history the names of those who despised death, for he tells the tales of Mucius, who displayed bravery by putting his hand in fire, and one of the Scipios, who while he was dying at sea was able to say to his men, "All is well with the

---

lete's crowns abound in Basil's consolations: Eps. 5, 101, 139, 206, 256, 257. Also Gr. Naz. Ep. 238.

[1]Cicero Tusc. 3.26.63, Plutarch Cons. ad Apoll. 116C, Jerome Ep. 60.14.

[2]Cicero Tusc. 3.24.58, Plutarch Cons. ad Apoll. 118EF, Jerome Ep. 60.5.

[3]Seneca Helv. 16.7 (trans. Basore, II, 475).

commander!"[1]

There were at the disposal of the Christian writer a number of scriptural personages fit to be held
up as exemplars of equal stature. To the wife of
Nectarius, appropriately, the mother of the Maccabees
is described:

> [She] beheld the death of seven sons, and
> neither groaned nor shed an ignoble tear.
> Rather she gave thanks to God that she be-
> held her sons, albeit by fire and sword
> and by the most cruel tortures, set free
> from the bonds of the flesh; and thus she
> received commendation in the sight of God,
> and everlasting renown in the sight of
> men.[2]

It was, predictably enough, ὁ μέγας ἀθλητὴς Ἰὼβ
who most typified the patience and steadfastness
prized by Christian consolers.[3] Like the self-evident
paramythetic passage from 1 Thessalonians, Job was
the natural hero for those who sought in the biblical
writings the models for endurance of grief and tragedy. Though he could not be made into an Epicurean
wise man, laughing at the cruelest efforts of Chance
-- for Christians it was no random nor conspiratorial
power behind events -- Job was able to become for
these authors not only the righteous Hebrew undergoing testing at the hands of the High God, but also
a legitimized (i.e., scripturally-derived) example of
the kind of σοφός whom in various ways the Platonic
and Stoic tradition had held aloft, a man whose vir-

---

[1] Seneca Ep. 24 (trans. Gummere, I, 169-71).

[2] Basil Ep. 6 (trans. Deferrari, I, 43). See the
similar treatment in Basil De morte 10.

[3] Basil Ep. 6.

tue was not compromised by external things. Job and
his story had already become established as a consolatory example in earlier Christian writings (e.g.,
James 5.11). Cyprian used Job's case in a typical
manner to enforce his prohibition of murmuring against
events like the famine which occurred during his
episcopate; believers were to emulate "a man without
complaint, a true worshipper of God."[1]

The treatments of Job in the Cappadocian writings are not uniform. Basil's epistolary references
are abbreviated, but they contain the core ingredients
of this particular consolatory argument-by-example.
He writes of this man whose life was a lesson in bearing misfortune:

> ...we ought to revere God's loving kind-
> ness and not repine, remembering that
> great and famous saying uttered by the
> great combatant Job when he saw his ten
> children in a brief moment of time slain
> at a single meal: 'The Lord gave, and
> the Lord hath taken away: as it hath
> pleased the Lord, so is it done.'[2]

In a sermon entitled On Grief and Despondency, he
provides another glimpse of the long-suffering hero,
this time indicating that he did not meet his trials
at all in the Stoic mood. He did not display an
"adamantine" or stony heart, but cried out because
of his tribulations. Μὴ ἀσυμπαθὴς ὁ ἄνθρωπος ![3]   On

----

[1]Cyprian De mortalitate 14.

[2]Basil Ep. 5 (trans. Deferrari, I, 37). See
also Ep. 300.

[3]Basil De tristitia et an. dej. 3: Basil argues
here that Jesus' weeping was not ἐμπαθής, but ped-
agogical -- i.e., for the disciples' sake.

the other hand, he, like Jesus at the tomb of Lazarus, did not capitulate to uncurbed lamentation, nor
show the fondness for grief (φιλόλυπον) so often
met among the weak.[1] Job's struggle with Satan is
considered in Basil's work On Detachment, where the
hero is declared to have repulsed the Evil One's
attempts to call into question the dispensations of
God's wisdom. Because of his patience in adversity,
the author says, Job is guaranteed a place of prominence when the Judge gathers the universal church.[2]
Recounting Job's reaction to the news of the death
of his children, Basil argues that he knew that none
of the events which befell him warranted tears, but
that he tore his garments as a demonstration of
fatherly and natural affection. Even in that moment,
however, he kept his grief in check, gave his famous
response, and brought Satan to defeat.[3]

We find in Gregory of Nyssa's oration for Pulcheria an elaborate narration of the same event,
replete with details of the calamity claiming his
children's lives.[4] The reader/listener is urged

---

[1]Ibid.

[2]Basil Quod mund. adhaer. non sit 10.

[3]Ibid.

[4]Gr. Nyss. Pulch. (Opera, IX, 469, ll. 20ff.):
"Full were the vessels, ample the provisions of the
table, drinking cups were lifted, there were enter-
tainments for them as is proper and musical pieces
and all kinds of amiable fellow-revellers. Also
toasts, friendly greetings, games and laughter:
every refinement that one expects to find in a
gathering of youths at the hearth. What followed
upon these things? At the peak of the enjoyment of
these pleasures, when the ceiling quaked above them,
the banquet hall becomes a grave for the ten chil-

to imitate the athlete Job, letting him become a
"trainer by his own example with a view to steadfastness and manliness, anointing the soul for the
time of close struggle with testings":

> You do not think, do you, that he delivered
> himself of something low-minded and paltry,
> or made a display of it by his bearing,
> either scratching his cheek with his nails,
> or tearing out the hairs of his head, or
> covering himself with dust, or pounding the
> breast with his hands, or throwing himself
> to the ground, or surrounding himself with
> mourners, or invoking the names of those
> who have passed away, and wailing over their
> memory? He did not one of these things!
> But the one bringing word of the evil events
> described in full the calamity involving the
> children, and he [i.e., Job] at the same
> time both heard and immediately sought to
> probe (ἐφιλοσόφει) concerning the nature
> of the things which are, asking whence
> came the things which are, and from what
> they are brought to birth, and what things
> it is reasonable to expect that we know of
> the things which exist. 'The Lord gave,
> the Lord has taken away.'[1]

The passage reveals a Job with philosophical interests and terminology one might have difficulty dif-
ferentiating from those of Gregory himself! Similarly, he is able to make the account of the
restitution of children and properties to Job a

---

dren, and the vessel mixes with the streams of blood
from the youngsters and provisions of the table are
utterly defiled by the gore from the bodies" (trans.
by author).

[1]Ibid., trans. by author.

transition to the subject of resurrection only because of a theological proposition of which he is
particularly fond. The point of connection is the
idea of restoration: as Job's life was restored to
its original condition, so also resurrection is the
reconstitution of the original nature of man. This
formula, which is thoroughly Platonic,[1] is one of
the prime features of Gregory's theology of resurrection, and we shall have something more to say about
it later. What needs to be mentioned here is the
Cappadocian introduction of a biblical hero in the
place of an exemplary figure from the classical consolation tradition. The figure of Job, appearing in
Basil's writing as the prototype for patience in
suffering, and in Gregory of Nyssa's orations as the
one who turned misfortune into an occasion for
philosophical insight, has been fashioned by authors
who, like Philo and the Alexandrian Christian teachers before them, cannot avoid making historical
persons into personifications of virtues or models of
the philosophic life. Traces of the biblical
themes implicit and explicit in the Job story are
not missing from the consolatory example of the Cappadocians -- sight is not lost of his commitment to
the proposition that all things happen in accordance
with the will of a beneficent God. Job, however, no
less than Anaxagoras, becomes in the consolation
writings an example of a σοφός coping with misfortune, and the Hellenic hues of the portrait are
clearly discernible. He experiences tragedy, and it
evokes questions of ontology; he is threatened by
incapacitating grief, but by the exercise of reason
avoids both insensibility and excessive mourning.
The biblical personage, that is to say, is introduced into consolation by products of Greek education
and letters, and it shows.

---

[1]Ibid., (Opera, IX, 472, l. 10). ἡ εἰς τὸ
ἀρχαῖον τῆς φύσεως ἡμῶν ἀναστοιχείωσις. See also
Gr. Nyss. Anim et res. (NPNF, V, 464).

One gains from Gregory of Nyssa's introduction of Abraham and Sarah into his funeral oration the same impression of the thorough mixture of biblical and Greek ideas and concerns. Abraham is presented as one who is willing to sacrifice Isaac because he sees that his departure would be both better and more providential (πρὸς τὸ κρεῖττόν τε καὶ θειότερον). Leaving behind his wife, τὸ ἀσθενέστερον μερός τῆς ἀνθρωπίνης φυσέως, the patriarch meets his test. But Sarah, rather than Abraham, is the focus of the passage, for Gregory speculates how she might have conducted herself, being subject to motherly affections, and stirred by sumpathy. He imagines her pleadings, and her insistence that Abraham's knife must first remove her from in front of Isaac if the deed is to be done: "One stroke will suffice for the two of us; let the burial mound be the same for both; let one grave-stone give the tragic account of the common misfortune."[1] But Sarah said and did none of these things, Gregory writes, because "she saw those things which are unseen by us...she realized that the end of mortal life is the beginning of the more divine life for those who have departed."[2] Sarah knew, according to our author, that for the departed there is no deceit, desire, arrogance, or "any other such passion of the kind which vex the soul," and this knowledge enabled her to give her child over to God. The passage represents the playing-out of a distinction between manliness (ἀνδρεία) and womanish weakness (γυναικισμός), a contrast which figures prominently in the Alexandrian writings, and is a familiar consolation theme. Gregory, addressing both parents of a deceased child, portrays both Abraham and Sarah as having avoided the feminine, weaker instinct, and to have proven,

---

[1] Gr. Nyss. _Pulch._ (_Opera_, IX, 468-9). Trans. by author.

[2] _Ibid._

like Job, their ὑπομονὴ καὶ ἀνδρεία.[1] The same
counsel is given by Basil, who exhorts Elpidius to
become an "example of manliness," and by Seneca, who
denies his mother the use of her womanhood as an
excuse for persistent grief, since her virtues set
her apart from such weakness.[2]

Beyond the provision of historic examples of
grief courageously borne, and the transmission of
tales of heroism, the Christian consolations also
had in common with their classical precursors the
quotation of authoritative writings. For the Cappadocians, the wisdom of the poets, philosophers
and playwrights, though commendable when directed to
virtues and the pursuit of the good, were not appropriate to this task. Basil and the Gregories fill
their consolatory writings with biblical references
and allusions, and with but few exceptions, spurn
the sayings which were undoubtedly familiar to them
from the Greek letters and orations.[3] In the place
of references to Socrates' speech to the judges, or
the texts from Pindar, Sophocles, Euripides, etc.,
by which the author of the Consolation for Apollonius, for instance, supports his arguments, the
Cappadocian consolers supply a number of scriptural
sayings and allusions. Not infrequently, one sus-

---

[1]Ibid., (Opera IX, 470, ll. 14ff). Note that
in Gr. Naz. Or. 8.4-5 (for his sister Gorgonia)
Gregory refers to their parents Gregory and Nonna
as the Abraham and Sarah of the day.

[2]Basil Ep. 206, Seneca Helv. 16.

[3]There are in Basil's consolation letters no
references to pagan authors. The topoi are not
attached to names, though occasionally a reputable
wise man from the Hellenic tradition is mentioned,
as for example in Gregory of Nazianzus' reference to
Plato in Ep. 31.

pects that some effort has been made to match a known saying from the Hellenic literature, an utterance of Plato or a well-known slogan, with something of similar import from the Bible. It will not advance our case greatly to discuss all of the quotations and allusions which are found in the consolations under consideration. A proliferation of such texts occurs in the longer writings, and not all of them serve a consolatory purpose. There are, however, beyond the mention of the Maccabean heroine, the trials and sayings of Job, and the Abraham-Sarah episode, several texts which recur in Basil's letters and are taken up by his fellow consolers -- these warrant brief discussion.

Like the examples of Job and Abraham, most of the biblical quotations which occur in the consolations are hortatory, and hold out encouragement to the afflicted. There was in Hebrew and early Christian writings an ample supply of statements directed to circumstances of oppression and persecution, and these travelled easily to consolations. In a literature which urged its readers to regard what befell them as a test of loyalty to the deity, and spoke of misfortunes as contests and trials for which they were to be rewarded "crowns of glory" (1 Peter 5.4), the assurance of Paul was necessary: that God would not let his people be tempted beyond their strength, and would provide an escape from trials which makes them endurable. This remark from 1 Corinthians 10.13 appears in three of Basil's letters, and is designed to spur on communities suffering hostilities at the hands of Arians.[1] Something like Paul's guarantee that whatever happens is capable of being endured seems to be evoked by the consolation situation itself. We see that Cicero has recourse to some lines from Euripides' Orestes which make a very similar point:

---

[1] Basil Eps. 139, 140, 256.

No speech so terrible in utterance-
no chance, no ill imposed by wrath of
heaven, which human nature cannot bear
and suffer.[1]

The heartbeat behind biblical (and particularly
the New Testament) exhortations to remain steadfast
in tribulations is the fervent eschatology which envisions not only a God who tolerates the works of a
tempter, but a God who is shortly to preside over a
time of judgment in which persistence of faith and
hope among believers will be determinative for salvation. And there is no reason not to take Basil's
words at face value when this sense of impending
κρίσις enters his consolations. He urges the haras-
sed Christians of Alexandria to bear the present
testing (πειρασμός), and "await the revelation from
heaven and the epiphany of our great God and Savior,
Jesus Christ," knowing that they, like the rest of
creation, will be dissolved.[2] The same combination
of warning and solace is found in a personal letter,
where he reminds the wife of Briso that "the preparation of our defence before our Lord Jesus Christ,
and our zeal to be numbered among those who love
Him, are sufficient to overshadow our grief."[3] It
is entirely in keeping with these theologoumena that
certain explicitly eschatological passages from the
New Testament should secure places in the consolation
writings. One finds in Basil's Ep. 139 the combination of Hebrews 11.36-7 (about faithful witnesses

---

[1]Cicero Tusc. 4.29.63 (trans. King, 401). The
passage from Euripides Orestes 1 reads:
    οὐκ ἔστιν οὐδὲν δεινὸν ὧδ' εἰπεῖν ἔπος,
    οὐδὲ πάθος, οὐδὲ συμφορὰ θεήλατος,
    ἧς οὐκ ἂν ἄροιτ' ἄχθος ἀνθρώπου φύσις.

[2]Basil Ep. 139 (trans. Deferrari, II, 329).

[3]Basil Ep. 302 (trans. Deferrari, IV, 235).

who were "sawn in two" and "killed with the sword")
with the celebrated statement from Romans 8.18 ("the
sufferings of this present time are not worth com-
paring with the glory that is to be revealed in us").
Habakkuk's promise of the one who is coming in "a
little while," cited in Hebrews 10.37 for those who
have "need of endurance," appears in Basil's epistles,
along with several more dramatic passages depicting
the fire and destruction of the day of judgment.[1]
Apparently Basil and his colleagues found such themes
applicable to any situations of distress, and used
them unsparingly in their consolations directed either
to individuals grieving over deaths or communities of
Christians beleaguered by lack of leadership and
oppression from Arian foes.

The most prominent of the biblical passages
which repeatedly emerge in consolationes, as mentioned above, is Paul's injunction to the church in
Thessalonica that they should not, out of their concern for those who had "fallen asleep," conduct themselves like "the rest" (non-Christians) who are
without hope. We have already noted one of the
reasons the text appealed to Christian consolers (in
this they were faithful to Paul's intent) -- it chal-
lenged believers to demonstrate to the surrounding
culture that their faith enabled them to transcend
the sorrows which attend disasters and deaths. The
text would have been read and heard as more than
παραίνεσις by Christians of the fourth century,
however, for we must assume that the entire passage,
as well as the single sentence, was known to them.

---

[1]Hebrews 10.37 is referred to in Eps. 238 and
140. See 2 Peter 3.7, Luke 18.7 in Ep. 256, Luke
18.8 in Ep. 257, 2 Thess. 3b-4a in Ep. 139. References to the "kingdom" based on biblical imagery are
not uncommon: reminiscences of Isaiah 35.10, 51.11
and Matthew 25.34 are seen in Gr. Nyss. Placill.
(Opera, IX, 486-7).

The citation of 1 Thessalonians 4.13-14 in a consolation must surely have been an abbreviated way of con-
juring in the minds of the correspondents or listeners
the whole Pauline vision of the sounding of the trump,
the progression of the saints of the past and present
"to meet the Lord in the air and...always be with the
Lord" (1 Thess. 4.17). It, too, is one of the eschatological passages which entered Christian consolation -- perhaps chief among them. When a preacher
made this the text for his funeral oration, or the
letter writer positioned it strategically in his
missive, the Christian hope was being stated in short-
hand. For the Cappadocians, as for Paul, this ἐλπίς
was a categorically different brand of confidence
than that available to non-believers, for it was
grounded in the belief of Jesus' resurrection, his
expected parousia, and the judgment in which, as
Basil writes, "the Lord will not abandon his holy
ones."[1] In Basil's letter to Nectarius, the consolatory import of the saying from Thessalonians is
made explicit:

> ...it is God's command that those who put
> their trust in Christ shall not grieve
> for those who have been laid to rest, be-
> cause of their hope of the resurrection....[2]

Similarly, at the end of the sermon for Pulcheria, a
discussion of the fact that death was necessary as
the beginning of a "metamorphosis towards the better"
is "sealed" by the quotation of Paul's word about
hope to the church in Thessalonica.[3]

It is not surprising that Paul's famous passage

---

[1] Basil _Ep._ 257 (trans. Deferrari, IV, 35).

[2] Basil _Ep._ 5 (trans. Deferrari, I, 35).

[3] Gr. Nyss. _Pulch._ (_Opera_, IX, 472, ll. 15-17).

on resurrection in the fifteenth chapter of 1 Corinthians also appears in the consolations. Again, the mention of a line, or an allusion to the seed-analogy is seen to be sufficient to call to the audience's mind the resurrection-teaching which is the substance of the hope shared by Christians. When Gregory of Nazianzus speaks of "the last trumpet" in the midst of his tribute to Caesarius, and Gregory of Nyssa argues that Job's contemplation of "the things which are" led him to see that the life to come is not like the kernel, but the beauty of the ear of grain, they are both invoking images which have become the commonplaces of Christian speech.[1] The passages from Thessalonians and Corinthians, the allusions to Job's courage, even the references to "our hope" and the "promise of the future" which do not receive particular emphasis in the literature, function as topoi in the Christian consolations. They are the mutually understood touchstones upon which the composer of the paramythetic letter or oration could reply. This is not to say that the virtual elimination of quotations from the Greek writers in favor of scripture utterly transformed (as some have argued) the consolation argumentation, or effectively removed from pictures of death and the future life all influences of the Hellenic tradition. This anxious concern to distinguish between the biblical and Greek notions of death and afterlife, and the inclination to dissociate the teachings of Jesus and Socrates on the question, though clearly an important issue for some recent scholars, did not weigh so heavily upon the Cappadocians.[2]

---

[1]Gr. Naz. Or. 7.21, Gr. Nyss. Pulch. (Opera, IX, 472).

[2]See Oscar Cullmann's 1955 Ingersoll Lecture "Immortality of the Soul or Resurrection of the Dead?" in Immortality and Resurrection, ed. by Krister Stendahl (New York: The Macmillan Company, 1965),

Our consideration of these few among the biblical texts which Christian consolers found "topical"
permits us to return somewhat naturally to the themes
with which consolers, pagan and Christian, occupied
themselves in their closing sentences: afterlife,
the end of souls' bondage, and the life "beyond."
We encounter in the Cappadocian consolations a healthy
mixture of biblical and Christian doctrinal language,
on the one hand, and Greek and Platonic imagery, on
the other. Indeed, the two strains of thought so
interpenetrate one another that it would be misleading, in this instance, to propose that any unbridge-
able opposition is seen to exist between ideas of
immortality and resurrection. Having taken two
accounts of creation, the Genesis account and the
Platonic scheme of fallen souls, and run them together,[1] the Cappadocians, like Origen before them,
likewise were obliged to produce a resolution or
finale of the process which combined in a single
eschatology motifs stemming from both the biblical
and the Greco-Roman traditions. We see in the
attempts of the fathers of the early church to say
which doctrines of the Greeks (transmigration, palin-
genesis, etc.) are most proximate to the resurrection
belief of Christians a real attentiveness to the
points of congruence and conflict.[2] It is as if these
theologians are, with extreme care, shuffling together

---

pp. 9-53. (Volume hereafter cited as Stendahl,
Immortality).

[1]For the resultant problems in defining sin,
see the treatment by Brooks Otis, "Cappadocian Thought
as a Coherent System," DOP XII (Cambridge, Mass.:
Harvard University Press, 1958), pp. 109-16.

[2]For discussion and references see Harry A.
Wolfson, "Immortality and Resurrection in the Philosophy of the Church Fathers," Stendahl, Immortality,
pp. 54-96.

two different, but equally familiar decks of playing
cards -- both had been required in the age of the
Apologists, and by the fourth century the close proximity, even the melding, of ideas from the Phaedo and
from St. Paul is a usual and natural phenomenon in
theological writings.

This is no less true from the spelling-out of
the hopes for the departed (and those soon to follow)
which occur in the consolations of Basil and the Gregories. Death is repeatedly termed the separation
of soul from body, or liberation of the life of the
human being from the bonds of flesh (τῶν δεσμῶν τῆς
σαρκὸς), as in Basil's sixth letter. Basil's remark
in Ep. 101 is typical:

> If the hope of Christians were limited to
> this life, the early separation from the
> body would reasonably be thought hard; but
> if for those who live according to God the
> beginning of the true life is the release
> of the soul from these bodily bonds, why
> then are we sorrowful even as 'those who
> have no hope?'[1]

Gregory of Nazianzus is not at all hesitant to
announce kinship of this notion of the separation
of soul from body with the ideas of Plato. He con-
soles a man named Philagrios by telling him that
his misfortune affects only the body and things corporeal, and urges him to live for the time to come,
making this life a preparation for death (again,

---

[1]Basil Ep. 101 (trans. Deferrari, II, 189).
Other references to release from the body occur in
Eps. 301, 302. In the passage in question, we note
Basil's appropriation of the "life according to..."
formula, familiar to us from the philosophical
schools. Christians are those, Basil says, who
locate the true life in τὸ κατὰ θεὸν ςῆν.

Phaedo 64A), since, as Plato said, the soul is to be released from the body, or the Prison.[1] The much-used Platonic play on the words σῶμα and σῆμα was available to our authors, who thought the idea perfectly compatible with the Pauline yearning in Philippians to "depart ("the flesh," as he says in the next verse) and be with Christ."[2] Gregory of Nyssa searched out a passage from Psalm 148 to support the same theme. He asks rhetorically in the funeral sermon for Flacilla whether David did not cry out to the Lord, "deliver my soul from prison" (ἐξάγαγε ἐκ φυλακῆς τὴν ψυχήν μου) and whether the ancient holy ones did not recognize "the departure from the body [to be] preferable for the soul."[3]

The use of the motif of the soul's separation from the body at death as a solacium is common in

---

[1]Gr. Naz. Ep. 31.4: καὶ ζῆν ἀντὶ τοῦ παρόντος τῷ μέλλοντι, θανάτου μελέτην - τοῦτο ὁ φησί Πλάτων - τὸν τῇδε βίον ποιούμενον καὶ λύοντα τὴν ψυχὴν τοῦ εἴτε σώματος, εἴτε σήματος, κατ' ἐκεῖνον εἰπεῖν, ὅση δύναμις.

[2]Philippians 1.23. Basil recounts in Ep. 29 that he was often "moved to indignation against [Athanasius of Ancyra]...because, in the desire which came to possess him 'to be dissolved and to be with Christ,' he did not prefer, for our sakes, 'to abide still in the flesh'" (trans. Deferrari, I, 173). In Ep. 76, Gregory of Nazianzus combines the preparation theme from Phaedo 64A and the Philippians text in reference to Basil.

[3]Gr. Nyss. Placill. (Opera, IX, 484), trans. by author. See also Gregory's Pulch. (Opera, IX, 467) and Melet. (Opera, IX, 455), where Ps. 124.7 (the "snare is broken and the bird has flown away") is quoted in reference to the bishop of Antioch, who "has been freed from the bondage of the body."

the consolations of non-Christian authors, both before
and after the beginning of the Christian era. Steeped
in the writings of Plato and the poets, composers of
consolations spoke of the soul's divine origin, an
idea already found in the Axiochus,[1] and, like Pseudo-
Plutarch, drew from their reading of the Cratylus the
inference "that death is...nothing else than the
severing of two things, soul and body, from each
other."[2] We have already had occasion to discuss
the proposition with which Cicero wrestles in the
opening of his Tusculans -- that regardless of whether death means total extinction of life and intelligence or a migration of the soul to blissful
estates, consolation is possible. For the Atomists,
there was no evil in death because the soul was no
more. But for Plutarch, for Cicero in the Somnium
Scipionis, and for Seneca, death was deliverance in
a different sense. It was the release of the immortal soul into true life, or as Seneca wrote, "the
birthday of eternity" (aeterni natalis).[3] So it is
that Plutarch commends to his wife the law which

---

[1]Plato Axiochus 370B. Also Cicero Tusc. 1.25.
61-3, 68-70. Crantor is thought to have been the
"middle man" between the writer of the Axiochus and
Cicero and the Plutarchian consoler by Buresch,
Consolationum, p. 54.

[2]Plutarch Cons. ad Apoll. 121E (trans. Babbitt,
II, 211).

[3]Seneca Ep. 102. In the same letter he writes:
"It is no new thing for you to be sundered from that
of which you had previously been a part...This is
what ordinarily happens: when we are born, the
afterbirth always perishes. Why love such a thing
as if it were your own possession? It was merely
your covering. The day will come which will tear
you forth and lead you away from the company of the
foul and noisome womb. Withdraw from it now too as

forbids the mourning of infants, "those who have departed to a dispensation and a region too that is better and more divine."[1] And Seneca assures Marcia that only the image of her son has perished: "he himself is eternal and has reached now a far better state, stripped of all outward encumbrances....he has fled and wholly departed from earth...sped away to join the souls of the blessed."[2]

If pagan and Christian consolers in the Hellenistic period do not speak in very different terms of what happens to the soul at death, and the distinctions which might be expected to be kept sharp

---

much as you can...and ponder on something nobler and loftier. Some day the secrets of nature will be disclosed to you, the haze will be shaken from your eyes...Then you will say that you have lived in darkness, after you have seen, in your perfect state, the perfect light."

[1]Plutarch Cons. ad uxorem 612A (trans. De Lacy and Einarson, VII, 605). See also 611DF. Plutarch argues that the soul which is in the world only a short time regains its divine "posture" easily. Gregory of Nyssa makes a similar point in the oration for Pulcheria: "...are we vexed that she has not come to the experience of such things [i.e., the sufferings of old age]? No, it is fitting to rejoice together with those whose lives did not admit the experience of the saddened, did not feel griefs here, nor will discover anything of the saddened there. For this sort of soul, which having nothing for which it should come to judgment, does not fear Gehenna..." (Opera, IX, 465-6, trans. by author). See Seneca Marc. 23.

[2]Seneca Marc. 24-5 (trans. Basore II, 89). On the interesting combination of this immortality doctrine with vestiges of Stoic eschatology of conflagration, see the letter's conclusion.

between resurrection and immortality become blurred
in Cappadocian letters and orations, we are only
meeting further evidence of what can be seen in their
longer theological writings. They compress biblical
(particularly Pauline) and Platonic notions of the
soul (i.e., psychologies), and they assume that the
New Testament proclamation of resurrection was the
fulfillment of a vision of deliverance from mortality
which had been anticipated by the Greeks, but not
"ratified" by divine revelation until the advent
and triumph of Jesus.[1] In insistent discussions
Christian theologians, the Cappadocians among them,
propounded the uniqueness of the Church's belief in
resurrection and immortality, asserting that immortality, like life itself, is bestowed by a gracious
God, and does not belong naturally (or essentially)
to the soul (κατὰ χάριν , not κατὰ φύσιν), and that
the resurrected "body" is identifiable as in some
sense the body which had existed before. These
ideas are not given detailed explication, however,
in the consolations.[2]

---

[1]Werner Jaeger, "The Greek Ideas of Immortality,"
in Stendahl, Immortality, p. 112, writes: "The
Christian Fathers rejected the story of the transmigration of the soul, but they accepted the immortality of the individual soul, since they found it
reconcilable with Paul's notion of the resurrection
and with Jewish-Christian angelology, i.e., the existence of a world of immaterial beings. The most
important fact in the history of Christian doctrine
was that the father of Christian theology, Origen,
was a Platonic philosopher at the school of Alexandria. He built into Christian doctrine the whole
cosmic drama of the soul, which he took from Plato,
and although later Christian Fathers decided that
they took over too much, that which they kept was
still the essence of Plato's philosophy of the soul."

[2]See Wolfson, "Immortality and Resurrection in
the Philosophy of the Church Fathers," pp. 54-64,

Even if it is difficult to separate in these writings the resurrection from the immortality language and imagery, it is worthwhile to examine briefly the more striking of those passages in which resurrection is expressly mentioned as a source of consolation. This will enable us to assess the extent to which this Christian solacium, presumably the church's most compelling offering in this context, assumed a place of importance among the argument utilized. It should also put us in a position to appreciate what particularly Cappadocian "twists" were given to the received descriptions of the Christian hope and the life enjoyed by the heavenly company.

Explicit reference to the resurrection occurs in only two of Basil's nineteen consolation letters, though in both instances the doctrine is recommended as that argument "above all" (ἐπὶ πᾶσιν) capable of bringing comfort.[1] The infrequent appearance of the word ἀνάστασις in the letters does not suggest, it must be supposed, an indifference on Basil's part to this particular Christian topos, even if, when it does appear it is set among many others. Rather, the doctrine is presupposed in his many references to "hope," his quotation of Paul's words to the Thessalonians, Romans, and the like. Basil's treatment in this instance is analogous to his arguments, discussed earlier, to the effect that all events have their place in a providential scheme -- he assumes the God of the Christians, rather than Tyche, to be director. So also in his assurances of eternal life and rewards for those who persevere, Basil assumes ἀνάστασις in Christ to be the ground of hope for survival of death, even if it goes unnamed.

---

for argument and references.

[1]Basil Eps. 5 and 301. In the latter epistle, the phrase is πρὸ πάντων.

The shape of resurrection belief is more fully articulated in the orations of Gregory of Nazianzus. A striking passage occurs in his panegyric for Caesarius. Gregory claims to be adding a more powerful remedy (φάρμακον) to the string of solacia already offered, and he proceeds to speak of the liberation of the God-beloved soul from prison and its rush to meet its Lord (I Thess. 4.17). He continues:

> Then, a little later, it receives its kindred flesh (τὸ συγγενὲς σαρκίον) which once shared in its pursuits of the things above, from the earth which both gave and had been entrusted with it, and in some way known to God, who knit them together and dissolved them, enters with it upon the inheritance of glory there. And, as it shared, through their close union, in its hardships, so also it bestows upon it a portion of its joys, gathering it up entirely into itself, and becoming with it one spirit and mind and God. (ἕν καὶ πνεῦμα καὶ νοῦς καὶ θέος).[1]

We note several things about the passage. It issues, first of all, from a series of statements which reveal the Platonic view of the soul -- most specifically its separability from the body,[2] -- but asserts the reception by this soul of the flesh appropriate to it. Gregory, like Origen,[3] appears to be

---

[1]Greg. Naz. Or. 7.21 (trans. from NPNF, VII, 236-7, except for the last phrase, which cannot be rendered "one in spirit and in mind and in God").

[2]Wolfson, "Immortality and Resurrection in the Philosophy of the Church Fathers" in Stendahl, Immortality, p. 79.

[3]Origen De prin. 2.2.2, Cels. 5.18-24.

framing Paul's notion of the pneumatic body in terms
of incorruptible and divine "substance" - a body
suitable for heavenly existence. However qualified
this "flesh" might seem to be, the clear point of
the passage is to give voice to the Christian proposition that the whole being, as part of the creation
which God pronounced good, is "to inherit the glory."
There is a sense in which it is a doctrine which
strives to give up as little of the Platonic soul and
as little of the resurrected body as possible, but it
is a compromise of each position. The closing sentence describes the resurrected being, the fleshly
element gathered entirely into the psychic, as becoming spirit, mind and God. Here we meet Gregory's
conception of θέωσις, the process by which the
Christian became a participant in the divine life.
To this favorite theme of Gregory we shall want to
return in the next chapter.

Let us consider the passage, mentioned earlier,
in which Gregory of Nyssa uses the restoration of
goods and family to Job as a springboard for his
resurrection solacium:

> ...death deprives the departed not at all
> as far as being is concerned. For death
> is nothing else for men than a purifying
> of evil. Since our nature was established
> in the beginning by the God of the uni-
> verse like a vessel capable of receiving
> good things and, when the enemy of our
> souls had infused evil in us through cun-
> ning, the good was displaced, for this
> reason, so that the implanted evil would
> not be eternal in us, the vessel is dis-
> solved temporarily in death by a superior
> Providence, so that when the evil flowed
> out, man might be formed anew and be re-
> stored to the original life, untainted by
> evil. For this is the resurrection, the
> re-formation into the original state of
> our nature. If then it is impossible for
> human nature to be reconstituted for the

better without resurrection, and if resurrection is not able to take place unless death goes before, then death would
be a good, becoming for us a beginning
and a way of change towards the better."[1]

We see in the passage Gregory's persistent theme,
also an inheritance from Origen, that evil, rather
than matter, is the pernicious element in man. It
stems from the view, fundamental to Origenist cosmology (and theodicy), that fleshly encasement is the
result of the error, the falling away of souls
from the divine life -- not the cause. Gregory of
Nyssa explains the purpose of the temporary separation of soul and body to which his colleague had
referred: it is necessary for that purgation of
evil which must precede the restoration of man to
the purity he enjoyed before the Fall, the restoration of the "image of God." Again we observe the
concern of Christian theology to reclaim the whole
man, or rather to assert that the "God of the Universe" intends to be accountable for all that he
created. It is only the dross of evil and evil
inclinations which death is designed to eliminate.
But the assertion of an only temporary separation of
soul and body by these theologians doubtless contains a renunciation of the ultimate severance up-
held in Platonism, and a corrective of the emphasis
on the separability of the two spied in Origen.[2]
Biblical eschatology and the Pauline treatment of
the resurrection, however spiritualized, required

---

[1]Gr. Nyss. Pulch. (Opera, IX, 471-2). Trans.
by author.

[2]Milton McC. Gatch, Death: Meaning and Mortality in Christian Thought and Contemporary Culture
(New York, The Seabury Press, 1969), pp. 62-3, makes
this point in connection with Gregory's treatise On
the Soul and Resurrection.

some scheme for the incorporation of soul and body
(to be sure, an incorruptible body) in the restitution of man's primal nature. With that qualification, Gregory of Nyssa was willing, even eager, to
use Platonic as well as New Testament language to
describe the final restoration. For when he says
that the resurrection is ἡ εἰς τό ἀρχαῖον τῆς φύσεως
ἡμῶν ἀναστοιχείωσις, his favorite formula for this
Christian dogma, he is echoing Plato's Symposium.[1]

Our findings indicate, then, that for Basil,
resurrection (as the basis of the hope peculiar to
Christians) functions very much like other topoi,
and takes its place among many other solacia which
can be traced to the Hellenic consolation tradition,
or to texts and examples from the Bible which suggested themselves to the consoler. It may be that
the Bishop of Caesarea composed such epistles with
the particularity of the Christian ἐλπίς taken for
granted. It remains true, however, that the explicit reference to resurrection as a παραμυθία was
not considered by him to be a necessary ingredient
of the letter of condolence. It occurs infrequently,
and in those two instances where it appears, the
theme of resurrection does not dominate in the sense
that other argumenta slip into the background or are
said by the author to be obviated. A comparison
with letters of Jerome and Augustine in the West,
and those of Theodoret, an Eastern Christian consoler who belongs to the next generation after Basil,
highlights the point being made here, for the resurrection gains fuller treatment and more prominent
placement in the consolatory epistles written by
these men.[2] The situation is different in the

---

[1]Specifically, Plato Symposium 192E-193D, as
noted in Gregory of Nyssa, NPNF, V, 464. The phrase
appears in Gregory's De an. et res., Pulch., In
Eccles., De virg., De mortuis. Cf. Origen Cels. 5.23.

[2]Indicative of this is Theodoret's Ep. 43, in

orations of the two Gregories, which represent resurrection as one of the chief sources of solace. Often,
as in the two works we have just discussed, the doctrine is, in effect, the capstone of a tower of topoi,
and leads the authors to exclaim that it is the most
powerful remedy for grief, or that death can, in the
light of the resurrection, be welcomed as the beginning of the ascent to something better -- the regaining of the image of God. As the resurrection idea
appears in the sermons, it is more than a slogan or
by-word, for we have seen that even in the capsule
presentations of the doctrine in these works we are
encountering something more than mere recital --
there are clear signs of the theologians' own interests and interpretations. It comes as no surprise
that Christian writers have recourse to the resurrection-teaching in their paramythetic efforts. This
principal solacium of the Christian community was
clearly capable, like quotations from scripture and
ecclesiastically-colored eulogy, of asserting itself
in a genre which was highly controlled in terms of
both form and ideas. The further question we shall
need to ask is whether the Cappadocians were able
to be inventive consolers beyond the selection of
already available topoi, Greek and Christian --
whether, in fact, the Tendenz of a particular writer, or of "Cappadocian thought" gained voice in
these most formalized writings.

In the usual consolation epistle or treatise,
whether pagan or Christian, discussions about death,
or the soul's separation from the body, or the many
evils of the world that are better left behind,
move purposefully to the point at which the deceased
can be pictured in a paradise of some description.
Menander had tutored those who desired to compose a
proper παραμυθητικὸς λόγος to conclude their

---

which the resurrection theme takes up half of the
letter. Only Ep. 65 among his consolatory letters
fails to take up this topos. See also Jerome Ep. 60.
2-4.

arguments and examples with beatitude motifs. The orator, he says, should persuade his audience that the deceased abides happily in the Elysian Fields, that he or she looks down upon the mourners and responds to their lamentations with a reproach. The soul, returned to its divine home, needs no mourning. They warrant mourning, rather, who are left below.[1] Menander's suggestions are taken up in several writings. We see Lucian in his work On Grief[2] imagining a dead man rising in his casket to ridicule his mourners, and Sulpicius writes in the same vein, though more cautiously, to Cicero that "if there be any consciousness even among the dead, such was your daughter's love for you and affection for all her family, that this [i.e., mourning] at any rate is not what she would have you do."[3] Similarly, Gregory of Nyssa's Oration on Meletius begins and ends with declarations that the departed bishop has joined the apostles, enlarging their number. He now intercedes for his friends and followers left behind, among whose "negligences and ignorances," no doubt, is their mourning for one now in bliss.

We see in the treatises of Seneca and Plutarch that these climactic visions of the happy state of the departed were thought to be significant consolatory motifs, and the language is appropriately vivid. Marcia is treated to a description of her son's welcome by a "saintly band" including the Scipios and Catos and Marcia's own father, who has become the boy's guide as they wander happily "throughout the free and boundless spaces of eternity," capable of mingling with the stars.[4] Invoking the Stoic doctrine

---

[1] Menander De demonst., Spengel, Rhetores III, 414.

[2] Lucian De luctu 16, Cicero Fam. 4.5.

[3] Aristeides Or. 11.

[4] Seneca Marc. 25-26. Here, Marcia's father

of the ἐκπύρωσις , Seneca relates how all the created
order, including those "who have partaken of immortality" will ultimately be part of the "mighty destruction," reverting to the antiqua elementa. The
knowledge of this eschatological mystery adds to the
happiness which Marcia's son is enjoying.[1] Plutarch's
words to his wife about their daughter Timoxena are
simpler:

> That she has passed to a state where there
> is no pain need not be painful to us; for
> what sorrow can come to us through her,
> if nothing now can make her grieve?[2]

Our Cappadocian consolations provide ample evidence that the Christian author had no intention of
being outdone in the pictorialization of the felici-
ties enjoyed in paradise. The heavenly landscape is
not populated by the Dioscuri, Heracles, and other
heroes, but with the giants of virtue of the Old
Testament, and the band of martyrs and saints waiting
to greet those passing from the world of change and
temptation to life in the presence of God. Further,
the entry of the redeemed into paradise is not thought
to be postponed until the Great Resurrection, as one
learns quickly from these writings. Basil writes en-
thusiastically of the reception to be had in heaven
by those who are worthy, especially those who died

---

tells her, "minds are uncovered and hearts revealed
and our lives are open and manifest to all, while
every age and things to come are ranged before our
sight" (trans. Basore, II, 91-5). On contemplation
of the stars as the occupation of the blessed, see
Cumont, After Life, ch. 8.

[1]Seneca Marc. 26.6-7.

[2]Plutarch Cons. ad uxorem 611E (trans. De Lacy
and Einarson, VII, 601).

young and avoided the corruptions of earthly existence, and those who, when their faith and orthodoxy
were tested, proved themselves "noble athletes."
"Earth has not covered your beloved," Basil assures
the parents of children who have died, "but heaven
has received him."[1] (As Plutarch had comforted his
wife that their daughter's soul had not been long
enough in the world to become "warped," so also
Gregory of Nyssa argues that the princess Pulcheria
passes from life without reason to fear Gehenna.)[2]
It belongs to the Gregories to provide the grand
detail of the beatitude of the elect. Celestial
food from the "angelic board," eternal hymning and
praise to the Triune God, contemplation of the unseen
realities, life free of all disturbances of the passions, limitless joy -- all of these are part of the
μετουσία θεοῦ, which the saints experience in eternity. Nor is it too much for those left behind to
hope that the ones taken from them now intercede with
God on their behalf.[3] Gregory Nazianzus imagines
that his father, having shaken off his bodily chains,
"holds intercourse naked with the nakedness of the
prime and purest mind, being promoted...to the rank
and confidence of an angel."[4] The same writer ends
his oration for his sister Gorgonia by addressing
these words to her:

> Better is your present lot...the throng of
> angels, the heavenly host, the vision of

---

[1]Basil Eps. 5, 300 (trans. Deferrari, I, 37 and
IV, 223).

[2]Plutarch Cons. ad uxorem 611E, Gr. Nyss. Pulch.
(Opera IX, 466).

[3]Gr. Naz. Or. 18.4.

[4]Gr. Naz. Or. 18.4 (trans. from NPNF, VII,
256).

glory, and that splendor, pure and perfect
beyond all other, of the Trinity Most High,
no longer beyond the ken of the captive
mind, dissipated by the senses, but entirely contemplated and possessed by the
undivided mind, and flashing upon our
souls with the whole light of the God-
head.[1]

This theme of heavenly contemplation of the God whose
essence cannot be plumbed is a particularly striking
feature of Cappadocian consolations, and stands out
all the more because in this literature it follows
upon a number of solacia which emphasize the frustrations of life in the world and the limitations of
minds, still, as our authors like to say, obscured
by clay.

Such glimpses of the glorified ones represent
more than a change in mood effected by proficient
rhetors. Two orders of existence come into view in
the consolation: the life of those destined to
mourn others and die themselves, and those who have
been delivered from corruptibility and live in the
presence of things beyond mortal vision. In perhaps
no other kind of writing is the distinction and gra-
dation of "sarkic" and "pneumatic" existence reduced
to such bald contrast. The literature is addressed
to those who struggle vainly against a life of contin-
gencies and fall prey to passions they cannot control,
but it dramatizes the glorified life of beings for
whom there is no more instability of soul, no remaining uncertainties. So it is that in these consolations one finds portraits of humanity at both
extremes: man subject to evil and death, and man the
holy one, liberated from the turmoil of mundane
captivity. In the context of the genre, they are
images of the suffering mortal and the escapee to

---

[1]Gr. Naz Or. 8.23 (trans. from NPNF, VII, 244).

paradise, but for our consoler-theologians they are
more, for they suggest the old man and the new, the
life of everyman, and the life of those who have
commenced in its perfect form τὸ τῷ θεῷ ζῆν.   In
these contrasting pictures there are more issues
at stake than is immediately apparent -- because
for the Cappadocians philosophy itself is taken up
with the movement from estrangement to communion, the
transformation of man from mourner to beholder of God.
This purpose, they believe, is at the heart of the
divine economy, with the result that παραμυθία and
θεολογία become one and the same enterprise.   It is
a theological point of genuine importance, then, in
addition to being the solacium to which depiction of
the heavenly life led, when the Cappadocians take
up an ancient theme, that death is wrongly feared
and in fact wrongly named.   Gregory of Nazianzus
ends the consolatory portion of the oration for his
father with these words about life and death:

> One takes its rise from the corruption
> which is our mother, runs its course
> through the corruption which is the dis-
> placement of all that is present, and
> comes to an end in the corruption that
> is the dissolution of this life; while the
> other which is able to set us free from
> the ills of this life, and oftentimes
> translates us to the life above, is not
> in my opinion accurately called death,
> and is more dreadful in name than in
> reality; so that we are in danger of ir-
> rationally being afraid of what is not
> fearful, and courting as preferable what
> we really ought to fear.   There is one
> life, to look to life.   There is one
> death, sin, for it is the destruction of
> the soul.   But all else, of which some
> are proud, is a dream vision, making
> sport of realities....What grievance can
> we find in being transferred hence to the
> true life?   In being freed from the vicis-

situdes, the agitation, the disgust, and
all the vile tribute we must pay to this
life, to find ourselves, amid stable things,
which know no flux, while as lesser lights
we circle around the great light?[1]

It is on this note that the Cappadocians conclude
their consolatory arguments, imparting to a yearning
shared by the whole of Hellenistic culture the particular impress of a religion which saw revealed in
an incarnate God the means of deliverance which was
ἔξοδος, a way out, but even more ἄνοδος, a way
upwards.

　　If the attention we now give to the epilogue of
the consolatio seems anticlimactic, that is itself
faithful to the conventions of the genre. Examination
of two of the motifs which serve to close the letters
and orations will make this clear. It is usual for
the consoler to deliver some practical advice to the
bereaved about worthy duties which can distract the
person from the lingering pangs of grief. Basil,
like many before him, counsels a widow to pay heed
to the rearing of her children, an occupation which
he promises will "divert [her] soul from its sorrows."[2]　A different kind of advice urges the mourner
to find consolation in the memory of the dead, and
to call to mind the privilege of having lived with
such a man or woman, in contrast with which the

---

[1]Gr. Naz. Or. 18.42 (trans. from NPNF, VII, 268-
9). The same theme is found in Basil Ep. 101 and
De morte (M1266-1268), and in Nyssa's Pulch., Placill., Melet. (Opera, IX, 469, ll. 10-14; 484, ll.
3-19; 455, ll. 2-3, resp.).

[2]Basil Ep. 302 (trans. Deferrari, IV, 235).　Cf.
Plato Menex. 248D, Seneca Marc. 16.7, Helv. 19.3.

loss does not seem an exorbitant toll.[1] Basil combines the two topoi in his advice to the wife of Briso: let your sons "stand as living images, giving consolation for the absence of him for whom you yearn."[2] The other set of exhortations which characteristically appear in our consolations are not without precedent in the Hellenic writings, for we recall from the Menexenus the heroes' speech left as a legacy for their survivors, with its injunction that "they will best forget their ill fortune and live a life that is nobler and truer and more pleasing in our eyes."[3] There is about the Christian consolers' presentation of the same idea a more abrasive tone, for it is couched in the language of eschatology and issues from the conviction that encounters with the devil's warfare are meant to lead on to perfection (πρὸς τὴν τελείωσιν).[4] It is appropriate to end our examination of the topoi employed in the paramythetic writings of Basil and the Gregories with the word with which the bishop of Caesarea concludes his letter to the Nicopolitan presbyters:

---

[1]This popular theme is found in Basil Ep. 302, Gr. Naz. Eps. 76, 197.7, and in Seneca Ep. 99, Polyb. 10.3, Marc. 4-5. Basil writes in Ep. 301: "...For a husband to grieve over his separation from his wife is itself no small gift among the gifts of God, to those who look at the matter reasonably; for many have we known who have accepted the dissolution of an incompatible marriage as a relief from a burden" (trans. Deferrari, IV, 229).

[2]Basil Ep. 302 (trans. Deferrari, IV, 233-5).

[3]Plato Menex. 248D (trans. R.G. Bury, LCL, VII, 1952, p. 377).

[4]Basil Ep. 101.

The more numerous trials you experience,
the more perfect reward you must expect
from the just Judge. Do not, then, be
impatient with the present situation, nor
grow weary of hope. For yet a little and
a very little while, and He who assists
you will come to you, and will not delay.[1]

The preceding pages have been taken up with an
examination of the relationship of Cappadocian consolation methods and arguments to the larger Greco-
Roman tradition of the consolatio. It is a relationship of heavy indebtedness in which numerous lines
of reasoning, images and examples are traceable to
a common stream of topoi created and embellished
over several centuries. But it is doubtful that our
authors had any sense of being purloiners as they
appropriated these items from the general treasury.
The tradition was theirs, and as they viewed the
matter, its flowers were there for the visiting by
any diligent and discriminating bee. Our comparisons have revealed the degree of impact of Christian
teachings and traditions upon inherited Hellenic
consolatory ideas and models: the turning of eulogy
in the direction of attributes and deeds prized
within the church, the displacement of classical quotations and heroes by correlate biblical materials,
the traces of Christian theological tenets in discussions of providence and eschatology, the attempt
to connect the doctrine of μετριοπάθεια with the
Jesus-tradition (and with current Christological
assertions), and the combination of resurrection
teaching with already avilable notions of immortality
and beatific existence.

Cappadocian consolation, as we have treated it
to this point, represents the utilization and adaptation of materials familiar to us from non-Chris-

---

[1]Basil Ep. 238 (trans. Deferrari, III, 415).

tian writings of the genre, with the addition of elements from the Christian tradition which are <u>topoi</u>
in their own right (resurrection doctrine, the examples of biblical personages, the exhortations of Paul,
etc.). It remains to be shown whether and to what
extent theological themes and emphases which "counted"
for Basil and the Gregories and figured prominently
in what might be called "Cappadocian thought" are
discernible in their consolatory writings, and this
is the subject of the concluding chapter.

CHAPTER 5:
CAPPADOCIAN θεολογία AS παραμυθία :
DEATH AS SEPARATION FROM THE WORLD AND
ASCENT TO GOD

The purpose of our examination of the solacia
which predominate in the consolatory writings of the
Cappadocians is by now transparent. We have been
conducting, through scrutiny of a single literary
genre, what amounts to a case-study of the thesis
that for these writers the Greek paideia and the
Christian paideia functioned as complementary
resources, both indispensible for the full articulation of their φιλοσοφία. In tracing the "gene-
alogies" of several of the argumenta and citing the
parallels of consolatory motifs and topics in other
writings, we have managed to identify among the
paramythetic ideas used by Basil and the Gregories
two sources which, even though they influence and
interpenetrate one another, remain distinguishable.
The first, carrying the burden of the consolatory
task, are those solacia developed over hundreds of
years by Hellenic "physicians of the soul," philosophers of all schools who turned their minds to the
problem of death and the therapy of grief. When one
of the Cappadocians drew from this storehouse of
commonplaces, he did so naturally, neither as an
interloper nor borrower, for this tradition was his.
To these nuggets of the Greek literature of condolence our authors added sayings, images and insights
from the substance of their Christian education --
from the Bible and from the teachings of the church.
We have noted some of the results: Job became the
ideal of patience in the face of adversity; tribulations were proclaimed the testing ground for those
soon to be rewarded or penalized by the divine Judge,
and resurrection was inserted as the Christian version of the confidence in afterlife. These motifs
deriving from the life of the church are analogous

219

to the topoi of the Greek philosophical tradition, for they were firmly established in the lore and literature of the Christian movement as principles and doctrines which gave definition to the religion. Of these teachings Basil and the Gregories believed themselves not only heirs but consecrated protectors.

We have concluded that the consolation arguments of the Cappadocians are made up of a thorough mixture of topoi selected from both Greek and Christian sources. We could let this be our final word, as more than one commentator on the consolations has,[1] were it not for the unique and striking conception which we know our authors to have had of the relation of the two παιδεῖαι. Not content to view the Christian philosophy as a balanced blend of cultural inheritances, they subjected both the Greek and the Christian theologies to a particular μόρφωσις which left neither the Hellenic pursuit of the good nor the Church's aspirations after God quite the same as they had been before.[2] The logical question to be put to the literature under consideration takes this shape: beyond the use of Greek solacia and the Christian symbols and quotations whose prominence in Christian writings make them comparable as topoi, are there any traces of the theologoumena for which the Cappadocians, as a distinctive group of ecclesiastical thinkers, are known? Is there a Cappadocian παραμυθία which is recognizable not only as Christian theology, but as the articulation of the brand of θεωρία which is the earmark of their doctrinal

---

[1]See Stanislas Giet, Les Idées et L'Action Sociales de Saint Basile (Paris: J. Gabalda et Cie, 1941), pp. 412-7, and David Amand, L'Ascèse Monastique de Saint Basile (Maredsous: Editions de Maredsous, 1948), pp. 17-18.

[2]Jaeger, Early Christianity and Greek Paideia, pp. 68-102.

system?[1] It is our intention to test this question in two ways: by attempting to discover in other Cappadocian writings the kinds of theological ideas and concerns to which their consolation language and thought bear the closest resemblance, and by examining more closely those few consolation arguments, particularly in the orations of the Gregories, which seem to be their own constructions, the contributions of these theological artisans to the philosophy of consolation.

Ἑκούσιαν ποιήσατε τὸ κατηναγκασμένον. These words (the final utterance of the Cappadocian martyr, Gordius, according to Basil) could be made the inscription over the remarkable labors and ideas of the Archbishop of Caesarea. "As we all must die, let us through death win life. Make the necessary voluntary...Exchange the earthly for the heavenly."[2] Though the fourth-century consoler needed to address himself to the issue of the necessary death, the inevitable fate of the creature, he lived in a world in which the word "death" had more than this single application. Plato and Paul discuss, in ways more obviously different to moderns than to the Cappadocians, the two deaths of men. Plato speaks of the true philosopher's practice in dying, through which

---

[1]For the contention that there is such a "system," see the article by Brooks Otis, "Cappadocian Thought as a Coherent System," DOP XII, pp. 97-124. Otis writes at the beginning of his study: "Cappadocian thought can be defined as an attempt to unite the doctrine of God with the doctrine of angels and the doctrine of man in a way which would equal the logical consistency of the system of Origen without involving its heretical consequences" (p. 98).

[2]Basil Homilia in Gordium mart. (M 31.505BC).

the soul anticipates its liberation from the body, which is a hindrance to the pursuit of truth. The apostle extolls the willing death by means of which Christians crucify "the flesh with its passions and desires," removing the sting of the final mortality. Both are sounding the theme which is the theological basis and rationale for the ascetic communities which Basil founded and promoted, and the conviction, we want to argue, which underlies his attempts to provide παραμυθία for the bereaved and persecuted: "make the necessary voluntary!"

The language by which Basil offers consolation and that by which he seeks to enlist Christians in the ascetic life is, upon close examination, identical. The one literature treats unwelcome death and the other encourages dying to the world. A single theology serves both. Counting death as a necessary separation of the soul from that which stands in the way of its reunion with the divine life, this theology argues that those who desire to approach the deity have it within their power to commence this sanctifying pilgrimage by ἄσκησις, by the practice of dying before their "necessary" deaths. So it is that Basil's exhortations to retreat from the cares of the world have a very familiar ring to one who has read the consolationes. The long list of entanglements which make it impossible for a person to "keep the mind in tranquility" are a case in point:

> He who is not yoked in the bonds of matri-
> mony is greatly disturbed by violent de-
> sires...while he who is already bound in
> wedlock is seized by yet another tumult
> of cares; if childless, by a longing for
> children, if possessing children, by
> solicitude for their nurture, by keeping
> watch over his wife, by the management of
> his household...losses on contracts,
> quarrels with neighbors, contests in the
> law courts...Every day brings with it

some particular cloud to darken the soul;
and the night takes over the cares of
the day, deluding the mind with the same
cares in fantasy.[1]

Now presented as that which must be renounced in
order to find a divine ἡσυχία, this catalogue of
the ills of earthly existence stems from consolation
literature, where it appeared initially in the pseudo-
Platonic Axiochus. We have met lists like this in
the later consolations, where they make up the topos
which contrasts the heavenly benefits of the deceased
with the hardships he or she left behind -- the difficulties of marriage, the anxieties of child-rear-
ing, the distresses of political and economic life,
and all those things which have made the life of man,
as one consoler has it, "an uncertain sea, turbulent
winds, a fickle dream...smoke dispersing."[2]

---

[1]Basil Ep. 2 (trans. Deferrari, I, 11).

[2]See the pseudo-Basil Homilia consolatoria ad
aegrotum (aegr.) (M 31.1717). In the same treatise,
we read: "The rich man is alarmed by all things:
the days, as the times of court appearances; the
evenings, as the opportunities of robbers; the nights,
as the scourges of anxieties; the dawn, as the onset
of flatterers. And he fears not time alone, but
place as well. He dreads the housebreaking of robbers, the plots of thieves, the slander of the vio-
lent, the accusations of those who were treated
violently by him, plunderings at the hands of the
more powerful, the villainies of the domestics, the
meddling of informers...the rottenness of walls, the
collapse of houses, the approaches of barbarians...
the losing utterly after having gained, deprivation
after the acquisition. O man, if such is the storm
of possession, where is the spring of enjoyment?"
(trans. author). Stig Y. Rudberg, Études sur la
tradition manuscrite de saint Basile (Uppsala: AB
Lundequistska Bokhandeln, 1953), pp. 117-8, writes:

The solace given to those who mourn the dead
and the solution offered to those who would cheat the
inevitable by embracing "the sentence of death" are
at root one and the same. The seminal idea is caught
up in verbs and nouns which have in view separation
(χωρίζω, χωρισμός) and withdrawal (ἀναχωρέω, ἀναχώρησις, ἀναχωρητής). The term χωρισμός is familiar
in Platonic and in early Christian writings as a
description of physical death, which results in the
separation of the soul from the body. It is the term
used in the famous passage in Phaedo 67D (λύσις καὶ
χωρισμὸς ψυχῆς ἀπὸ σώματος), and taken up by Clement,
Origen and others to express the same idea.[1] In the
face of the ensnarements of life enumerated above,
Basil holds out to his friend Gregory, whom he is
trying to induce to join him in holy retreat "the one
escape -- separation from the world altogether" (μία
φυγή, ὁ χωρισμὸς ἀπὸ τοῦ κόσμου παντός).[2] In Basil's
speech, the term ἀναχώρησις, with its connotations
of retirement (from battle, or from public life, as
in self-exile) and the term χωρισμός have become
interchangeable. He uses the word χωρισμός to speak
of retirement from the world in the monastic sense,
and he refers to the death of Briso as his withdrawal
or ἀναχώρησις, urging his widow to accept the fact
that God has beckoned that noble soul "to depart from

"Bien que l'Hom. cons.--malgré le témoignage unanime
des mss--ne provienne pas de Basile, elle est toute-
fois interresante comme échantillon de la manière
propre de Proclos et de l'éloquence réligieuse qui,
vers la moitié du cinquieme siècle, était à la mode
dans la capitale de l'Empire." For the topos under
consideration, see also Gr. Nyss. Pulch. and Placill.
(Opera, IX, 465ff., and 486-9, resp.).

[1]Clement Strom. 4.3, Origen Jo. 28.6, Methodius
Res. 1.57, 2.8.

[2]Basil Ep. 2 (trans. Deferrari, I, 11).

life" (ἀναχωρῆσαι τοῦ βίου).[1] Clearly the death
which came unexpectedly to the successful officer by
the legislation of God (νομοθεσία τοῦ θεοῦ), and
the death to the world which Basil urges upon Gregory of Nazianzus as the "one escape" are conceived
along similar lines: death and the practice of
death convey the deceased and the monk to a better
χώρα. The character of this more propitious "place,"
in the case of the person who has died, is known to
us from the consolations, where it gains its definition by the things which are missing, by the absence
of those things which beset earthlings. Gregory of
Nyssa speaks of Flacilla's migration to an undefiled
existence where there is no flattery or slander, no
pleasure or pain, no poverty or plenty, no servant-
hood or lordship -- all these are banished to make
room for bliss (μακαριότης), for contemplation of
the unseen realities (θεωρία τῶν ἀοράτων), and for
an unending happiness (εὐφροσύνη τέλος οὐκ ἔχουσα)
which is surely, we may say, "beyond the pleasure
principle."[2] Likewise, the place of retirement for
the one who seeks, while still alive, "to sever the
soul from its sympathy with the body" (τῆς πρὸς τὸ
σῶμα συμπαθείας τὴν ψυχὴν ἀπορρῆξαι)[3] introduces
him to an existence which can be spoken of only in
terms of what has been left behind. To portray the
life of one who, while yet in the world, has embraced
the practice of dying, a string of words is needed
which feature the alpha-privative (ἄπολιν, ἄοικον,
ἀνίδιον, ἀφιλέταιρον, ἀκτήμονα, ἄβιον, ἀπράγμονα,
ἀσύναλλακτον).[4] Each kind of death is depicted
as a boon, not only because it signals the soul's

---

[1]Basil Eps. 2 and 302 (trans. author).

[2]Gr. Nyss. Placill. (Opera, IX, 486, ll. 4-15).

[3]Basil Ep. 2 (trans. Deferrari, I, 11).

[4]Ibid.

separation from myriad evils, but because each of
the two mortalities is the commencement of the soul's
purification (ἀρχὴ καθάρσεως τῇ ψυχῇ) and the beginning, as well, of the acquisition of "the eternal
goods" (τῶν αἰωνίων ἀγαθῶν).[1]

One grows accustomed to seeing Basil depicted in
secondary literature as "le legislateur de la vie
monastique"[2] who was responsible for the organization
of monastic communities, while the theoretical underpinnings awaited the writings of the two Gregories.
It would be possible, one must suppose, to argue
along similar lines that the bishop of Caesarea was
a businesslike and conventional consoler, content to
piece together various combinations of the topoi delivered to him by the genre itself. But it must be
wondered whether either of the issues is that simple.
Is there not within Basil's writings evidence of an
overarching theological scheme which can be seen to
inform both of these activities and is it not possible to sketch the larger tapestry against which
the vocabulary of consolation and ascetic life not
only "work," but are shown to be of a piece with
Basil's θεολογία?

Basil's treatise On the Holy Spirit addresses
neither the special circumstances which summon
forth a consolation nor the special audience eager
for counsel about the ascetic life. As a discussion of the role of the Spirit in the formation and
nurture of Christians, this writing yields an outline of that portion of "the Cappadocian system"
concerned with the redemption of mankind.

---

[1]Ibid., (trans. Deferrari, I, 13, 15).

[2]Jean Daniélou, Platonisme et Théologie Mystique:
Doctrine Spirituelle de Saint Grégoire de Nysse
(Aubier: Editions Montaigne, 1944), p. 87.

The divine οἰκονομία for humanity, Basil declares, is a recalling (ἀνάκλησις) from the fallen
state, a return to proper relationship with God from
the alienation brought on by disobedience. To this
end Christ made his sojourn in the flesh (ἡ μετὰ
σαρκὸς ἐπιδημία), providing the race of men with an
example of perfection of life.[1] An essential part
of the limitation is sharing Christ's death, for
the following reason:

> It is necessary that the continuity of the
> old life be cut. And this is impossible
> unless a man be born again, according to
> the Lord's word; for the regeneration, as
> indeed the name shows, is a beginning of a
> second life...in making a change in lives
> it seemed necessary for death to come as
> mediator between the two, ending all that
> goes before, and beginning all that comes
> after.[2]

Here it is in reference to Baptism and the common
life of Christians that we find the insistence on
dying, the willing anticipation of the end of the
old life in order to commence the new. What is the
process, we are led to ask, by which the soul returns
to relationship with God? Basil acknowledges that
the approach of the corporeal to the incorporeal
(the Spirit) is problematic. The intimate relationship, he says:

> ...results from the withdrawal of the
> passions (ὁ χωρισμὸς τῶν παθῶν)
> which, coming afterwards on the soul
> from its friendshp to the flesh, have
> alienated it from its close relation-

---

[1] Basil Spir. 15.35.

[2] Ibid., (trans. from NPNF, 2nd series, V, 21).

227

ship with God.[1]

The passions, then, must be removed from the soul in order for restoration to occur. When man has returned to his primal beauty, "cleaning the Royal Image and restoring its ancient form," he is able to approach the deity.[2] The rewards in store for those who, in response to the summons and assistance of the Spirit, advance towards perfection are many, and for their portrayal Basil has reserved some arresting language. The promise is held out that as the aspirant approximates the Christ-like existence through imitation, he will position himself to behold the ineffable beauty of the archetype, God himself, for he becomes visible (as the fourth evangelist wrote) to those who have seen the Son, his image. Illuminated by the Spirit, souls become themselves spiritual (ψυχαὶ πνευματικαὶ) and are initiated into life in which the future is known, mysteries come clear, and all the benefits of heavenly citizenship are enjoyed. The climax, Basil writes is:

> ...joy without end, abiding in God, being made like to God (ἡ πρὸς θεὸν ὁμοίωσις), and highest of all, being made God (θεὸν γενέσθαι).[3]

---

[1] Ibid., 9.23 (trans. from NPNF, V, 15).

[2] Ibid.

[3] Ibid., 9.23 (trans. from NPNF, V, 16). Much of the thought of Basil's Spir. 9 was taken from Plotinus, as P. Henry demonstrated in his Les états de texte de Plotin (Brussels: n.p., 1938), p. 160. Jaeger argues that the ideas were borrowed from Basil in turn by Gregory of Nyssa in his De Instituto Christiano, in Two Rediscovered Works of Ancient Christian Literature: Gregory of Nyssa and Macarius (Leiden: E.J. Brill, 1954), pp. 100-3. The pertinent

Such, in very brief compass, is the pattern of the divine rescue operation undertaken for man, as Basil conceives it. One sees within the scheme clear signs of the two mythic structures firmly implanted in the minds of Greek Christians: the Platonic vision of the falling away of the souls with the plan for their eventual return, and the biblical vision of the breach in relationship caused by man's disobedience and repaired by the providential actions of the loving God. In its elaborated form it is more than the wedding of two world-views. It represents those elements from the Greek παιδεία which illuminated and strengthed the church's advocacy of the new spiritual training, the παιδεία τοῦ χριστοῦ. Whether the Cappadocians were completely successful in their attempt to produce a cosmology, theology, angelology and anthropology "which would equal the logical consistency of the system of Origen without

---

passages are in Plotinus En. 6.9, in which we read: "...here what we love is perishable, hurtful...our loving is of mimicries and turns awry because all was a mistake, our good was not what we sought; There only is our veritable love and There we may unite with it, not holding it in some fleshly embrace by possessing it in all its verity. Any that have seen know what I have in mind: the soul takes another life as it draws nearer and nearer to God and gains participation in Him; thus restored it feels that the dispenser of true life is There to see, that now we have nothing to look for but, far otherwise, that we must put aside all else and rest in This alone, This become, This alone, all the earthly environment done away, in haste to be free, impatient of any bond holding us to the baser, so that with our being entire we may cling about This, no part in us remaining but through it we have touch with God." The translation is from Stephen MacKenna, trans., Plotinus: The Enneads (3rd ed., London: Faber and Faber Limited, 1962), p. 623.

involving its heretical consequences"[1] is another
question, and not our immediate concern. We must,
rather, turn once again to Cappadocian consolatory
efforts and seek to discover what elements within
them are put in a different perspective when viewed
against the broader backdrop of what they termed their
φιλοσοφία.

There emerges, in the first place, a rather
glaring inconsistency when Basil's (and the Gregories',
for that matter) endorsement of μετριοπάθεια as the
proper treatment for those who grieve is compared
with the prescription in a work like De Spiritu
sancto for the soul which seeks sanctification. The
clear indication in the latter is that the severance
of passions (ὁ χωρισμός τῶν παθῶν) is being called
for, and the riddance of the πάθη, considered unfor-
tunate accretions to man due to his fleshliness,
appears to be prerequisite for the virtuous life.
In Basil's writings which pertain to monastic practice we meet repeatedly the language of the Stoic
ideal, the insistence that ἄσκησις results in the
extirpation of passions. In the Longer Rules, Basil
asserts that "perfect renunciation consists in a
man's attaining complete impassivity" (ἀπροσπαθὲς),
and that detachment from wealth and external things
can bring "freedom from anger, grief, worries, and
...from all the harmful passions of the soul."[2] A
passage in the Ascetic Discourse reflects the same
theological basis for this ideal which we encountered in Basil's work on the Spirit. Originally in
the image of God, man surrendered this pristine
nature and was dragged into ἐμπαθεῖς.[3] The solution

---

[1]See above, note 1, p. 221.

[2]Basil Reg. fus. 8 (trans. from W.K.L. Clarke,
The Ascetic Works of Saint Basil (London: SPCK,
1925), p. 167). Emphasis added by author.

[3]Basil Ascet. 1 (M 31.869). Clarke, Ascetic

is clear: "he that has imitated in his own life, so
far as is possible, the passionless character of the
divine nature (τὸ ἀπαθὲς τῆς θείας φύσεως) has restored in his soul the image."[1]

The Christological basis for the ideal of
ἀπάθεια was somewhat trickier for Basil. We noted
in the last chapter that in the interest of asserting the true humanity of Jesus, his πάθη were not
only admitted but emphasized, and the result was an
example of μετριοπάθεια -- a Lord who showed his
affection and grief, but μηδὲν ἄγαν.   This was not,
of course, the only way in which the Christian savior
might be depicted. Clement of Alexandria, in a celebrated passage, portrayed Christ as "entirely impas-
sible (ἀπαθής); inaccessible to any movement of
feeling, either pleasure or pain," and likewise
urged upon his imitator, the true gnostic, "impassibility, not moderation of passion (ἀπάθειαν ... οὐ
μετριοπάθειαν) ...the complete eradication of desire
[which] reaps as its fruit impassibility."[2]

To this view of the Son, and to its implications,
Basil is no stranger. It is taken for granted in a
redemptive scheme in which imitation of Christ is
understood in conjunction with χωρισμός τῶν παθῶν,
which in turn enables the aspiring soul to behold the
archetype. Basil has reservations, however, about
the denial of πάθη of any kind to Jesus, and apparently wishes to draw back from the "Stoic" Christ
on the grounds that this portrait suppressed a full

Works, p. 11, doubts the authenticity of the sermons
on the grounds of scarcity of biblical quotations,
vocabulary, and differences in style and materials
found in undisputed works by Basil.

[1]Basil Ascet. 1 (trans. Clarke, p. 133).

[2]Clement Strom. 9 (trans. from ANF, II, 496).

definition of his human nature. The qualification
he puts on the attribution of πάθη to Jesus in Ep.
261 bears this significance. God the Father is understood to be ἀπαθής in two senses of the word (that of
impassibility or immutability, and of passionlessness). While, Christ, in his human nature, is subject to change and suffering. The ἀπάθεια of Christ
is ethical and consists of sinlessness. So it is
that Basil distinguishes between the natural affects
(τὰ φυσικά πάθη), which support claims of the Son's
full humanity, and the affects arising from wickedness (τὰ ἀπὸ κακίας πάθη) which Jesus "thrust aside
as unworthy of his unsullied divinity."[1] In the end,
the Christological aspect of the problem is not
entirely ambiguous, for the two natures preserve both
the ideal of μετριοπάθεια and ἀπάθεια, both being
in effect frozen in what passes for a divine paradox.

Where these two ethical and psychological constructs apply to other parts of Basil's thought,
the resolution is not so tidy, and unclarity remains.
In the same document which defines restoration of the
soul's pure image as attainment of the likeness of
the divine apatheia we read that the best rule of
the continent life is "to aim neither at luxury nor
ill-usage of the flesh, but in both directions to
avoid excess."[2] Even if it is true that language
of the doctrine of ἀπάθεια is systematically avoided
or criticized in consolations, we are not justified
in concluding that only in situations in which the
problem of grief is at issue does Basil adopt the
ethical suppositions of the Academy. In his homily

---

[1]Basil Ep. 261 (trans. Deferrari, IV, 81). For
an informative treatment of the πάθη in Basil's
writings, see August Dirking, "Die Bedeutung des Wortes Apathie beim heiligen Basilius dem Grossen," Theologische Quartalschrift (1954), pp. 202-12.

[2]Basil Ascet. 1 (trans. Clarke, p. 136).

on anger, for example, we meet the familiar argument
that wrath, the product of the irascible part of the
soul, has its positive counterpart in courage -- reason, like a bridle, is able to keep this πάθος under
control.[1] Mixed in with assurances that solitude
can bring about the suppression of the chief πάθη
(including λύπη), are a curious series of remarks
about grieving.[2] We read in the Longer Rules that
ἐγκράτεια "destroys sins, quells the passions (παθῶν
ἀπαλλοτρίωσις), and mortifies the bodies even as
to the natural affections," and yet we are also
advised in the Rules that there is a legitimate mourning and grief -- not only over those who have committed sins, but also with those who are afflicted.[3]

---

[1]Basil Hom. 10.5 (M 31.365).

[2]Basil Ep. 2 (trans. Deferrari, I, 13): "For
just as animals are easily subdued by caresses; so
desire, anger, fear and grief, the venomous evils
which beset the soul, if they are lulled to sleep by
solitude and are not exasperated by constant irrita-
tions, are more easily subdued by the influence of
reason." Dirking, "Die Bedeutung des Wortes Apathie
beim heiligen Basilius dem Grossen," pp. 207-8,
writes: "Ganz im stoischen Fahrwasser schwimmt B.
[Basil], wenn er den echten Steuermann beschreibt
(Hom in princip. proverb. 15), 'der immer sich selbst
gleich bleibt, ohne sich durch die Begierden zu erhe-
ben, und ohne niederzusinken im Unglück' ...B. Fährt
an der angegebenen Stelle fort: 'Wenn die flei-
schlichen Leibenschaften, wie Zorn, Furcht, Freude,
Trauer die Seele besturmen, dann muss die Seele wie
der Steuerman oberhalb der Leidenschaften sitzen und
die Vernunft beherrschen.'Damit erhebt B. die
ἀταραξία und die ἀπάθεια in Sinne der Beherrschung
der schlechten Leidensschaften zur sittlichen For-
derung."

[3]Basil Reg. fus. 17.2 (trans. from FOC, IX, 272).
See also Basil Reg. br. 192, 194, Mor. 52.1, 70.20.

In the ascetic writings as well as the consolations, the figure of Jesus and certain biblical teachings ("Weep with them that weep...," etc.) seem to have exercised a moderating influence upon the more stringent and harsh ethical precepts of the Stoic tradition.

One suspects, furthermore, that practical experience contributed to Basil's reticence about the kind of unchecked rigorism which might issue from an asceticism grounded exclusively in the ideal of "apathy." The Cenobitic model is itself a consciously designed instrument for the control and moderation of ἄσκησις, and as such it is the social expression of Basil's disenchantment with the excesses and errors which were endemic to solitary retirement. Only in community can the perils of assumed perfection and untested humility be avoided. "In comparison with whom will you be the lowest if you live alone?"[1] Basil wonders how the solitary will "give evidence of his compassion, if he has cut himself off from association with other persons."[2]

Scrutiny of quite different kinds of writings reveals in an unmistakable way that Basil mixes the two ethical traditions with bewildering freedom, placing μετριοπάθεια- and ἀπάθεια- teaching side by side in single compositions. And even if this unstrained combination is one of the marks of Stoicized-Platonism of the Hellenistic era, one is tempted to conclude that we are dealing with an author who simply possesses no ground rules in the matter.

---

[1]Basil Reg. fus. 7 (trans. from FOC IX, 252). It is noteworthy that although Gregory of Nyssa advocates purity to the point of ἀπάθεια he warns against excessive austerity (Virg. 2, 5, 22).

[2]Basil Reg. fus. 7 (trans. from FOC IX, 251).

There is, nevertheless, a general coherence and rationale which informs Basil's juxtaposition of these two ideals -- one that is important to the redemption scenario in his theology, and one which sheds light as well on his consolation philosophy.

In the soteriological scheme which envisions the soul's return to its original nature, a progressive ascent is assumed, a movement which includes purification, illumination and perfection of the reclaimed ψυχή .[1] The Cappadocian fathers chose well when they fastened upon a Pauline text as the motto for this dynamic of the interior life, for nothing was more apt than the image taken from the games of a (Christian) runner "forgetting what lies behind and straining forward to what lies ahead...toward the goal for the prize of the upward call of God in Christ Jesus" (Phil. 3.13-14). The passage is quoted or echoed in several passages worth considering here. Basil, treating Jesus' designation as ὁδός in the mode of Alexandrian exegesis, looks to the loftier insight (πρός ὑψηλοτέραν ἔννοιαν), and concludes:

> We understand by Way that advance (προκοπή)
> to perfection which is made stage by stage,
> and in regular order (εἱρμῷ καὶ τάξει),
> through the works of righteousness and 'the
> illumination of knowledge;' ever longing
> after what is before, and reaching forth
> unto those things that remain, until we
> shall have reached the blessed end, the
> knowledge of God (τὴν θεοῦ κατανόησιν).[2]

---

[1]Basil Spir. 9.23. See also Gr. Naz. Or. 2.76, Or. 20.4, and the remarks by I.P. Sheldon-Williams in Armstrong (ed.), Later Greek and Early Medieval Philosophy, pp. 427, 444, 452.

[2]Basil Spir. 8.18 (trans. from NPNF, VII, 12). According to Gregory of Nazianzus (Or. 43.25), Basil

In an epistle to Chilo in which the life of the monastic is the subject of discussion, we get a closer look at what this journey involves practically, that is, in the daily existence of one beset by various trials and temptations. After ringing in the admonition from the Epistle to the Philippians, Basil warns that the soul cannot depend on "yesterday's virtue" nor rush directly to the height of discipline (εἰς ἀκροτῆτα ἀσκήσεως). He proceeds to outline a strategy for combat with the πάθη :

> It is better to advance a little at a time.
> Withdraw then by degrees from the pleasures
> of life and obliterate every habit, lest you
> bring on yourself a crowd of temptations
> by irritating all your passions at once.
> When you have mastered one passion, then
> begin to wage war against another, and in
> this manner you will in good time get the
> better of them all.[1]

Basil appends to this advice some words of just the sort he customarily places at the conclusion of a consolatio:

---

rose to the episcopate by a natural spiritual progress. Sheldon-Williams, drawing from Gregory's account, writes: "Basil attained the episcopate (which, according to the ps.-Dionysius, corresponds to perfection in the Ecclesiastical Hierarchy) 'not by receiving baptism and instruction at the same time, as is the case with most of those who nowadays aspire to that office, but in accordance with the order and law of the spiritual ascent' (τάξει καὶ νόμῳ πνευματικῆς ἀναβάσεως)." Armstrong, Later Greek and Early Medieval Philosophy, p. 444.

[1]Basil Ep. 42 (trans. adapted from NPNF, VII, 144).

> Seek continence...and accustom your soul
> to trials. Considering the separation of
> soul from body as deliverance from every
> evil, accept only the enjoyment of the
> blessings which are eternal, the enjoy-
> ment of which all saints have shared.[1]

What can be deduced from these accounts of the rationale and strategy of spiritual advancement? It
is apparent that we are in the presence of a scheme
which is extremely sensitive to stages of ἀνάβασις,
to what is possible for a given aspirant in a given
situation. Although Basil speaks of the completed
journey, "the blessed end," as knowledge of God, or
beholding the archtype, or τελείωσις, the soul's
condition at the completion of the ascent is one of
passionlessness. The journey's task, dynamic, and
completion consist in the χωρισμός τῶν παθῶν. The
ethics of moderation logically stands at the earlier
stage of the progression, aiding the aspiring soul
at numerous points along the Way, serving as preparatio in the sense that "mastery"of a πάθος must be
antecedent to its elimination. Basil, for reasons
we have already mentioned, demonstrates a modest
resistance to the explicit declaration that ἀπάθεια
prevails at the summit. He opts instead for biblical
imagery concerning knowledge and intimate kinship
with God. Nonetheless, perfection means for him, no
less than for Gregory of Nyssa (who is not nearly so
reticent about the terminology of passionlessness),
a purification from corporeality and its accompanying πάθη .[2] Even if there were critical elements in
the Christian doctrines of creation and resurrection
which forced qualification of Greek notions of the
drama enabling the soul's return "home," the Cappadocian system is alert at every turn to all the

---

[1]Ibid., (trans. Deferrari, I, 253-5).

[2]Basil Spir. 8, 9, 15, Hex. 1.6.

ramifications of the truth that ψυχή and θεός are kindred as "intelligibles and not sensibles,"[1] as pneumatic rather than sarkic existences. This worked itself out ethically in a way which reflects a tiered, rather than an opposing relationship of the doctrines of μετριοπάθεια and ἀπάθεια: the practice of the first leads to the control of the "affects," at which point the more practical contemplative may undertake the rigorous practice of ἀπάθεια. The scheme is firmly established in the writing of Philo, who distinguishes in his exegetical profiles of virtue between the μετριοπάθεια of Aaron and the more perfect ἀπάθεια of Moses,[2] and also in the thought of Clement of Alexandria, who declares that the person who requires moderation in order to retain control over desires is "not yet pure [like ὁ γνωστικός], but subject to passions."[3] Nemesius of Emesa, a contemporary of the Cappadocians, has left us perhaps the clearest statement of the moral perceptions and accomplishments which distinguish the "contemplative" from the "worthy man" in a passage which concerns the problem of grief:

> Every form of grief, by its essential
> nature, is an evil. For even though it
> may chance to be the grief of a worthy

---

[1]Armstrong, Later Greek and Early Medieval Philosophy, p. 426.

[2]Philo Leg. alleg. 3.129-34. See above, Chap. 3, p. 121, n. 2.

[3]Clement Strom. 6.9: τίς δὲ καὶ σωφροσύνης ἀνάγκη, μὴ χρῄζοντι αὐτῆς; τὸ γὰρ ἔχειν τοιαύτας ἐπιθυμίας, ὡς σωφροσύνης δεῖσθαι πρὸς τὴν τούτων ἐγκράτειαν, οὐδέπω καθαροῦ, ἀλλ᾽ ἐμπαθοῦς.
See Walther Völker, Der wahre Gnostiker nach Clemens Alexandrinus (Berlin and Leipzig, n.p., 1952), esp. pp. 188-94, 524-40.

man (ὁ σπουδαῖος) at the destruction of
good men, or at the deaths of children,
or at the ruin of a city, yet he does not
grieve for the sake of grieving, nor of
deliberate choice, but as driven thereto
by circumstances. But when such things
occur, an actual contemplative (ὁ
θεωρητικὸς) will be completely unmoved
(ἀπαθὴς παντάπασιν), seeing that he has
severed himself from present things, and
cleaves to God; while any worthy man is
schooled to be affected by such griefs
only in due measure, not excessively
(μετριοπαθὴς ... οὐχ ὑπερβαλλόντως),
nor so as to behave as their captive,
but rather as battling for the mastery
of them.[1]

It has been argued that this distinction came to
Nemesius from the Plotinian, Porphyry,[2] which it well
may have, but what is more fundamental to note is
that some such stratification of pursuers of virtue
had become, so to speak, the Hellenistic thinker's
philosophical class-structure. What had in an earlier epoch been a tension and opposition between
conflicting ethical schemes was now turned on end,
resulting in a conception of the soul's progress in
which the aspirant, as H. Chadwick wrote, "must
learn to rise through the 'moderation' of Aristote-
lian ethics to achieve the passionlessness (apatheia)
of the Stoics."[3]

---

[1]Nemesius Nat. hom. 19 (trans. from LCC, IV,
359-60).

[2]B. Domanski, Die Psychologie des Nemesius,
cited in William Telfer, ed., Cyril of Jerusalem and
Nemesius of Emesa, LCC, IV (Philadelphia: The West-
minster Press, 1955), pp. 359-60.

[3]Chadwick, Early Christian Thought, p. 63.

Nemesius' treatment of λύπη has brought us full-circle to the question of consolation. If, as is being argued here, Basil maintains a view of the soul's progress which assumes the ethics of moderation as the base and platform for a further and ultimately total purification of the πάθη , the juxtaposition of the two vocabularies is not so problematic as we supposed. Μετριοπάθεια and ἀπάθεια are ideas which work in tandem, and appear side by side even in that literature addressed to monastics, for in these circles particularly is there awareness of the gradations which separate novice from ὁ τέλειος ἐγκρατής. This mixing of two ethical strategies makes it all the more stiking, however, that in the consolationes one never finds the counsel of ἀπάθεια being given. When the notion surfaces in connection with grief, it is roundly criticized. How are we to account for this? Several explanations suggest themselves. We have already spoken of the Jesus-tradition and its moderating influence upon those who were tempted to advocate Stoic hardness in the face of the loss of friends and family. This church interest meshed nicely with the Crantorian doctrine already firmly fixed in the consolation literature, a position embraced by Stoics and Platonists alike in the Hellenistic period (e.g., Posidonius and Plutarch). Some have been tempted to conclude that there was in the Christian community a basic and distinctive spirit of sympathy and compassion which simply would not tolerate, especially in a situation of mourning, Stoic "savage impassivity."[1] As a generalization, the point may have some merit, but we have observed that the assumption of a fundamental incompatibility of this kind fails to appreciate the range and diversity of early Christian thought,

---

[1]This kind of contrast is envisioned by F.J. Foakes-Jackson, The History of the Christian Church to A.D. 461 (7th ed., New York: George H. Doran Company, 1924), p. 193.

and cannot account for Clement's "apathetic" Christian gnostic, or for the persistence of the strain
of thought personified in that figure -- an energy
which runs through the mystical and ascetical thought
developed by the Alexandrians and the Cappadocians.

The key reason for the uniform espousal of the
"lower" ethic in the consolation writings is, we
suspect, simpler and less theoretical than any of
these. It has to do with the nature of the genre
itself. The canons which control even the personal
epistolary consolations derive, demonstrably, from
rhetorical practice, and specifically, from the
public oration. As a result, the consolatio reveals,
both in form and argumentation, an awareness of its
audience, which is a general audience. The topoi
emerged from and returned to the public. The genre
itself, in addition to other assumptions a theologian
might have had about distinctions between pneumatic
and sarkic believers within the church, dictated to
the composer of a consolation that arguments were to
be directed (and accomodated) to the larger audience.
The consolatio conceives of its audience as, to use
Nemesius' categories, "worthy people" rather than
"contemplatives," and it is reasonable that the
ethic of moderation receives full voice in this
literature. In considering the Cappadocian consolation we are in touch with the ethical and spiritual
double standard which is not unfamiliar in the patristic writings. In reference to Clement of Alexandria, Henry Chadwick has commented:

> Side by side...with instruction for his
> educated and even wealthy converts liv-
> ing in the world, married, active in
> commerce, perhaps entrusted with posi-
> tions of civil authority, there are ele-
> ments that point forward towards the
> spirituality of the monks, withdrawn
> from society and devoted to contempla-

241

tion in solitariness.[1]

We recall Basil's letters to the families of Arinthaeus, Nectarius, and Briso as well as Gregory of
Nyssa's "command performance" funeral orations delivered for members of the imperial family. But
beyond that we see the control which the consolatory
genre, by its very nature and purpose, exercised
over the content of the individual works, particularly
in letters written to leaders of the churches and
monastics. In these latter consolations one finds
no evidence that different solacia have been framed
to suit a more "advanced" readership. Whomever it
addresses, then, the consolatio understands its
audience to be humanity, man in his distress and
vulnerability, not the philosopher. It is for this
reason that Basil and the two Gregories, though
obviously no strangers to the ethic and ideal which
counsels and culminates in ἀπάθεια, consistently
urge, in their capacity as consolers, μετριοπάθεια.
As a literature which treats the fate of all mortals,
it could read no other way.[2]

As a consequence of the demands and purposes of
the genre, the Cappadocian consolation is a writing
of stark contrasts and polarities. In an important
sense, it is a literature which did not lend itself
to the theological scheme which our three writers
were intent upon articulating. Because it is
addressed from beginning to end to humanity in
extremis, abject man, the consolation does not provide any "middle ground" through which the authors
might trace the steps of those who were advancing,

---

[1]Chadwick, Early Christian Thought, pp. 63-4.

[2]Cicero's recorded deliberations on the problem
of death and consolation show his consciousness of
the audience for which such teachings are meant.
See Cicero Tusc. 1.49.117-9.

gradually removing themselves from the injuries dealt
by worldly events. Missing from the consolatory writings, or so it seems, is that terrain so important
to Cappadocian thought which allows for gradual
ascent and the purificatory pilgrimage of the soul.
Only two orders of being are in view: the mortal
in his pain and the delivered saint in beatitude.
Perceived from this angle, the consolation's abrupt
change of mood as the consoler breaks off lamentation
and visualizes the departed in heavenly company has
theological repercussions for the Cappadocians -- it
pushes to the extremes the "depth" and the "height"
which can be reached by the human soul.

We have attempted to develop in this chapter the
correspondence of certain of Basil's consolation
arguments to theological axioms which his other writings show to be decisive for his thought: Especially
pertinent has been the idea of death as separation
from the world either in actuality or in ἄσκησις --
the death which marks the beginning of the soul's
migration to God. Although it is apparent that
Basil has turned philosophical and theological tenets
having to do with "dying to the world" to his considerations περὶ θανατοῦ in the consolations, the evidence is more implicit than explicit. His references to resurrection and heavenly reward are, for
the most part, merely references, and they gain
definition only in the light of his other writings.
It may be expected that recognizably Cappadocian
theologoumena, insofar as they assert themselves in
the collection of consolatory topoi, come into
clearer focus in the lengthier funeral orations.

In turning to the examination of two themes
which appear in the orations of Gregory of Nyssa
and Gregory of Nazianzus, two objectives are in
view. There is a need to examine the extent to which
these writers sought to insinuate their own favorite
themes into this literature already crowded with
well-tested argumenta, and how much the basic unit
of the consolation, the brief and self-contained

topos, yielded to the intentions of men whose religion was a finely-wrought and elaborate φιλοσοφία.

At the conclusion of his funeral oration for
Meletius, Gregory of Nyssa assures the congregation
that the departed bishop of Antioch now intercedes
"face to face" with God for those left in the world,
having passed through the veil (Heb. 6.20), and
having left "behind him the curtain of the flesh."[1]
He adds these words as the conclusion of his παραμυθία:

> He has left Egypt behind, this material
> life. He has crossed, not this Red Sea of
> ours, but the black gloomy sea of life.
> He has entered upon the land of promise,
> and holds high converse with God upon the
> mount. He has loosed the sandal of his
> soul, that with the pure step of thought
> he may set foot upon that holy land
> where there is the vision of God.[2]

As a single solacium, this likening of Meletius to
Moses appears to be relatively innocent. It is,
however, the compression into a few lines of Gregory's entire theology of the ascent of man to the
life of virtue (ὁ κατ᾽ ἀρετὴν βίος), as we know from
other of his ascetical writings, In Cantica, De
instituto Christiano, De virginitate, and most directly, Vita Moysis. It is not our purpose here to
treat in detail the distinctive marks of Gregory's
interpretation and re-definition of the Christian
life of perfection, inspired as it was by the mystical strain in Origen's writings and by the attempt
to elaborate upon several of the themes we have
already noted in Basil's thought. This has been

---

[1]Gr. Nyss. Melet. (trans. from NPNF, V, 516).

[2]Ibid. (trans. from NPNF, V, 517).

244

done by others, and with unusual insight and subtlety by W. Jaeger, who declared that Christianity means for this thinker "the mystery of the separation and liberation of the soul from all material bondage to the senses and its ascent and return to God."[1] Moses had been fashioned by Gregory into the model aspirant, the symbol of realized spirituality whose life could be presented not only historically, but also by an exegetical and theological θεωρία as a means of laying bare the stages of advance towards perfection (τελειότης), towards the summit in which God is beheld (ἐν ᾗ καθορᾶται θεός).[2]   In accordance with the Platonic substructure which is operative in the works of his teachers Origen and Basil, Gregory takes it as axiomatic that man's innate desire of the good is potentially stronger than his inclinations to sensuality -- his fascinations with and attachment to material things -- and so depicts man's return to God and the restoration of his authentic image as growth in perception of being (γνῶσις τῶν ὄντων). So it is that Moses, or the philosophic person, gaining mastery of the passions, learns to discriminate between those tangible phenomena which seem to exist, and those intelligible realities which, as Paul wrote, (I Cor. 2.9) "no eye has seen, nor ear heard, nor the heart of man conceived." A movement from the prosaic

---

[1]Jaeger, Two Rediscovered Works of Ancient Christian Literature: Gregory of Nyssa and Macarius, p. 74. On this theme, see the same work, pp. 70-142, and Jaeger's Early Christianity and Greek Paideia, pp. 68-102.

[2]Gr. Nyss. Vita Mos. is divided into two sections: a recounting of the outline of the Moses story, and the larger portion, which is θεωρία, or spiritual exegesis of the same events. In the same author's Melet. (Opera, IX, 455, 1.11-456, 1.1) we find the reference to the summit, where Moses holds "lofty conversation" with the deity.

to the mysterious, from the coarse to the sublime, the
process culminates in the contemplation of the transcendent nature, the God who is the source of being
and beauty.[1]

A single aspect of this rather elaborate drama
requires our investigation, since it is prominent
in the scaled-down version which Gregory employs as
a consolatory argument. As he approached the holy
terrain of God, Moses "loosed the sandal," an image
which for Gregory suggested a great deal. The the-
ophany at the bush, and specifically the order to
remove the sandals, takes on a significance directly
related to the theme of χωρισμός when we read the
incident through Gregory's eyes. He writes in his
Life of Moses:

> From that light we are taught what is re-
> quired if we shall stand within the beam
> of truth, and that it is not possible with
> bound feet to go up to that height in
> which the light of the truth is seen un-
> less the dead and earthly covering of
> skins is loosened from the foundations of
> the soul, which was put around our nature
> in the beginning, when we were naked
> through disobedience of the divine will.
> And thus the same knowledge of the truth

---

[1]Gregory frequently refers to God as the archetype or the prototype of beauty. See the remarks of
Jaeger, Two Rediscovered Works of Ancient Christian
Literature: Gregory of Nyssa and Macarius, p. 76,
where he points to the use of such language in the
treatises In Cant., Virg., Vita Mos., and Anim. et
res. Plotinus speaks of the One as τ'αγαθόν and
ὑπεράγαθον in En. 5.5.13.1 and 6.9.6.40-42. Danielou
has shown the closeness of Gr. Nyss. Virg. 11 to Plotinian terminology and thought in "Gregoire de Nysse
et Plotin," Congrès de Tours et Poitiers (Paris: n.p.,
1954), pp. 259-62.

when it manifests itself will follow when
these things happen to us. For the full
knowledge of being results in purification from mere opinion concerning non-
being.[1]

Ascent to God is an impossibility until the "dead
covering" of the soul is removed -- until "this fil-
thy life" (τὸν ἰλυώδη βίον) is abandoned. In the
treatise on Moses, as in the oration on Meletius, the
idea stands in close relationship to the familiar
treatment of the clothing bestowed upon Adam and Eve
in consequence of their disobedience.[2] The garments

---

[1]Gr. Nyss. Vita Mos. (Opera, VII, pt. 1, 39, 11.
21ff.). Trans. author.

[2]Gr. Nyss. Vita Mos. (Opera, VII, pt. 1, 39, 98),
Melet. (Opera, IX, 454-5). The clothing of Adam and
Eve in Genesis 3.21 receives allegorical treatment in
Philo Leg. Alleg. 2.53-58, 3.69. The notion that
the body is the soul's clothing has a long history
in non-Christian writings, e.g., in Empedocles (frg.
126), Porphyry De abst. Signs of an early debate
among Gnostic and Catholic Christians about "coats
of skins" and bodily "coverings" or "tunics" of
souls are found in Tertullian Adv. Valent. 24, De
res. mort. 7, and Irenaeus Adv. haer. 1.5.5. The
dispute about somatic existence (this time in reference to the resurrection body) continued in Origen
De prin. 2.3, 2.8-10, 3.6 and in Methodius De res.
2ff. For a helpful analysis of this problem, see
R.M. Grant, Miracle and Natural Law in Graeco-Roman
and Early Christian Thought (Amsterdam: North-Holland
Publishing Company, 1952), pp. 232-4, 254-5.
    Of particular interest, due to evidence of Cap-
padocian familiarity with his writings, is the passage
in Plotinus En. 1.6.7.5, which combines the themes of
ascent to the good with "stripping" or "undressing"
(ἀπόδυσις): "Therefore we must ascend again towards

are understood to signify the corporeality of mortals,
from which issue the passions. Gregory's treatment
of the theme elsewhere takes a number of forms. He
argues in De mortuis that τοὺς δερματίνους χιτῶνας
were a gift designed to preserve the freedom of
man, whose ultimate disgust with the sensate world
would prompt him to choose instead the regaining of
his original nature.[1] In several other writings, the
skins, representative of man's mortal condition,
assume an important place in the process of purification because in the dissolution of the bodily part
of man there is opportunity for the destruction of
the evil which adheres so closely to somatic existence.[2] It was this theological motif in a capsulized

---

the Good, the desired of every Soul. Anyone that
has seen This, knows what I intend when I say that it is
beautiful. Even the desire of it is to be desired
as a Good. To attain it is for those that will take
the upward path, who will set all their forces towards
it, who will divest themselves of all that we have
put on in our descent: so, to those that approach
the Holy Celebrations of the Mysteries, there are
appointed purifications and the laying aside of the
garments worn before, and the entry in nakedness --
until, passing, on the upward way, all that is other
than the God, each in the solitude of himself shall
behold that solitary-dwelling Existence, the Apart,
the Unmingled, the Pure, that from Which all things
depend, for Which all look and live and act and know,
the Source of Life and of Intellection and of Being."
(Trans. by MacKenna, pp. 61-2).

[1]Gr. Nyss. Mort. (M 46.522-4). See the remarks
in Jean Danielou and Herbert Musurillo, From Glory
to Glory (New York: Charles Scribner's Sons, 1961),
pp. 12-3.

[2]Gr. Nyss. Anim. et res. (trans. from NPNF, V,
464-5): "Seeing then, that all the infusions of the

version which Gregory inserted as a _solacium_ in the
funeral oration for Pulcheria, arguing that the evil
implanted in the sentient part of man would not be
eternal: the "vessel is dissolved temporarily by
death" as part of the divine plan, "so that when the
evil spill[s] out, humanity may be formed anew and
restored to the original life."[1] There is a sense

---

life of the brute into our nature were not in us
before our humanity descended through the touch of
evil into passions, most certainly, when we abandon
those passions, we shall abandon all their visible
results. No one, therefore, will be justified in
seeking in that other life for the consequences in
us of any passion. Just as if a man, who, clad in
a ragged tunic, has divested himself of the garb,
feels no more of the disgrace upon him, so we too,
when we have cast off that dead unsightly tunic made
from the skins of brutes and put upon us (for I take
the 'coats of skins' to mean that conformation be-
longing to a brute nature with which we were clothed
when we became familiar with passionate indulgence),
shall, along with the casting off of that tunic,
fling from us all the belongings that were round us
of that skin of a brute; and such accretions are
sexual intercourse, conception, parturition, impuri-
ties, suckling, feeding, evacuation, gradual growth
to full size of life, old age, disease, and death."
See also Gr. Nyss. _Virg._ 12.

[1]Gr. Nyss. _Pulch._ (_Opera_, IX, 472, ll. 1-11).
Trans. author. The same set of ideas is found in
Anim. et res. (NPNF, V, 451ff.), and Basil approaches
the same idea, even though he does not employ the
same language in _Ep._ 261. The phrase of which Gregory is particularly fond (ἡ εἰς τὸ ἀρχαῖον τῆς
φύσεως ἡμῶν ἀναστοιχείωσις) has Platonic origins:
see Plato _Symp._ 193D. For a critique of the uneasy
melding of Gregory's doctrine of the simplicity of

in which Gregory's invocation of the theme of death
as a welcome dissolution, as well as the image of the
stripping of skins and garments, simply prepare the
way for his particular contribution to the theology
of perfection. This Gregorian _Tendenz_ is not missing
from the brief argument in the _oration_ on Meletius.
Moses, freed from the sandal, the dead skin which has
no place in the presence of God, moves "with pure
step of thought" up the mount toward the deity. The
language which best describes the life of the Christian philosopher is language of being. He is the one
who is dedicated to penetration beyond appearances to
the highest knowledge: γνῶσις τῶν ὄντων. Job, as
we recall, responded to the tidings of his children's
death philosophically -- that is, he reflected περὶ
τῆς τῶν ὄντων φύσεως,[1] and Sarah likewise did not
resist the demand for Isaac's sacrifice, for she
knew that beyond death there was no deceit, error,
desire or any of the passions. Moses is celebrated
by Gregory as the moral hero who conquered θυμός
and ἐπιθυμία. The result was ἐλευθερία, freedom
from all the πάθη, which are "accretions [to the
soul] from without, because in the Beauty which is
man's prototype no such characteristics [i.e., anger,
fear, grief, etc.] are to be found."[2] 'Απάθεια is
the goal of the Christian philosopher's ἄνοδος. It
is the fruit of leaving behind the seeming good (τὸ
φαινόμενον ἀγαθόν) and rising to the authentic good

---

the soul and the dogma of corporeal resurrection, see
the remarks of Cherniss, _The Platonism of Gregory of
Nyssa_, pp. 49-58.

[1]Gr. Nyss. _Pulch._ (_Opera_, IX, 470, ll. 26-31).

[2]Gr. Nyss. _Anim. et res._ (trans. from NPNF, V,
411). For a good discussion of ἀπάθεια in the writings of Gregory, see Walther Völker, _Gregor von
Nyssa als Mystiker_ (Weisbaden: Franz Steiner Verlag
GMBH, 1955) pp. 259-64.

(τὸ ὄντως ἀγαθόν). Gregory displays no wariness of the term and its philosophical implications, and he follows the lead of Clement and Origen in calling Christ the "founder of passionlessness" (ἀρχηγός τῆς ἀπαθείας)![1] At the summit of the mount to which man, the lover of beauty, has been drawn by his desire to behold God, τὸ ἀρχέτυπον κάλλος, he exists in a state of "passionless blessedness" (τὴν ἀπαθῆ μακαριότητα),[2] a life consummately noetic and contemplative. Here the restored man, image purified, participates in the life of the Divine Mind. All of this, the monument wrought by his "hazardous attempt to intellectualize the supraintellectual,"[3] stands behind the brief solacium inserted by Gregory at the end of his consolation on Meletius. Surely it is justified to regard this as a piece of παραμυθία which possessed special significance for our author.

The "loosening of the sandal of the soul" by Moses and its analogous image of the stripping of the garment of skins are heavily freighted, though abbreviated, expressions of this thinker's most cherished notions of the life of perfection. Equally applicable to the theory of the ascetic life and to the discussion of death and resurrection, it is a theological motif capable of conveying both encourage-

---

[1] Ἀπάθεια was one of the features of heavenly life described in Gr. Nyss. Placill. (Opera, IX, 486, 1. 13). On the mixture of this and other Stoic terms with Platonic concepts and vocabulary, see the comments by Jaeger, Two Rediscovered Works of Ancient Christian Literature: Gregory of Nyssa and Macarius, pp. 79-80.

[2] Gr. Nyss. Anim. et res. (NPNF, V, 464).

[3] Jaeger, Two Rediscovered Works of Ancient Christian Literature: Gregory of Nyssa and Macarius, p. 73.

ment and consolation. To those familiar with Gregory's thought, the mention of Moses in a funeral sermon injected an element crucial to Cappadocian theology and yet not easily addressed in the <u>consolatio</u>, for it reminded the mourners by the example of the deceased that it was the duty of Christians "to make the necessary voluntary," to be attentive to that life-long process of purgation and illumination which promises to the spiritual athlete ἀπάθεια and assimilation to God.[1]

Our purpose in isolating this single argument among many in Gregory's consolations should be clear.

---

[1]In Gregory's theology of ascent, restoration of the image does not result in a consummation of the journey, or in any sort of absorption into God. Sheldon-Williams writes in Armstrong, <u>Later Greek and Early Medieval Philosophy</u>, pp. 455-6: "In Plotinus' philosophy transcendent and immanent coalesce in the divinity of the soul and 'the transfiguration of the soul consists in the realization of its most pure activity, not in addition to itself....Therefore transcendence and immanence imply each other.' But for Gregory the soul is the image of the Divine, not the Divine itself, and the mutual implication of transcendent and immanent is never realized in the soul, but in the consubstantiality of the Son. This remains a mystery: but though inaccessible to the intellect, it is grasped by faith, which reveals the Third Heaven as an insatiable joy, insatiable because the distance between the soul and God is infinite, joy because the soul has become one with her Beloved, who is one with God." Gregory has taken a favorite precept -- that one can know that God is, but not what he is -- and pushed the proposition further. The battle with Eunomius is influential here, for this neo-Arian claimed that the essence of God was knowable: it consisted of the ungenerateness of the Father. Cf. Gr. Naz. <u>Or</u>. 28.10.

If one perceives "through" this miniature solacium of Gregory the theological structure which invests the reference to Moses' ἔξοδος and ἄνοδος with its substance and significance, it becomes apparent that we are confronted by something other than a self-explanatory consolatory topos of the kind met throughout these writings. In a manner corresponding to Basil, but quite his own, Gregory has turned the theology of ascent to the purposes of παραμυθία, and has in the process positioned in this most controlled literature, in a nutshell, his paradigm of Christian φιλοσοφία. This is his declaration of why Christians must hear Paul's exhortation, and "Sorrow not as others who have no hope."[1]

In the ninth chapter of De spiritu sancto, Basil concluded his account of the soul's stage-by-stage journey from this world to the world of God with a striking phrase: there awaits the purified and illumined soul "abiding in God (ἡ ἐν θεῷ διαμονή), being made like God (ἡ πρὸς θεὸν ὁμοίωσις), and highest of all, being made God (θεὸν γενέσθαι)."[2] That deification should be the τέλος of his paideia was an ancient notion seized upon by Christian, especially Greek Christian, thinkers. Though these theologians were careful to note that the soul's immortality, by nature man's before he surrendered it, had become a χάρις -- something to be restored by the grace of the Creator who alone is immutable being -- they did not loosen their grip on the Platonic assumption that soul is kindred to the divine intelligence and that it is attracted to the deity as like to like. The notion of θεοποιήσις or θέωσις, with its already substantial history in

---

[1]Gr. Nyss. Melet. (Opera, IX, 457, ll. 3-4).

[2]Basil Spir. 9.23.

253

both Christian and non-Christian circles,[1] was particularly attractive to the Cappadocian fathers. Seeking through the attainment of ἀπάθεια to become ἰσάγγελος ,[2] the ascetics withdraw from the world to become God-like, to cleanse and repair the image and likeness which contact with the sensible world had so seriously corrupted. But the idea possessed an even broader theological background: θέωσις represented the meeting point of man in his infinite ascent to the source of his life, and the divine condescension, God's gracious cooperation in humanity's yearning for restoration to true being. The reversal of man's drifting from his natural purity and the impetus for growth in the direction of God was revealed in his providential οἰκονομία , the advent and work of Christ, the Son ὁμοούσιος τῷ πατρί who, as Athanasius' formula expressed it "became man in order that we might become Gods" (ἐνανθρώπησεν ἵνα ἡμεῖς θεοποιηθῶμεν).[3] Divine contact with mortal life is the basis for "recalling" man to what Basil termed kinship with God (οἰκείωσιν θεοῦ). Hence man, as the "image of the image" is able to participate in the life of God himself.

It is a measure of Gregory of Nazianzus' enthusiasm for the idea of θέωσις that it is on display in his consolations. We mentioned in the last chapter his presentation of the doctrine of the resurrec-

---

[1]For example, Plato Tht. 176B, which has to do with the concept of ὁμοίωσις θεῷ , Plotinus En. 1.2., 12.3-7, Clement Strom. 6.15, Protr. 11, Origen Jo. 2.2, Mart. 25, Athanasius Inc. 54.3, Gr. Naz. Or. 8.23, Or. 7.21, Carm. 1.2.34.161, Gr. Nyss. Virg. 1. See Völker, Gregor von Nyssa als Mystiker, pp. 274-82.

[2]Gr. Nyss. Hom. I in Cant.

[3]Athanasius Inc. 54.3.

tion, a vision of the reception of a purified "flesh" by the soul in a close union or "growing together" (συμφυΐαν) which renders a reconstituted being "one spirit and mind and God."[1] As part of this solacium, which Gregory describes as a more powerful consolatory φάρμακον than the others he has offered, he speaks of the paradox, true of man throughout his life, inescapably sharp for him in the face of death, that "though we are gods, we die like men the death of sin."[2] But because the creature of God, when he has taken "the narrow path," is glorious by virtue of his λόγος, νόμος and ἐλπίς, there can be no distress or grief:

> What is this new mystery which concerns me
> (τὸ καινὸν τοῦτο περὶ ἐμὲ μυστήριον)? I
> am small and great, lowly and exalted,
> mortal and immortal, earthly and heavenly.
> I share one condition with the lower world,
> the other with God; one with the flesh, the
> other with the spirit. I must be buried
> with Christ, become the son of God, yea God
> himself (υἱὸν γενέσθαι θεοῦ, θεὸν αὐτὸν).[3]

If from the beginnings of consolation there was a drive to change the mood of man from dread to desire of death, here is Gregory's foundation for such a change of mind! In substantial debt to the Platonic proposition that the human being is capable, by emulating the perfect righteousness of God, to become like him, Gregory (and other theologians before him) proclaimed that θέωσις was the prize towards which the Christian athlete strained (τῆς ἀρετῆς ἆθλον

---

[1]Gr. Naz. Or. 7.21. See Chap. 4, p. 204, n. 1.

[2]Ibid., (trans. from NPNF, VII, 237).

[3]Ibid.

θεὸν γενέσθαι).[1] Strong traces of Plato's assumption of the essential affinity between ψυχή and θέος are seen everywhere the Greek fathers expound either the creation of man in God's image and likeness, or map out strategies for returning the image to its former spotless condition. It is striking, however, that the theme of θέωσις appears in rather bold relief in the consolation thought of Gregory of Nazianzus, for his other writings show him to have been a devotee of this concept not only in its application to the interior life, but as a persistent motif informing the entire structure of his soteriology.[2]

---

[1]Gr. Naz. Ep. 178.

[2]This is the argument developed in Donald F. Winslow, The Dynamics of Salvation: A Study in Gregory of Nazianzus, soon to be published by The Philadelphia Patristic Foundation, Ltd. Winslow writes: "It is impossible...to avoid the conclusion that Gregory's soteriologically oriented christology is centered upon his concept of theosis. 'In the incarnation of the Son, human nature was not only annointed with a superabundant overflowing of grace, but was assumed into an intimate and hypostatical unity with God himself' [So Georges Florovsky, "The Lamb of God," SJT, 4 (1951, p. 17)]. And, most important, the theosis of Christ's humanity is, for Gregory, the paradigm of the theosis of all humanity. It is the fundamental postulate upon which rests the whole unfolding "work' of Christ. What Christ achieves in his God-manhood is not the work of a 'spiritualized' or 'adopted' humanity, but the work of the 'humanity of God' [Or. 45.22]. The theosis of Christ's human nature is not the disappearance of his humanity; it is neither the total absorbtion of the lower into the higher nor some kind of metaphysical 'transubstantiation.' Rather, it is the participation so complete, so intimate and interpenetrating, that to call the 'deified' human nature 'God' is not a

The paradox and contrariety marking the difference
between what man was created to be and what he,
through his willfullness, had become, was mediated,
Gregory asserted repeatedly, by the God-Man. Christ
took upon himself man's "denser nature, having con-
verse with flesh by means of mind," and "his inferior
nature, the humanity, became God, because it was
united to God...in order that [man] too might be made
God so far as he is made man."[1] Even in the abbreviated treatment of θέωσις in the consolatory sermon
the Christological point does not go unmentioned.
Deification, "the great mystery which concerns [us],"
has as its goal the transformation of fear of death
into longing for it as the entrance into life shared
with God:

> This is the purpose for us of God, who for
> us was made man and became poor, to raise
> our flesh, and recover his image, and re-
> model man, that we might all be made one in
> Christ, who was perfectly made in all of us
> all that He Himself is, that we might...bear
> in ourselves only the stamp of God.[2]

This, according to Gregory, is the special consolation
for Christians: for those who are steadfast in their
love for God through joys and hardships alike, and
grow in virtue, the future holds the promise of becoming sons of God, of participating in God's life
through ἄσκησις.

Like Gregory of Nyssa, then, Gregory of Nazianzus

---

semantic trick but a description of reality [See
Florovsky, Eastern Fathers of the Fourth Century
(Paris: YMCA Press, 1931), p. 116.]."

[1] Gr. Naz. Or. 29.19 (trans. from NPNF, VII, 308).

[2] Gr. Naz. Or. 7.23 (trans. from NPNF, VII, 237).

adds to the plethora of consolation argumenta a capsule version of one of the theologoumena central to
his vision of the Christian life. It is too much to
say that the addition of motifs from the Cappadocian
theological scheme utterly transforms the shape of
Hellenistic consolation, for we have seen that these
teachings take their place among the other topoi, and
never become alternatives which make all the preceding solacia irrelevant or unappreciable. Surely
those who have depicted the difference between Christian and non-Christian consolation by comparisons
of bold, confident hymns with fearful dirges have
under-estimated both traditions -- the former for
the seriousness with which it confronted death and
its consequences, the latter for its resources of
spirit in the face of mortality and absurdity. More
than the differences in argumentation, our study has
brought to light the similarities: Plutarch, no
less than Basil, trusts in the soul's survival of
death and journey to a place of bliss, though their
"mechanics" of rescue are distinguishable, and Gregory of Nyssa, as a part of his call for the soul's
ascent of the holy mountain, shares with Epictetus a
thorough disdain for the things the world values.
As fashioners of philosophies for consolation, these
writers, Christian and non-Christian, have more in
common than we might have supposed initially, for
theirs is an age in which the most serious men in the
culture are training for death while they live.

* * * * * *

    The consolatory writings of Basil and the two
Gregories are signals and examples of the attitude
of the Cappadocian fathers to Greek παιδεία . It
is the long and revered history of the Greco-Roman
consolatio which one sees and hears in their letters
and funeral sermons, evident both in the structure
preserving the dynamic of antiquity's confrontation
with death, and in the solace and exhortations

originating from sages of the past. Throughout this study, we have encountered testimonies to the power of the genre. The structural demands of the literary type and the received tradition of <u>solacia</u> have been seen to exercise persistent influence over expressions of condolence by these three fourth century theologians.

It may be an overstatement to say that the Cappadocians' obedience to the rhetorical conventions of their era is slavish, at least as this is shown in their handling of the <u>consolatio</u>. However, their dependence upon the norms and canons observed by the rhetors is definitely more striking than the literary freedom sometimes claimed for them. The Cappadocians do not display revolutionary or even boldly innovative tendencies when adopting Hellenic modes of expression and it is not obvious from their consolatory writings that they are intent upon redeeming or transforming the genre.

Because Basil and his colleagues were exact and self-conscious practitioners of the New Sophistic, students of their thought can scarcely afford to assess their ideas without taking into full account the shape and requisites of the genres which became for them the vehicles of the Christian <u>paideia</u>. Failure to perceive the demands put upon an ancient consoler by the structure and history of the literary type itself can only result in misreadings and misjudgments of Cappadocian thought. It is not accurate, for example, to conclude from a stylized expression of empathy in a <u>consolatio</u> that the writer disavows a thoroughgoing doctrine of ἀπάθεια or somehow holds a qualified view of the heavenly life as free from "affects."[1] His sympathetic utterance is simply

---

[1]In the context of a claim that Gregory of Nyssa has attenuated the doctrine of ἀπάθεια, and is not so dedicated to that ideal as Origen, Völker in his

259

dictated by the context of lamentation which must
open a proper consolatio. The consolation is, in
short, a controlled and controlling genre -- this
fact has pressed itself upon us at virtually every
point in the study. Radical departures from the
format of the consolatio are not to be found in the
Cappadocian samples. These writers, like their predecessors and contemporaries, are dutiful in their
observation of the established elements of proem,
eulogy and lament, consolatory arguments and examples, attempts to depict the beatified existence of
the "dead," and epilogue.

We have seen that Cappadocian indebtedness to
the established and tested tradition of consolation
was limited to form alone. The great majority of
consolatory arguments advanced in Basil's letters
and in the orations of the Gregories are paralleled
in earlier and contemporaneous non-Christian literature of the same type. In many instances these topoi
are simply taken over unchanged and offered as
solacia worthy of any philosopher practicing "therapy
of the soul." The numerous insights about the
common destiny of mortals, counsels concerning the
power of reason to bring grief into check or anticipate misfortune, the "logic" of untimely deaths, and
suggestions for busying oneself while the sense of
loss is sharpest -- these pieces of consolation and
others like them appear to have been the common
property of consolers of all persuasions. In other
cases, we have taken notice of the adaptation of
ancient paramythetic motifs and arguments to the
experiences and teachings of the Christian community:

---

influential study cites as an example an exclamation
from one of Gregory's funeral orations. Völker, Gregor von Nyssa als Mystiker, p. 263: "Nicht ohne einen
gewissen Tadel ruft der Prediger aus: τίς οὕτως
ἀπαθὴς τὴν ψυχὴν , dass er nicht über den Tod der
Pulcheria weinen sollte!"

eulogy receives a Christian turning, ideas of the
survival of death and assertions of the soul's immortality are infused with and elaborated from resurrection dogma, and the heavenly landscape, like the
list of heroic endurers of misfortune, is peopled
with figures from the Christian tradition. Essentially, the function of biblical literature in the
consolatio is adaptive and improvisational, for it
represents the replacement of the genre's required
philosophical utterances, literary allusions and
renowned historical examples with samples from the
writings counted authoritative by Christian thinkers.
Similarly, the tension between the philosophical
ideas of μετριοπάθεια and ἀπάθεια which came to
such sharp focus in consolatory writings can be seen
to survive and at the same time undergo significant
redefinition. Μετριοπάθεια as a consolatory "strategy" is deduced from the figure of Jesus, whose
temperance in grief is proposed as the paradigm, with
the result that moderation, the less stringent of
the two therapies, is endorsed by the Cappadocians as
a concession to natural feeling and to the lesser
spiritual-philosophical capabilities of the common
man. On the other hand, ἀπάθεια is trumpeted as a
divine attribute, a characteristic of that heavenly
existence enjoyed by those who are (wrongly) mourned,
and the goal of those contemplatives who aspire,
even while in the world, to put themselves beyond
the reach of its attachments and cares.

The Cappadocian father's practice of consolation
is confirmation in the concrete instance of the principle Basil espoused in his treatise on the value of
pagan literature: they are not "religious despisers
of culture;" nor do they believe that a fundamental
opposition exists between that παιδεία which is the
fruit of the Hellenic intellectual journey and the
revelation which has been made accessible in the
παιδεία τοῦ χριστοῦ. From the riches of Greek
literary and rhetorical models and from that storehouse of ideas, in spite of criticism from some of
their Christian contemporaries, they drew fully and

unabashedly.[1] Ultimately, the Cappadocians' view of paideia, as it informs and makes itself apparent in the consolatory writings, is not compromised by those peculiarly pregnant theological solacia which they range alongside the others. Fastening upon the conviction that the "necessary" death of man, the inevitable mortality separating soul from body, might be anticipated (and conquered!) by "voluntary" withdrawal from the world, the Cappadocians seek to address both consolation and ascetic practice from a single theological platform. It is a theology of the soul's ascent patterned after Christ the Logos, who is also the "Way" to the Father. Basil and the Gregories hold that the ascent of the deceased and of the contemplative is enabled by the severance of the soul from the πάθη, and climaxes in the restoration of the unspoiled image which God's saving condescension in the "economy" of Christ has made it possible for man to reclaim.

The two counsels or strategies for treating the "affects," we have noted, have correspondences at

---

[1]Basil's treatise Ad adolescentes de legendis libris suggests a setting in which some defense of study of pagan literature was necessary. And Gregory of Nyssa's attention to the Egyptian wisdom which was part of Moses' preparation for knowing truth and the true deity is clearly directed at opponents of Christian employment of non-biblical and non-Christian learning. Jaeger, Two Rediscovered Works of Ancient Christian Literature, pp. 133-4: "...the author defends himself against the criticism that he is trying to substitute Greek philosophy for the wisdom of the Bible. He maintains his position by proving that his philosophical theology is in full harmony with the Scriptures. Thus he does attribute some value to the combination of Christian religion with the paideusis of the outside world, and that is precisely his attitude in the Vita Moysis."

several levels. Μετριοπάθεια is the moral counsel best suited for the masses who, unliberated from worldly attachments, must strive to hold the passions within reasonable limits, while ἀπάθεια is the practice prescribed for the spiritually elite. Moderation is likewise the fitting philosophic advice for the world's mourners who are incapable of viewing sorrow, misfortune and death as indifferentia. It is also the tutor's suggestion for the neophyte ascetic who is urged to bring himself to purity of mind gradually -- moderating one πάθος at a time. Ἀπάθεια, on the other hand, is the state of being of the deceased who has been delivered to the band of saints, and it is the goal of the aspirant attempting to approach the divine life "before the time" through asceticism. For both brands of philosophical therapy the Cappadocians naturally enunciated theological and christological warrants: for μετριοπάθεια in the sinless πάθη possessed by Christ as evidence of his genuine humanity (epitomized in the modulated sympathy displayed at Lazarus' death), and for ἀπάθεια in the restitution of the original nature of man in that work of the Son which prompted Gregory of Nyssa to call him the "founder of passionlessness" (ἀρχηγός τῆς ἀπαθείας).

It is intrinsic to the consolatio to bring into sharp juxtaposition the extreme conditions of man -- both as mourner trapped in a hostile environment, and as a delivered soul in beatitude. The correlate descriptions of the soul's condition, compressed and thus contrasted in the letters and funeral orations, represent the two boundaries of a more expansive theology of gradual advance and ascent which is the mark of the Cappadocian scheme of salvation. It is only against this larger landscape of ideas that it has been possible to isolate and distinguish παραμυθία especially significant for the Cappadocians from the many solacia which came to them already well-wrought from the Greco-Roman and Christian practice of consolation. We have seen that Basil's own contributions to the craft of consolation, his variously stated assurances that death and separation

signal the beginning of life, are not at all incidental to what we might call his "working theology"
-- the same assertion runs through the center of
his descriptions of the process of sanctification
begun in baptism and of the journey of the mind's
progress in purification undertaken by the monastic.
The same holds true for those solacia which awareness
of the thought of the Gregories throws into relief
as ideas which "count" in a special way for them (and
presumably for their correspondents and audiences).
When Gregory of Nyssa likens the departure of a
popular bishop to the mountain-ascent of Moses, and
speaks of the removal of the skins which enables
"pure step of thought" toward the ineffable God, he
offers as consolation his own θεωρία of what has
been wrought in the Logos. And when Gregory of Nazianzus turns his favored soteriological theme of
deification to the purposes of consolation, he too
seeks to transform fear of death and mourning of the
dead by invoking the promise which constitutes the
παιδεία τοῦ χριστοῦ .

Cappadocian θεολογία is παραμυθία. If it
does not supplant all the answers and insights
which have found their way into Greek παιδεία and
into the consolatio as one of its fruits, this
θεολογία is nevertheless offered by them as the
fulfillment of profound and ancient human yearnings
for salvation and illumination.

ABBREVIATIONS

ANF	The Ante-Nicene Fathers
DOP	Dumbarton Oaks Papers
FOC	Fathers of the Church
GCS	Die griechischen christlichen Schrift- steller der ersten drei Jahrhunderte
LCL	Loeb Classical Library
M	Migne, Patrologiae Cursus Completus
NPNF	A Select Library of Nicene and Post-Nicene Fathers of the Christian Church
Opera	Gregorii Nysseni Opera (W. Jaeger edition)
SVF	Arnim, Stoicorum Veterum Fragmenta

BIBLIOGRAPHY

Amand, David. L'Ascèse Monastique de Saint Basile.
Maredsous: Éditions de Maredsous, 1948.

Armstrong, A.H., and Markus, R.A. Christian Faith and
Greek Philosophy. New York: Sheed and Ward,
1960.

Armstrong, A.H. The Cambridge History of Later Greek
and Early Medieval Philosophy. Cambridge:
Cambridge University Press, 1967.

Arnim, Johann von. "Krantor." Paulys Realencyclopädie
der classischen Altertumswissenschaft. Vol.
11.2, cols. 1585-1588.

Arnim, Johann von. Stoicorum Veterum Fragmenta. 4
vols. Stuttgart: B.G. Teubner, 1968.

Arnold, E.V. Roman Stoicism. New York: The Human-
ities Press, 1958.

Balas, David L. ΜΕΤΟΥΣΙΑ ΘΕΟΥ, Studia Anselmiana,
Fasciculus LV. Romae: I.B.C. Libreria Herder,
1966.

Barbel, Joseph, editor. Gregor von Nazianz: Die Fünf
Theologischen Reden, Testimonia: Schriften der
altchristlichen Zeit. Dusseldorf: Patmos-Ver-
lag, 1963.

Bardy, Gustav. "Apatheia." Dictionnaire de Spiri-
tualité Ascétique et Mystique. Vol. 1. Paris:
G. Beauchesne, 1932, 727-46.

Basil. Ascetical Works. Translated by Sister M.
Monica Wagner. The Fathers of the Church, Vol.
9. New York: Fathers of the Church, Inc., 1950.

Basil. The Ascetic Works of Saint Basil. Translated
  by W.K.L. Clarke. New York and Toronto: The
  Macmillan Co., 1925.

Basil. Exegetic Homilies. Translated by Sister
  Clare Way. The Fathers of the Church, Vol. 46.
  Washington: The Catholic University of America
  Press, 1963.

Bauer, Johannes. Die Trostreden des Gregorius von
  Nyssa in ihrem Verhältnis zur artiken Rhetorik.
  Marburg: Universitäts-Buchdruckerei, 1892.

Bevan, Edwyn. Stoics and Sceptics. Oxford: Clarendon Press, 1913.

Beyenka, M.M. Consolation in St. Augustine. Washington, D.C.: Catholic University of America
  Press, 1950.

Blumenthal, H.J. Plotinus' Psychology: His Doctrines
  of the Embodied Soul. The Hague: Martinus
  Nijhoff, 1971.

Boulenger, F. Grégoire de Nazianze: Discours Funè-
  bres. Paris: n.p., 1908.

Bréhier, Émile. The Hellenic Age. The History of
  Philosophy. Translated by Joseph Thomas.
  Chicago: University of Chicago Press, 1963.

Bréhier, Émile. The Hellenistic and Roman Age, The
  History of Philosophy. Translated by Wade
  Baskin. Chicago: University of Chicago Press,
  1965.

Bréhier, Émile. Les idées philosophiques et reli-
  gieuses de Philon d'Alexandrie. Paris:
  Librairie Philosophique J. Vrin, 1925.

Buresch, Carolus. Consolationum a graecis romanisque
  scriptarum historia critica. Leipzig: J.B.
  Hirschfeld, 1886.

Campbell, J.M. The Influence of the Second Sophis-
    tic on the Style of the Sermons of St. Basil the
    Great. Washington, D.C.: Catholic University
    of America, 1922.

Campenhausen, Hans von. The Fathers of the Greek
    Church. Translated by Stanley Godman. New
    York: Pantheon Books Inc., 1959.

Cavallin, Anders. Studien zu den Briefen des Hl.
    Basilius. Lund: Gleerupska Universitetsbok-
    handlen, 1944.

Chadwick, Henry. Early Christian Thought and the
    Classical Tradition. New York: Oxford Uni-
    versity Press, 1966.

Chadwick, Henry. "Origen, Celsus, and Stoa." Jour-
    nal of Theological Studies, 48 (1947), 34-49.

Cherniss, Harold Fredrik. The Platonism of Gregory
    of Nyssa, University of California Publications
    in Classical Philology, Vol. 11, No. 1.
    Berkeley, Calif.: University of California
    Press, 1930.

Cicero. Cicero: De Finibus Bonorum et Malorum.
    Translated by H. Rackham. The Loeb Classical
    Library. New York: The Macmillan Co., 1914.

Cicero. Cicero: De Natura Deorum and Academica.
    Translated by H. Rackham. The Loeb Classical
    Library. New York: G.P. Putnam's Sons, 1933.

Cicero. Cicero: Letters to Atticus. Translated by
    E.O. Winstedt. 3 vols. The Loeb Classical
    Library. New York: The Macmillan Co., 1912.

Cicero. Cicero: The Letters to His Friends. Vol.
    1. The Loeb Classical Library. New York:
    G.P. Putnam's Sons, 1927.

Cicero. Cicero: Tusculan Disputations. Translated
    by J.E. King, The Loeb Classical Library. Cam-
    bridge, Mass.: Harvard University Press, 1966.

Clarke, W.K.L. The Ascetic Works of Saint Basil.
    London: S.P.C.K., 1925.

Clemens, Titus Flavius. Clemens Alexandrinus. 4 vols.
    Die griechischen christlichen Schriftsteller der
    ersten drei Jahrhunderte. Leipzig: J.C. Hin-
    richs, 1905-36.

Cochrane, Charles Norris. Christianity and Classi-
    cal Culture. New York: Oxford University Press,
    1957.

Copley, Frank O. Latin Literature. Ann Arbor, Mich.:
    University of Michigan Press, 1969.

Courtonne, Yves. Saint Basile et l'Hellénisme.
    Paris: Firmin-Didot et Cie., 1934.

Cumont, Franz. After Life in Roman Paganism. New
    York: Dover Publications, 1959.

Daniélou, Jean and Musurillo, Herbert. From Glory
    to Glory. New York: Charles Scribner's Sons,
    1961.

Daniélou, Jean. "Grégoire de Nysse et Plotin."
    Actes du Congrès de Tours et de Poitiers. 1953,
    259-62.

Daniélou, Jean. L'Être et le Temps chez Grégoire de
    Nysse. Leiden: E.J. Brill, 1970.

Daniélou, Jean. Platonisme et Théologie Mystique:
    Doctrine Spirituelle de Saint Grégoire de Nysse.
    Aubier: Éditions Montaigne, 1944.

Dehnhard, Hans. Das Problem der Abhängigkeit des Basilius von Plotin. Berlin: Walter De Gruyter & Co., 1964.

De Lacy, Phillip H. "The Stoic Categories as Methodological Principles." American Philological Association, Transactions and Proceedings, 76 (1945), 246-263.

De Labriolle, Pierre Champagne. "Apatheia." Reallexikon für Antike und Christentum. Vol. 1. Stuttgart: Hiersemann Verlags- G.M.B.H., 1950, 484-7.

De Mendieta, Emmanuel A. The "Unwritten" and "Secret" Apostolic Traditions in the Theological Thought of St. Basil of Caesarea. Scottish Journal of Theology, Occasional Papers, 13.

De Vogel, C.J. Greek Philosophy. 3 vols. Leiden: E.J. Brill, 1953-1959.

Dill, Samuel. Roman Society from Nero to Marcus Aurelius. Cleveland: The World Publishing Co., 1969.

Dio Chrysostom. Dio Chrysostom. Translated by J.W. Cohoon. Vol. 2. The Loeb Classical Library. Cambridge, Mass.: Harvard University Press, 1939.

Diogenes Laertius. Diogenes Laertius: Lives of Eminent Philosophers. Translated by R.D. Hicks. The Loeb Classical Library. New York: G.P. Putnam's Sons, 1931.

Dirking, August. "Die Bedeutung des Wortes Apathie beim heiligen Basilius dem Grossen." Theologische Quartalschrift (1954), 202-12.

Dodds, E.R. The Greeks and the Irrational. Boston: Beacon Press, 1957.

Epictetus. _Epictetus: The Discourses as Reported by Arrian, the Manual, and Fragments_. Translated by W.A. Oldfather. 2 Vols. _The Loeb Classical Library_. Cambridge, Mass.: Harvard University Press, 1966-67.

Favez, Charles. _La Consolation Latine Chrétienne_. Paris: Librairie Philosophique J. Vrin, 1937.

Fern, Sister Mary E. _The Latin Consolatio as a Literary Type_. St. Louis, Mo.: St. Louis University Press, 1941.

Festugière, André-Jean. _Antioche Paienne et Chrétienne_. Paris: Éditions E. de Boccard, 1959.

Festugière, André-Jean. _Personal Religion Among the Greeks_. Los Angeles: University of California Press, 1960.

Foakes-Jackson, F.J. _The History of the Christian Church to AD 461_. 7th ed. New York: George H. Doran Company, 1924.

Gatch, Milton McC. _Death: Meaning and Mortality in Christian Thought and Contemporary Culture_. New York: The Seabury Press, 1969.

Giet, Stanislas. _Les Idées et L'Action Sociales de Saint Basile_. Paris: J. Gabalda et Cie, 1941.

Grant, Robert M. _Miracle and Natural Law in Graeco-Roman and Early Christian Thought_. Amsterdam: North-Holland Publishing Company, 1952.

Greene, W.C. _Moira_. Cambridge, Mass.: Harvard University Press, 1944.

Gregory of Nazianzus. _Gregor von Nazianz: Briefe_. Edited by Paul Gallay. Die griechischen christlichen Schriftsteller der ersten Jahrhunderte. Berlin: Akademie-Verlag, 1969.

271

Gregory of Nyssa. Gregorii Nysseni Opera. Edited
by Werner Jaeger, et. al. Leiden: E.J. Brill,
1958-.

Grillmeier, Aloys. Christ in Christian Tradition.
London: A.R. Mowbray & Co. Limited, 1965.

Hagendahl, Harold. Latin Fathers and the Classics,
Studia Graeca et Latina Gothoburgensia VI. Göte-
borg: Göteborgs Universitets Arsskrift, 1958.

Hannan, M.L. Thasci Caecili Cypriani: De Mortalitate.
Washington, D.C.: Catholic University of America Press, 1933.

Higginbotham, John, editor. Greek and Latin Literature. London: Methuen and Co., Ltd., 1969.

Holl, Karl. Amphilochius von Ikonium in seinem Verhältnis zu den grossen Kappadoziern. Tübingen:
Mohr, 1904.

Homer. The Iliad. Translated by Richard Lattimore.
Chicago: University of Chicago Press, 1951.

Hultin, Neil. "The Rhetoric of Consolation: Studies
in the Development of the Consolatio Mortis."
Unpublished Ph.D. dissertation. Johns Hopkins
University, 1965.

Jaeger, Werner. Early Christianity and Greek Paideia.
Cambridge, Mass.: Belknap Press of Harvard University Press, 1961.

Jaeger, Werner. Nemesios von Emesa: Quellenforschung-
en zum Neuplatonismus und seinen Anfängen bei
Poseidonios. Berlin: Weidman, 1914.

Jaeger, Werner. Two Rediscovered Works of Ancient
Christian Literature: Gregory of Nyssa and
Macarius. Leiden: E.J. Brill, 1954.

Jaeger, Werner. *Paideia: The Ideals of Greek Culture*. Translated by Gilbert Highet. 3 vols. New York: Oxford University Press, 1943-45.

Jerome. *Select Letters of St. Jerome*. Translated by F.A. Wright. *The Loeb Classical Library*. Cambridge, Mass.: Harvard University Press, 1963.

Johann, Horst-Theodor. *Trauer und Trost: Eine quellenund strukturanalytische Untersuchung der philosophischen Trostschriften über den Tod*. Studia et Testimonia Antiqua V. Munich: Wilhelm Fink Verlag, 1968.

Julian. *The Works of Emperor Julian*. Translated by Wilmer Cave Wright. 3 vols. *The Loeb Classical Library*. New York: G.P. Putnam's Sons, 1913-23.

Kassel, Rudolf. *Untersuchungen zur Griechischen und Romischen Konsolations-literatur*, Zetemata, Heft 18. Munich: C.H. Beck'sche Verlagsbuchhandlung, 1958.

Ladner, Gerhart B. *The Idea of Reform*. New York: Harper & Row, Publishers, 1967.

Lattimore, Richmond. *Themes in Greek and Latin Epitaphs*. Urbana, Ill.: University of Illinois Press, 1962.

Libanius. *Libanii Opera*. Edited by Richard Foerster. 11 vols. Leipzig: B.G. Teubner, 1903-27.

Libanius. *Libanius: Selected Works*. Translated by A.F. Norman. Vol. 1. *The Loeb Classical Library*. Cambridge, Mass.: Harvard University Press, 1969.

Lucian. *Lucian*. Translated by A.M. Harmon. Vol. 4. *The Loeb Classical Library*. New York: G.P. Putnam's Sons, 1925.

Lucretius. Lucretius: De Rerum Natura. Translated
    by W.H.D. Rouse. The Loeb Classical Library.
    New York: G.P. Putnam's Sons, 1931.

Marrou, H.I. A History of Education in Antiquity.
    Translated by George Lamb. New York: The New
    American Library of World Literature, Inc.,
    1964.

Martha, Benjamin Constant. Études morales sur l'an-
    tiquité. Paris: Hachette et cie., 1905.

McGuire, Martin R.P., editor and translator. Funeral
    Orations, Fathers of the Church, Vol. 22. New
    York: Fathers of the Church, Inc., 1953.

Merlan, Philip. From Platonism to Neoplatonism. 3rd
    ed. The Hague: Martinus Nijhoff, 1968.

Migne, Jacques Paul. Patrologiae Cursus Completus:
    Series Graeca. Paris: 1857-87.

Milligan, George. Selections from the Greek Papyri.
    Cambridge: Cambridge University Press, 1927.

Mossay, Julian. La Mort et l'Au-Delà dans Saint
    Grégoire de Nazianze, Recueil de Travaux d'
    Histoire et de Philologie, 4e Series, Fascicle
    34. Louvain: n.p., 1966.

Mullachius, G.A. Fragmenta Philosophorum Graecorum.
    Paris: Firmin-Didot et Sociis, 1881.

Nilsson, Martin P. Geschichte Der Griechischen Reli-
    gion. Vol. 2. Handbuch der Altertumswissen-
    schaft. Munich: C.H. Beck'sche Verlagsbuch-
    handlung, 1961.

Nock, Arthur Darby. "Orphism or Popular Philosophy?"
    Harvard Theological Review 33 (1940), 301-15.

Norden, Eduard. Agnostos Theos: Untersuchungen zur

Formengeschichte Religiöser Rede. Leipzig:
B.B. Teubner, 1929.

Norden, Eduard. Die Antike Kunstprosa. 2 vols.
Stuttgart: B.G. Teubner, 1958.

North, Helen. Sophrosyne: Self-Knowledge and Self-
Restraint in Greek Literature, Cornell Studies
in Classical Philology, Vol. XXV. Ithaca, N.Y.:
Cornell University Press, 1966.

Origen. Origenes Werke. Die griechischen christlichen Schriftsteller der ersten drei Jahrhunderte. Leipzig: J.C. Hinrichs, 1899-.

Otis, Brooks. "Cappadocian Thought as a Coherent
System." Dumbarton Oaks Papers, XII. Cambridge,
Mass.: Harvard University Press, 1958, 97-124.

Parke, H.W. A History of the Delphic Oracle. Oxford:
Basil Blackwell, 1939.

Pauly, August Friedrich von. Realencyclopädie der
classischen Altertumswissenschaft. Stuttgart:
J.B. Metzler, 1894-.

Pelikan, Jaroslav. The Shape of Death. New York:
Abingdon Press, 1961.

Philo. Philo. Translated by F.H. Colson and G.H.
Whitaker. 10 vols. The Loeb Classical Library.
Cambridge, Mass.: Harvard University Press,
1929-62.

Philostratus. The Life of Apollonius of Tyana.
Translated by F.C. Conybeare. 2 vols. The
Loeb Classical Library. New York: The Mac-
millan Co., 1912.

Plato. Plato: Euthyphro; Apology; Crito; Phaedo;
Phaedrus. Translated by H.N. Fowler. The
Loeb Classical Library. London: William
Heinemann, 1917.

Plato. Plato: The Republic. Translated by Paul
Shorey. 2 vols. The Loeb Classical Library.
London: William Heinemann, 1930.

Plato. The Works of Plato. Translated by George
Burges. London: Henry G. Bohn, 1854.

Plato. Plato: Timaeus; Critias; Cleitophon; Menexe-
nus; Epistles. Translated by R.G. Bury. The
Loeb Classical Library. Cambridge, Mass.:
Harvard University Press, 1952.

Pliny. Pliny: Letters. Translated by William Mel-
moth and revised by W.M.L. Hutchinson. 2 vols.
The Loeb Classical Library. Cambridge, Mass.:
Harvard University Press, 1963.

Pliny. Pliny: Letters and Panegyricus. Translated
by Betty Radice. 2 vols. The Loeb Classical
Library. Cambridge, Mass.: Harvard University
Press, 1969.

Plotinus. The Enneads. Translated by Stephen Mac-
Kenna. 3rd ed. revised by B.S. Page. London:
Faber and Faber Limited, 1956.

Plutarch. Plutarch's Moralia. Translated by Frank
Cole Babbitt, et. al. 16 vols. The Loeb
Classical Library. Cambridge, Mass.: Harvard
University Press, 1927.

Pohlenz, Max. Die Stoa: Geschichte Einer Geistigen
Bewegung. 3rd ed. 2 vols. Göttingen: Vandenhoeck and Ruprecht, 1959.

Pohlenz, Max. "Philosophische Nachklänge in altchristlichen Predigten." Zeitschrift für wissenschaftliche Theologie, 48 (1904), 72-95.

Prestige, G.L. God in Patristic Thought. London:
SPCK, 1964.

Prestige, G.L. St. Basil the Great and Apollinaris
   of Laodicea. London: SPCK, 1956.

Reilly, Gerald F. Imperium and Sacerdotium According
   to St. Basil the Great. Washington: Catholic
   University of America Press, 1945.

Rist, J.M. Plotinus: The Road to Reality. Cambridge:
   University Press, 1967.

Rist, J.M. Stoic Philosophy. Cambridge: Cambridge
   University Press, 1969.

Roberts, Alexander and Donaldson, James, editors. The
   Ante-Nicene Fathers. 10 vols. Grand Rapids,
   Mich.: W.B. Eerdmans, 1956 (reprint).

Robinson, T.M. Plato's Psychology. Phoenix: Journal of the Classical Association of Canada,
   Supplementary Volume VIII. Toronto: University of Toronto Press, 1970.

Rose, H.J. A Handbook of Greek Literature. New York:
   E.P. Dutton & Co., Inc., 1960.

Rose, H.J. A Handbook of Latin Literature. New York:
   E.P. Dutton & Co., Inc., 1960.

Rudberg, Stig Y. Études sur la Tradition Manuscrite
   de Saint Basile. Uppsala: AB Lundequistska
   Bokhandeln, 1953.

Schaff, Philip, and Wace, Henry, editors. A Select
   Library of Nicene and Post-Nicene Fathers of the
   Christian Church, Second Series. Vols. 3, 5, and
   7. Grand Rapids, Mich.: Wm. B. Eerdmans Publishing Company, 1969 (reprint).

Schenkl, K. "Ueber Benutzung der verloren gegangenen Schrift Ciceros 'De Consolatione' in der
   Zweite Rede auf Satyrus." Wiener Studien, 16
   (1894), 38-46.

Seneca. Seneca: Ad Lucilium Epistulae Morales.
   Translated by Richard M. Gummere. 3 vols.

The Loeb Classical Library. New York: G.P.
Putnam's Sons, 1918-30.

Seneca. Seneca: Moral Essays. Translated by John
W. Basore. 3 vols. The Loeb Classical Library.
New York: G.P. Putnam's Sons, 1932.

Sextus Empiricus. Sextus Empiricus: Against The
Physicists; Against the Ethicists. Translated
by R.G. Bury. Vol. 3. The Loeb Classical
Library. Cambridge, Mass.: Harvard University
Press, 1936.

Sikes, E.E. Lucretius: Poet and Philosopher. Cambridge: Cambridge University Press, 1936.

Sherwin-White, A.N. The Letters of Pliny. Oxford:
Clarendon Press, 1966.

Spengel, Leonard von. Rhetores Graeci. Vol. 3.
Leipzig: B.G. Teubner, 1856.

Stendahl, Krister, editor. Immortality and Resurrection. New York: The Macmillan Company, 1965.

Telfer, William, editor. Cyril of Jerusalem and
Nemesius of Emesa, The Library of Christian
Classics. Vol. 4. Philadelphia: The West-
minster Press, 1955.

Tertullian. De Anima. Edited with introduction and
commentary by J.H. Waszink. Amsterdam: J.M.
Meulenhoff, 1947.

Thraede, Klaus. Grundzüge griechische-römischen
Brieftopik, Zetemata, Heft 48. Munich: C.H.
Beck'sche Verlagsbuchhandlung, 1970.

Sykutris, J. "Epistolographie," Pauly Realencyclopädie der classischen Altertumswissenschaft.
Supplementband V. Stuttgart: J.B. Metzler,
1894-.

Treucker, Barnim. Politische und sozialgeschichtliche Studien zu den Basilius-Briefen. Bonn: Rudolf Habelt Verlag, 1961.

Völker, Walther. Der wahre Gnostiker nach Clemens Alexandrinus. Berlin and Leipzig: n.p., 1952.

Völker, Walther. Gregor von Nyssa als Mystiker. Wiesbaden: Franz Steiner Verlag GMBH, 1955.

Wagner, M.M. "A Chapter in Byzantine Epistolography: The Letters of Theodoret of Cyrus." Dumbarton Oaks Papers, IV. Cambridge, Mass.: Harvard University Press, 1948.

Winslow, Donald. The Dynamics of Salvation: A Study in Gregory of Nazianzus. Soon to be published. Philadelphia: The Philadelphia Patristic Foundation, Ltd.

Xenophon. Xenophon: Symposium and Apology. Translated by O.J. Todd. Vol. 4. The Loeb Classical Library. Cambridge, Mass.: Harvard University Press, 1968.

Zeller, Eduard. Outlines of the History of Greek Philosophy. 13th ed. Edited by Wilhelm Nestle and translated by L.R. Palmer. Cleveland: The World Publishing Company, 1931.

Zeller, Eduard. Plato and the Older Academy. Translated by Sarah Frances Alleyne and Alfred Goodwin. London: Longmans, Green and Company, 1888.

Zeller, Eduard. The Stoics, Epicureans and Sceptics. Translated by Oswald Reichel. New York: Russell and Russell, 1962.

INDEX OF NAMES

Ambrose, 33, 48, 49n.
Apollinaris, 173.
Apollonius of Tyana, 26, 27, 48.
Aristotle, 10, 102, 239.
Augustine, 49, 49n., 207.

Chrysippus, 11, 12, 20n., 39, 43n., 98, 99, 102, 104,
    104n., 105, 106, 107, 137.
Cicero, 11, 13, 14, 16, 17, 18, 33-40, 48, 49n., 83,
    85, 101, 102n., 103, 108, 117n., 137, 168, 192-93,
    200, 209.
Clement of Alexandria, 49, 50, 224, 231, 238, 241.
Crantor, 11-16, 48, 83-88, 107, 116, 160, 169n., 170,
    177, 240.
Cyprian, 48, 139n., 156, 186.

Democritus, 6, 6n., 28, 46.
Dio Chrysostom, 5, 63.
Diogenes Laertius, 11, 95, 96, 105, 106, 116.

Epictetus, 49, 161, 258.
Epicurus, 18-21, 46, 185.
Euripides, 2, 9n., 153, 180, 191, 193, 193n.

Himerius, 28, 32, 55-56, 59, 150.

Jerome, 10n., 48, 207, 208.
Jesus Christ, 125, 172-74, 186, 187, 193, 196, 202,
    240.
Job, 71, 162, 165, 182, 183, 185-89, 191, 192, 196,
    205, 219.
Julian, 28, 32, 55-56, 59, 104n., 145.

Libanius, 32, 48, 56-57, 63, 77, 148-150.
Lucretius, 18-20, 46.

Menander, 63-65, 68, 70n., 140, 209.
Moses, 244-47, 250-53.

Nemesius, 238-40, 241.

Origen, 49, 171, 171n., 197, 202n., 204, 224.

Paul, 69, 74, 126, 144, 153, 155, 155n., 173, 183n.,
    192, 194-96, 198, 199, 201-03, 205, 221, 222,
    253.
Philo, 49, 121-22, 126, 172n.
Plato, 7-10, 88-94, 102, 126, 181, 181n., 197-200,
    202, 202n., 207, 221.
Plutarch, 11, 12n., 13, 14, 20-27, 47, 48, 54-55, 117-
    21, 134, 135, 136, 164, 165n., 180, 180n., 200,
    201, 209, 210, 211, 240.
Pliny, 44-45, 48.
Plotinus, 121-22.
Posidonius, 11, 59, 112-17, 120, 240.

Seneca, 40-44, 47, 48, 146n., 148, 150, 161n., 162,
    165, 181, 184, 200, 210.
Sextus Empiricus, 12, 86.
Socrates, 7, 8, 32, 175n., 191, 196.

Theodoret, 155, 207, 207n.
Tertullian, 48, 48n., 156.

Zeno, 11, 41, 95, 96, 98, 99, 102, 106, 107, 108, 116.

INDEX OF BIBLICAL PASSAGES

Psalm 54: 134
Psalm 119.5 (LXX): 176
Psalm 148: 199

Proverbs 10.7: 175n.

Job 1.21: 60, 62, 162n.

Isaiah 35.10: 194n.
Isaiah 40.6: 176, 176n.
Isaiah 51.11: 194n.

Ecclesiasticus 38.16: 175n.

Matthew 19.14: 70
Matthew 25.34: 194n.

Luke 13.16: 149n.
Luke 18.7: 194n.
Luke 18.8: 194n.

Romans 1.11: 179.
Romans 8.18: 194.

1 Corinthians 2.9: 309.
1 Corinthians 10.13: 192.
1 Corinthians 15: 195-96.

2 Corinthians 12.7: 149n.

Philippians 1.23: 199, 199n.
Philippians 3.2: 144.
Philippians 3.13-14: 235.

1 Thessalonians 4.13: 69, 153-56, 185, 194-96.

2 Thessalonians 3b-4a: 194n.

Hebrews 10.37: 194, 194n.
Hebrews 11.36: 193.

James 5.11: 186.

1 Peter 5.4: 192.

2 Peter 3.7: 194n.

INDEX OF IMPORTANT GREEK TERMS

ἀδακρυτί, 145.
ἀλόγιστικον, ἀλόγιστον (part of soul), 90, 114, 118n.
ἀνάστασις, 203.
ἀναχωρέω, ἀναχώρησις, etc., 224-25.
ἀπάθεια, ἀπαθής, 11, 59, 81-123, 131, 145, 169-72, 231,
    232, 233, 234, 238, 239, 240, 242, 250, 251, 252,
    254, 259, 260n., 263, 267.
γενέσθαι θέον, 228, 253, 255, 256.
διηγήματα, 64, 70, 70n., 72.

ἐγκώμιον, 63, 65, 65n., 68, 72, 139, 142, 144.
ἐμπαθῶς, 135, 186n., 230.
ἐπιτάφιος, 29, 29n., 63, 66n., 79, 136.
εὐλογία, 60, 143, 144, 152.
εὐπάθεια, 11n, 106-09.

ἡγεμονικόν, 96-102, 114.

θεολογία, 213, 219, 226, 264.
θεοποιήσις, 253-54.
θεραπεία, 47, 104.
θεωρία, 131, 220, 225, 245, 245n., 264.
θέωσις, 205, 254-57.
θρῆνος, 4, 63, 65, 65n., 72, 139, 145, 152, 169.

λογιστικόν (part of soul), 90, 99, 114.
λύπη, 88, 89, 104, 104n., 108, 108n., 110, 119, 138,
    138n., 171, 174, 233, 240.

μετριοπάθεια, 81-123, 131, 135, 169-73, 216, 230, 231,
    234, 238, 240, 242, 261, 263.
μοῖρα θνητῶν, 25, 46, 163.
μονῳδία, 63, 68, 79.

οἰκείωσις, οἰκειότης, 126, 175n., 253, 254.
οἰκονομία, 167, 172, 227, 254.
ὁμοίωσις, 228, 253, 254n.

πάθος, πάθη, 11, 56, 56n., 68n., 81-123, 131, 167, 169,
    227, 231, 232, 236, 237, 240, 262, 263.
παιδεία, 127, 128, 131, 157, 222, 229, 258, 264.
παραμυθία, παραμυθητικός, 3n., 4n., 59, 60, 63, 64, 65,
    66, 68, 68n., 69, 71, 71n., 72, 75, 76, 77, 79,
    133-136, 140, 152, 153, 154, 156, 157, 167, 204,
    207, 208, 213, 220, 222, 244, 251, 253, 264.
περὶ πένθους (of Crantor), 13, 21, 35, 35n., 48, 83,
    88, 93, 104n.; (of Lucian), 32; (of Theophrastus),
    10.
προοίμιον, 72, 133.

σοφός, 55, 89n., 185, 189.
συμπάθεια, 135, 225.

ὑποδείγματα, 71, 182, 184.

φθόνος, 150, 151.
φιλοσοφία, 65n., 72, 130, 219, 230, 244, 253.

χιτών, 248.
χωρίζω, χωρισμός, etc., 224, 227, 230, 231, 237, 246.

ψυχή, 59n., 90, 94, 95, 99, 107n., 115, 118n., 119,
    168, 224, 225, 226, 228, 235.